Secure in Christ

Understanding Salvation for Unshakable Assurance

MATT PAVLIK

Christian Concepts
Centerville, Ohio

Secure in Christ

Copyright © 2025 Matt Pavlik

All rights reserved. No part of this book may be used or reproduced in any manner whatsoever without written permission except in the case of brief quotations embodied in critical articles or reviews.

Published in the United States of America by Christian Concepts (christianconcepts.com), an imprint of New Reflections Counseling, Inc. (newreflectionscounseling.com).

Although the author is a professional counselor, this book is not intended to be a replacement for professional counseling.

Pavlik, Matthew Edward, 1971-
Secure in Christ / Matt Pavlik.
ISBN: 978-1-951866-07-5 (softcover)

BISAC

REL067100 RELIGION / Christian Theology / Soteriology
REL067090 RELIGION / Christian Theology / Pneumatology
REL012120 RELIGION / Christian Living / Spiritual Growth
REL050000 RELIGION / Christian Ministry / Counseling & Recovery

Library of Congress

Salvation—Christianity
Assurance (Theology)
Faith and assurance
Bible—Theology—Salvation

Core Subjects

Soteriology, Assurance of Salvation, Faith, Regeneration, Union with Christ, Biblical Theology, Reformed Theology, Gospel-Centered Discipleship, Identity in Christ, The Gospel and the Christian Life, Overcoming Doubt, Renewal and Restoration, Hope and Perseverance, Spiritual Formation, Theodicy

Scripture quotations marked NLT are taken from the Holy Bible, New Living Translation, copyright © 1996, 2004, 2015 by Tyndale House Foundation. Used by permission of Tyndale House Publishers, Inc., Carol Stream, Illinois 60188. All rights reserved.

Scripture quotations marked (NIV) are taken from the Holy Bible, New International Version®, NIV®. Copyright © 1973, 1978, 1984, 2011 by Biblica, Inc.™ Used by permission of Zondervan. All rights reserved worldwide. www.zondervan.com. The "NIV" and "New International Version" are trademarks registered in the United States Patent and Trademark Office by Biblica, Inc.™

Scripture quotations marked ESV are from the ESV® Bible (The Holy Bible, English Standard Version®), copyright © 2001 by Crossway Bibles, a publishing ministry of Good News Publishers. Used by permission. All rights reserved.

Scripture quotations marked (CEV) are from the Contemporary English Version Copyright © 1991, 1992, 1995 by American Bible Society, Used by Permission.

2025 August: First Edition
2025 September: EPUB Edition

IMAGES

Cover and diagrams created by Matt Pavlik.

The name of the Lord is a fortified tower;
 the righteous run to it and are safe.
Proverbs 18:10 NIV

CONTENTS

PART 1: UNION IN CHRIST SECURES SALVATION 1
Chapter 1: What Problem Does Salvation Solve? 3
Chapter 2: What Is Salvation? 19

PART 2: STEADY GROWTH IN CHRIST CONFIRMS SALVATION 35
Chapter 3: What Are The Evidences Of Salvation? 37
Chapter 4: How Does A Fertile Heart Reveal True Salvation? 55
Chapter 5: How Sure of Salvation Can Believers Be? 77
Chapter 6: Can Believers Ever Lose Salvation? 97
Chapter 7: How Does Spiritual Growth Strengthen Assurance of Salvation? .. 113

PART 3: GOD'S GROUNDWORK SECURES SALVATION 129
Chapter 8: Who Causes Salvation? 131
Chapter 9: Who Chooses Salvation? 149
Chapter 10: What Freedom Does Salvation Secure? 167
Chapter 11: What Does Identity Teach Us About Salvation? 187

PART 4: GOD'S GUARANTEED VICTORY SECURES SALVATION .. 207
Chapter 12: What Is Evil's Role In Salvation? 209
Chapter 13: What is Suffering's Role In Salvation? 227
Chapter 14: No Plan B: Where Else Can We Go? 243

PREFACE

In this book, I use the singular "she" when referring to an individual person. This choice is not meant to exclude males but to avoid the repetition of "he or she" or the imprecision of the plural "they." Using "she" also creates a helpful distinction from the capitalized "He" used throughout for God, Jesus, or Holy Spirit.

Additionally, I refer to *Holy Spirit* without the definite article "the" to emphasize His personhood.

When I use "we" or "our," I am typically referring to myself together with other believers.

Citations from other works follow a numbered selected bibliography, formatted as:

SB#<number>, <author's last name>, p. <page number>

For example, a reference to the first source's page 27 listed in the bibliography would appear as:

SB#1, Gilmore, p. 27

I brought passion and insight to this book, God inspired me to understand His truth, and I used AI Copilot to edit, enhance, and clarify certain ideas, sentences, and paragraphs. All content and creative decisions are my own.

Why I Wrote Secure In Christ

God chose me on a Saturday evening in July 1991. God's causing of my spiritual birth was unmistakable. I was unable to believe one moment and I knew God was real the next. God opened my mind and heart so that I could see Him. I will always cherish this decisive and instantaneous transformation. When the reality of this world becomes confusing, it keeps me hopefully grounded in God's reality.

To put it plainly, my purpose is the same as John's:

> I write these things to you who believe in the name of the Son of God so that you may know that you have eternal life.
> 1 John 5:13 NIV

PART 1

Union In Christ Secures Salvation

From the moment we trust in Jesus, the cornerstone by which we measure everything, we are spiritually joined to His life, death, and resurrection. This union places us in Christ's righteousness and adopts us into God's family, securing our standing before the Father. Our salvation rests entirely on His perfect work, not on our own merit.

CHAPTER 1

What Problem Does Salvation Solve?

Salvation is the gift of spiritual life—a new birth that brings peace, joy, and an everlasting relationship with God. But what if worldly ideas have distorted your understanding of it?

Has Jesus rescued you from spiritual death into His life and light, only for you to live in fear of returning to darkness? Jesus cures spiritual blindness, making a return to darkness impossible.

When salvation is rightly understood, you can fully embrace the life-changing gift God has provided through Christ. It cannot be obtained or retained through human effort. Salvation is secure because it is entirely the work of Holy Spirit, who lives and works within every believer.

ASSURANCE OF SALVATION IS ESSENTIAL

Salvation is a matter of eternal life and death—its significance cannot be overstated. Because salvation is spiritual life, both awareness and assurance of that life confirm its authenticity.

Consider Steve, who believed he had to earn God's favor anew each day. Every misstep deepened his doubt in his salvation. He was consumed by fear—until he encountered the truth of God's grace. Once he realized that salvation is secure in Christ, he finally found peace, liberated from the exhausting cycle of performance-based faith.

How often do we live like Steve, even while believing differently? We affirm grace with our lips, but do we rest in it with our hearts? How many of us live under the shadow of fear, measuring ourselves against a standard we've already been freed from?

ASSURANCE: THE COMPANION OF SALVATION

Life is challenging enough without believing salvation is fragile. A wavering view of salvation undermines the peace and security of God's love. Imagine waking up each day with a knot of anxiety and doubt, wondering if you are "good enough" to keep your salvation. Now contrast this with rising each morning fully assured of God's unchanging love and faithfulness. That assurance flows from trusting that God's heart overflows with fierce love for you as His child.

Life often feels like a journey upstream. But salvation is not an uncertain midpoint between hell and heaven. God does not abandon us halfway home, watching from a distance as we paddle toward eternal life. Instead, He steps into the canoe with us, empowering and guiding us through life's currents. The journey may be turbulent, but with God leading, it cannot fail.

To be saved is to rest in God's complete rescue—to trust Him not only to **provide** the way, but to **be** the way. The alternative is a life marked by spiritual insecurity: fear and inadequate striving to gain His favor. We cannot fully trust God when we quietly suspect He may leave us behind.

ASSURANCE:
SALVATION PROTECTS THE MIND

God considers the security of salvation to be like a helmet—armor designed to protect the head from attack (Ephesians 6:17). Therefore, understanding salvation accurately is a defensive maneuver commanded by God. Too many people have holes in their helmet. But, because we are destined for eternal peace with God, we need not be plagued with daily anxieties. Instead, God wants us filled with hope.

> But since we belong to the day, let us be sober, having put on the breastplate of faith and love, and for a helmet the hope of salvation. For God has not destined us for wrath, but to obtain salvation through our Lord Jesus Christ.
> 1 Thessalonians 5:8-9 ESV

ASSURANCE:
THE GOSPEL HEALS INSECURITY

This book is a heartfelt journey into how the Gospel heals spiritual insecurity—a burden many people carry, despite God's unfailing love. The Bible's central message is simple yet profound: salvation is a free, irrevocable gift rooted in Christ's unchanging work, not in people's flawed efforts. The Gospel assures believers of God's steadfast love, no matter their fears, doubts, or struggles. This book seeks to illuminate the depth and permanence of God's love, dispelling the anxiety and uncertainty that often cloud faith.

Spiritual insecurity, guilt, and shame stem from flawed theology that misunderstands salvation. Many struggle with the fear that their imperfections could separate them from God. But shifting from trusting in self-effort to fully relying on the sufficiency of Christ's once-and-for-all sacrifice, produces assurance and joy.

As a professional counselor, I've witnessed how relying on self breeds fear, doubt, and insecurity. Motivated by a desire to showcase the incredible reality of God's love, I wrote this book to provide clarity and hope. With both theological depth and pastoral care, I want it to serve as a lifeline for those longing for peace and security in their relationship with God. Through scriptural evidence, theological insights, and practical examples, you will see how God's faithful solution to sin assures believers of their eternal salvation.

My prayer is that this book assures you of God's unwavering love, unbreakable promises, and irrevocable salvation. May it guide you to walk boldly in the joy and freedom of His grace. Together, let's explore how the Gospel transforms hearts, heals spiritual wounds, and brings lasting assurance to all who believe.

THE CONSEQUENCES OF MISUNDERSTANDING SALVATION

Misunderstanding salvation doesn't just lead to confusion—it brings life-altering consequences that ripple through every aspect of a believer's spiritual and emotional well-being. Pursuing the correct understanding of the Gospel should be a believer's top priority. Consider these two extreme distortions:

1. **Expecting more than the Gospel promises:** Assuming everyone will be saved or treating eternal life as an offer rather than a gift, can lead to a non-believer's false assurance of salvation. This view undermines God's initiative in choosing people for salvation.
2. **Expecting less than the Gospel promises:** Believing that salvation can be lost, or doubting its security, results in a weakened trust in God's love. This can leave true believers mired in uncertainty and fear.

Salvation is not conditional upon human effort to stay faithful; it is secured entirely by Christ. Doubting its permanence shifts the focus from God's faithfulness to our own performance, leading to unnecessary fear.

WHAT'S AT STAKE?

The quality of life and the believer's witness to God's kingdom are at stake. Weakened trust in God can manifest in the believer's life as any of the following:
- Compromised mental and emotional health: anxiety, low self-worth, shame, guilt, and despair.
- Distance from God: believing the lie that He is indifferent to believers' sense of well-being.
- Short-sighted perspective: prioritizing earthly matters more than eternal matters.

The negative consequences of believing that salvation can be lost are deeply concerning:
- Consuming fear and worry: "Does God accept or reject me?"
- Compulsive focus on performance: "Am I doing enough to earn salvation?"
- Continuous self-doubt: "Am I good enough?"
- Confusion over outcomes: "Am I responsible for saving people, or is God?"

A believer preoccupied with doubts about her salvation may fail to reflect the fullness of God's Good News to others. The Gospel isn't **okay-I-think-I-am-saved** news or **terrible-I-thought-I-was-saved-but-now-it's-too-late** news. The Gospel is **amazing-I-know-I-am-saved** news.

THEOLOGY AFFECTS EMOTIONAL HEALTH

Good theology is a correct view of God. Good emotional health is a correct view of self. Both are essential for victorious living.

Bad theology will lead to poor mental and emotional health. A lack of understanding what the Bible says combined with blindly trusting other people or institutions to interpret the Bible can lead to a negative self-worth. For example, beliefs like "God might terminate salvation", "God expects people to earn salvation", or "God doesn't care about people" can produce emotional conclusions like "I am alone in my journey toward salvation", "My situation is hopeless", or "I am unlovable." We should study the Bible individually and learn from other biblical teachers, but then test the spirit of the teaching by listening to Holy Spirit who helps us see the correct meaning.

Good theology starts with an accurate understanding of the Gospel. The Gospel is the foundation for understanding and interpreting other less-central passages. If the Gospel understanding is wrong, everything else will be wrong. If the Gospel has been interpreted correctly, it is difficult to misinterpret less-central passages.

When seeking to understand the main message of the Bible, it's important to see the big picture message. This is done by recognizing how the Bible speaks to foundational truths across many verses, chapters, and books. The Bible does not contradict itself, so passages that seem to be presenting differing ideas must be studied in context and reconciled to a coherent teaching.

The Gospel is the foundation for mental and emotional health. Accurate understanding of who God is leads to healthy thinking, feeling, and actions. But misguided understanding wastes precious effort. For example, believing that God's acceptance is conditional upon performance will encourage a fear-based relationship with God. This bad theology leads to a need to ask, "Have I performed sufficiently today to remain in good standing with God?" Then, because no one is perfect, it is easy for the next thought to be, "God is disappointed with me. My sin was too great today. My efforts were not enough. God will abandon me."

Notice the subtle, but significant, shift from relying on God's power to self-effort. One is cooperation with God's initiative, the other, operating alone.

The grave reality of this bad theology becomes even clearer when we consider the consequences of not performing. What happens if performance is not good enough? What is our official status before God? To have to seriously and continually ask this will become a source of debilitating anxiety. Have you ever found yourself feeling this way—wondering if God's love could run out? The Bible says that Jesus's sacrifice is sufficient to cover all sin and imperfections for all time (Hebrews 10:12-14).

Bad theology says that God might remove a person's salvation, so that she is no longer a child of God. Such a consequence would be traumatizing because it would mean being abandoned by God.

Bad theology also says that a true believer can remove her own salvation. This is impossible because no one, after knowing God's love, would want to end her relationship with Him.

Imagine believing that it's possible that God can change His mind, break His promise to never abandon us, and revoke His love. The consequences on our mental and emotional health would be devastating. Then, living in constant fear would be normal.

God is better than we are at dealing with how our hearts are both deceived and deceitful. He is gentler on us than we are on ourselves. He is the good shepherd that searches our hearts to find offensive ways (Psalm 23, 139). This is not to bring judgement and condemnation; it is to pull out sin splinters lodged in our hearts. Jesus came to save—to bring relief from the burden of sin (John 3:17-18).

EMOTIONAL HEALTH AFFECTS THEOLOGY

Negative life experiences might cause changes in personal theology. The depressed or anxious believer might start to doubt God's steadfast love for her. Despite the truth of God's Word, believers can adopt a distorted view of God when they are beaten down by traumatic events. For example, having an abusive father might result in a heart-felt belief "I am unlovable" which can produce bad theology like "God does not care about people" or "God cannot love a defective person like me."

Assurance of eternal life is a quality of life concern. The person who cannot feel assurance and know she is saved will suffer poor emotional and spiritual health.

Signs of spiritual sickness can start with feeling no choice but to compromise on biblical teaching to reconcile it with tragic life experiences. Unexplainable losses, such as the death of a spouse early in life, can turn hearts against God, causing people to doubt if God is real or that He cares. If this crisis of faith hasn't happened to you personally, chances are you know someone who seems like she has more to endure than she can bear.

Mental and emotional health concerns can significantly lower assurance, creating unnecessary suffering. The only way to heal is to apply correct theology with conviction, trusting God's truth more than negative experiences. As difficult as life can be sometimes, God expects us to hold fast to the truth of His integrity and faithfulness. To compromise on God is to lose everything.

Growing in truth about Jesus will increase assurance, while distance from Him will decrease assurance. This doesn't mean that low assurance is the believer's sole responsibility—as if an instant "fix" is available by working harder, being more disciplined, or simply thinking positively. Assurance is not earned through better discipline—it is received by resting fully in God's unchanging promises.

A believer should not compare her faith walk against other believers. She must run her God-appointed race. Everyone starts at a different place and faces different circumstances. Furthermore, appearances can be deceiving. Only God knows the depth of pain in each person's heart.

Low assurance indicates that God's love has not yet penetrated deeply enough into the believer's heart. To grow in assurance, she must cooperate with Holy Spirit to remove the barriers that block the truth from taking root. If her theology is solid, then personal wounds—such as experiences of abuse or neglect—may be preventing God's truth from fully shaping her perspective. What happens to us can feel more real than God's truth.

The problem isn't God's love but rather a misplaced focus away from God and onto self. This can lead to an incomplete train of thought:
1. God is powerful and perfect.
2. I am weak and inadequate.
3. God didn't fail, I did.
4. God rejects me because I am not good enough.

What Problem Does Salvation Solve?

While these statements contain truth, dwelling on personal inadequacy rather than God's sufficiency weakens assurance. We cannot save ourselves, so when our focus remains on sin and self instead of Christ's completed work, we struggle to recognize the high value God places on us. The Gospel completes the story by adding:

5. Christ's sacrifice reconciles my relationship with God, fully restoring His acceptance of me.

Spiritually, the enemy works to destabilize assurance—causing believers to doubt their relationship with God and feel uncertain about their salvation. He also deceives non-believers into a false confidence, leading them to presume salvation without genuine faith or surrender.

A believer can be saved yet allow lies and circumstances to interfere with assurance. Conversely, false assurance is possible—non-believers may assume they are saved when they are not. The key difference lies in trust: authentic assurance thrives when faith rests fully in God's sufficiency rather than human effort.

Anxiety And Doubt Are Optional

One of the ways God relates to us is by providing comfort. God does not want us to be afraid. He wants us to be confident in His strength. Doubt is related to fear; the person who doubts stops seeing God as strong and in control.

Many beliefs are implicit. This means it is possible to believe something strongly but, at the same time, not be fully aware of what you believe or why you believe it. You might think you know what you believe but it is your actions that reveal what you actually believe. For example, it is possible to know the truth that Jesus is gentle but live in fear of judgement because your heart has yet to fully grasp this truth.

When we verbalize what we believe, we expose hidden distortions and allow God's truth to correct them. This is why it is important to make beliefs explicit. This is done by externalizing them through writing, speaking or some other form of expression. When you put your beliefs into words, you become more aware of how the "truth" in your heart differs from the truth in the Bible.

God is always on your side, and His perfect love eliminates fear for the true believer. Anxiety is essentially fear. Because He is love, everything He does in your life is meant to reduce anxiety and increase trust in Him—even when trials make this hard to see. While suffering is inevitable for Christians, fear and doubt are not; God matures His children by driving away fear, providing unlimited peace through His presence (1 John 4:18). Scripture affirms that anxiety does not come from God—His desire is for His people to experience lasting peace and joy through Holy Spirit.

Insecurity is optional because God has given us everything we need to overcome it (2 Peter 1:3, 2 Timothy 1:7). Spiritual insecurity stems from misinterpreting the Bible's teaching on salvation. Salvation is not dependent on our perfection but on God's unchanging promises and perfect love. When lies take root in our hearts—whispering that our failures or sins outweigh God's grace—they distort the truth of the Gospel. To overcome insecurity, believers must reject these lies and realign their focus on the unshakable truth of God's character and the finished work of Christ

THE TRANSFORMATIVE POWER OF UNDERSTANDING SALVATION

Salvation is not simply one option among many—it is the ultimate and only solution to humanity's most profound problem. It goes beyond merely providing a potential fix; it is God intervening to rescue us from our desperate condition.

THE PROBLEM: HUMANITY'S SEPARATION FROM GOD

Everyone is born into a broken state:
- Enslaved to sin
- Spiritually dead and orphaned

What Problem Does Salvation Solve?

- An enemy of God

These realities highlight a serious and urgent problem: each person is born cut off from the only One who can save them. The consequences are fatal, leaving humanity spiritually adrift, without hope or purpose (Romans 3:23).

THE SOLUTION: A NEW LIFE UNITED TO CHRIST

Salvation is nothing less than a rescue—a deliverance from a life destined for destruction to a life that will endure forever. As Scripture assures:

> For the wages of sin is death, but the free gift of God is eternal life in Christ Jesus our Lord.
> Romans 6:23 ESV

Through salvation, believers are reborn into an entirely new existence:
- Freed from sin and enslaved to righteousness
- Spiritually alive and welcomed as God's child
- Brought into an eternal friendship with God

This transformation isn't partial or temporary; it is comprehensive and everlasting. Salvation addresses the problem of separation from God completely, providing reconciliation and restored relationship with Him.

When a person is born spiritually, she goes through a significant transformation. It might appear subtle on the outside, but it won't be subtle inside her heart and mind. To have God living with you and showing you His spiritual reality is a radical way of life.

Understanding the Gospel is the key to understanding all of life. It provides that sure and steady anchor for the soul. Every believer should be encouraged, her heart at rest, by answers to the following questions:
- Is God's love unconditional or conditional?
- Am I wanted by Him or unwanted?

- Is my existence intentional and significant, or random and arbitrary?
- Will I be in heaven, or might I still end up in hell?
- Does emphasizing free will become a liability or an asset to my spiritual journey?

The positive consequences of seeing that the Gospel teaches that believers are secure in Jesus Christ are profoundly amazing good news:
- God can be trusted.
- Knowing God's love provides secure emotional attachment.
- Significance and hope conserve energy to channel into God's kingdom agenda instead of wasting time worrying about how to be good enough for God.
- Consistent peace and confidence from knowing that only God has the power to save people, means sharing the Gospel message without worrying about outcomes.

Because salvation is unshakable, believers can confidently rest in God's love, knowing that their future is secure. This removes fear and provides the foundation for a life of peace and purpose.

Ultimately, anxiety and worry stem from weakened trust in God—consequences that vanish when believers embrace the Gospel's promise of eternal security. Believers who are confident in their faith in God will experience perfect peace. Worry is only possible when doubt weakens faith.

> You will keep in perfect peace those whose minds are steadfast, because they trust in you.
> Isaiah 26:3 NIV

By fully understanding and embracing the truth of salvation, believers can move past fear and doubt to live a life of steadfast peace and confident faith in God's unwavering love.

OVERVIEW OF TOPICS COVERED

This book defends the security of biblical salvation by exploring it from beginning to end in four parts. Together, they highlight God's purpose for salvation and how we can confidently trust in its permanence. The first half (Parts 1 and 2) focuses on the details of daily Christian living. The second half explores the bigger picture of eternity past (Part 3) and future (Part 4). The past and future must be understood correctly to comprehend God's complete intentions for salvation.

Each chapter focuses on a specific question with the overall goal to strengthen assurance of God's redemptive plan. The foundational questions in Part 1 establish the framework for understanding salvation. Part 2 explains how God leads believers to grow in Christ, confirming their salvation. Part 3 dives deeper, exploring the divine and human roles in salvation, the true nature of freedom, and the challenges posed by free will. Part 4 concludes with how God uses love, evil, and suffering to deepen our understanding of salvation. His complete solution to sin ensures we experience glory, not suffering, forever in the next life with Him.

FOR REFLECTION AND DISCUSSION

Read about Sarah's journey to find assurance of her salvation, then answer the questions at the end.

Sarah's Journey

Sarah had always struggled with feeling unworthy of God's love. As a child, she internalized the belief that her value was tied to obedience due to her parents' obsession with responsibility. As an adult, she carried that weight into her view of God as Father.

When her marriage began to falter, her sense of adequacy crumbled. Her thoughts weighed on her, an avalanche of doubt and insecurity, and soon, her uncertainty about herself became uncertainty about God. She thought, *If I was a better wife, maybe this wouldn't be happening. If I were a stronger Christian,* maybe God would bless my marriage. Was I ever truly saved? Maybe I only thought I had faith, but my failures prove I don't. The anxiety consumed her, making prayer difficult and Scripture confusing. Sunday's sermon on God's forgiveness seemed directed at others, not her. Fear shouted that she had somehow fallen outside of God's grace—that salvation was for those who had it together, and she clearly didn't.

One evening, while searching for something to hold onto, Sarah opened her Bible to Ephesians 2. She read the words,

> It is by grace you have been saved, through faith—and this is not from yourselves, it is the gift of God.

She read them again.

> It is by grace you have been saved, through faith—and this is not from yourselves, it is the gift of God.

Holy Spirit helped her understand this truth—not as an idea she had heard before, but as a reality she had not fully understood and embraced. God's grace had never been about her ability to perform. Salvation had never depended on her strength or perfection. It had always been entirely God's gift.

At first, this truth felt distant, almost too good to be true. Could she really trust it? The doubts didn't disappear overnight, nor did her fears. But the more she reflected on God's promises, the more she realized that doubts do not define her faith. Instead, God is the source of faith—He gave her the insight that faith is spiritual, not fleshly. She felt hope deep within. Instead of spiraling into uncertainty, she started bringing her questions to God rather than avoiding Him.

Day by day, Sarah began uncovering her faith, looking beyond her fluctuating emotions and failures, to the unshakable certainty of God's character. She wrote down scriptures about God's promises and reminded herself that His love was based on His nature, not her performance. She still struggled—she still had moments of fear—but now, she had a foundation to stand on when insecurity crept in.

What Problem Does Salvation Solve?

As weeks passed, her mindset changed. She no longer saw salvation as a fragile state she could lose. She began to experience true peace, not because life was perfect, but because she finally understood that God's love was unbreakable. She realized she had a real relationship with a Father who really cares. Slowly, she embraced the freedom that comes with trusting God completely, and joy followed.

Conclusion

Assurance does not mean being free from hardship; it means knowing that nothing—no doubt, no sin, no weakness—could undo the finished work of Christ. Without assurance, faith feels unstable—always dependent on performance rather than grace. But when salvation is fully understood as unbreakable, it leads to deep joy and lasting confidence. Like Sarah, you too can find freedom, strength, and assurance in the truth of the Gospel.

Questions

1. Are you afraid of losing your salvation? Why or why not, and how does that shape your relationship with God?
2. What problem does salvation solve?
3. What are some common misconceptions about salvation, and how can believers guard against them?
4. If salvation is a helmet meant to protect you, what condition is yours in? Is it strong and secure, or does it feel fragile?
5. In what ways have negative life experiences impacted your understanding of salvation or God's love?
6. Have struggles with mental or emotional health ever led you to doubt God's faithfulness? How have you worked through those doubts?
7. How can a solid theological foundation positively impact mental and emotional health?
8. In what ways does Satan attempt to undermine assurance, and how can believers resist his lies?
9. How much are you truly enjoying your salvation? What does it mean to fully embrace it, and how might fear or insecurity block that joy?

10. How could understanding salvation as a gift rather than an achievement change the way you live out your faith?
11. Why is assurance of salvation crucial for spiritual growth and personal peace?
12. How do you balance faith and feelings when doubts arise? What practices help realign your heart with truth?

CHAPTER 2

What Is Salvation?

Can you be certain of your salvation right now, or is it something you must wait until the afterlife to confirm? Is salvation a gift that is immediate and complete, or does it need to grow and mature before it becomes effective enough to save you? Is the process of gaining salvation reversible?

These questions stir fear and doubt in some believers, leaving them anxious about their standing with God. But Scripture proclaims a clear and comforting answer: salvation is synonymous with spiritual birth, a robust and instantaneous transformation. It is God's work alone, fully effective from the start and made to endure forever.

SALVATION IS RADICAL TRANSFORMATION

The Bible uses many terms to describe spiritual birth which highlight different aspects of salvation's miraculous transformation:

- being saved
- new birth, second birth
- becoming a new creation
- being born again, being born from above
- being adopted
- regeneration (being made spiritually alive)

New birth is something to be celebrated because it is a complete solution—it cannot be improved. Unlike human efforts that require progress, salvation is complete at the moment of spiritual birth because it originates entirely from God's work, not ours. Salvation solves humanity's sin problem but also provides so much more with eternal life.

SALVATION IS LIFE EVERLASTING

Being saved, having salvation, and possessing eternal life are all one and the same. The Greek word aionios in Romans 6:23 (and many other verses) means "everlasting," "unending," "forever," or "ceaseless."[1]

> For the wages of sin is death, but the free gift of God is eternal life in Christ Jesus our Lord.
> Romans 6:23 ESV

Salvation is for people in life-threatening danger who are helpless to do anything to provide their own rescue. From what threats do all people need to be saved?
- Death, sin, and evil
- Despair, fear, and anger
- Destruction of self and others

These are not isolated threats, but symptoms of separation from the Source of eternal life and goodness. Therefore, the primary danger is remaining forever trapped in temporary life.

God saves us from ourselves (Romans 5:6, 6:23, 7:24-25) for His purposes (Ephesians 2:9-10). We are saved from the death that we earned. We were helpless orphans (spiritually speaking)

---

1. https://biblehub.com/greek/166.htm

and enemies of God. But we rejoice because God chooses to save us in our weakness (1 Corinthians 1:26-31).

There are three perspectives of salvation from where we stand today, two thousand years after God resurrected Jesus:
1. **Past:** Jesus has already secured salvation for all who believe. He declared, "It is finished" immediately before His death (John 19:28-30).
2. **Present:** Believers experience eternal life today because Holy Spirit dwells inside of them (Ephesians 1:13-14).
3. **Future:** Holy Spirit is a deposit toward the future reality of heaven. Believers don't yet have all of the benefits of salvation, such as a new body that will last forever. But believers hope for them, waiting patiently (Romans 8:20-25).

Every believer must consider salvation as "I am already saved" (past), "I am being saved" (present), and "I will be saved" (future). From God's perspective outside of time, salvation is already completely finished. This is clearly presented by what is called the golden chain of salvation:

> For those whom he foreknew he also predestined to be conformed to the image of his Son, in order that he might be the firstborn among many brothers. And those whom he predestined he also called, and those whom he called he also justified, and those whom he justified he also glorified.
> Romans 8:29-30 ESV

Salvation is unbreakable because it is already accomplished (past tense). God foreknew, predestined, called, justified, and glorified believers. Salvation starts before the creation of the world and continues uninterrupted until it is completed. This means God works in the life of a person both before and after she believes. Before she believes, He works to bring about the circumstances which lead to her belief. This ensures that no one will "accidentally" be left out of heaven.

SALVATION IS A FREE GIFT

Salvation is a gift, not an offer. A gift has a specific giver and a specific recipient. An offer is available to all. A gift has an intended name written on it. A gift is initiated and fulfilled by the giver, requiring no effort to receive it. An offer is initiated by the giver but fulfilled by the recipient. An offer is worthless until it is claimed.

Many misunderstand salvation as something they must claim or activate, but Scripture shows that it is a direct gift from God, given without condition. Perhaps you have received one of those coupons in the mail addressed to both "previous owner" and "current resident"? The coupon is an offer that must be claimed and redeemed. Salvation is not like that. Salvation arrives as an announcement, "Welcome to God's family!"

Salvation requires faith to be of any benefit. Not everyone has the faith. That's why salvation is a gift. God gives the gift of salvation along with faith to enjoy it. Salvation and faith are inseparable. Having one means having the other. Therefore, God cannot grant them independent of each other. Salvation without faith would be like having a bank account without the password. The money is there, but never accessible. Faith without salvation would be like having the password without the bank account. Access is possible but there is no money.

> Faith is an extension of God's power rather than the exertion of human egos. Our faith in the Gospel, our commitment to Christ, is what God initiates in us. Faith is the result of divine action, a supernatural gifting.
> SB#1, Gilmore, p. 27

Faith is 100% spiritual; it originates solely from God, making it beyond human effort to manufacture. When Jesus tells people they have "so little faith", He is not blaming them for lack of effort, He is bringing awareness to their focus on the physical at the expense of the spiritual. To grow in faith means to grow as a *spiritual* being. Holy Spirit fosters spiritual growth by helping believers see Jesus as trustworthy because He is loving, powerful, and in control.

What Is Salvation?

Just as faith cannot be earned or manufactured, salvation also comes freely as a gift. Salvation must be free because no one can afford to buy it. Free means no payment is required now or ever (no strings attached). God, being a perfect loving Father, knows how to give good gifts (Matthew 7:9-11). Without God's generous gift, we will get what we deserve: death.

God knows that we cannot repay Him for His gift. His gift is unconditional; He will not, under any circumstances, take back His gift (John 6:37). God's gift is a well-thought-out plan. He does not experience buyer's remorse with respect to those He saves. That's because He knows everyone He creates and chooses them even before they are born (Ephesians 1:3-14; John 1:11-13).

SALVATION IS BEING A NEW CREATION

A human gift might be returnable, but God's gifts are life-altering and therefore non-returnable. The Bible speaks of the old becoming new, but never the new becoming old.

> **Therefore, if anyone is in Christ, he is a new creation. The old has passed away; behold, the new has come.**
> **2 Corinthians 5:17 ESV**

Becoming a new creation, made possible by Holy Spirit, is not just a change in status like a new job title; it is an infusion of God's spiritual life—His resurrection power—into a spiritually dead person. Once God reveals the reality of who He is, belief is instantaneous. Before salvation is like being blind with a light on; sight remains impossible. After salvation, Jesus has cured spiritual blindness, making sight automatic—no effort is required. If you have experienced this radical transformation, then Scripture assures that you:

- have crossed over from death to life, darkness to light (John 5:24, Colossians 1:13).
- have left behind perishable life to gain imperishable life (1 Peter 1).
- are alive to Christ and dead to sin (Romans 6:8-11).

Salvation is not only a one-time moment of renewal but an ongoing journey of transformation. Day by day, believers are inwardly renewed by God's Spirit, reflecting His glory and growing in likeness to Christ (2 Corinthians 4:16). This continuous renewal underscores the depth and permanence of the believer's new identity.

A New Identity And Purpose

As a new creation, believers are given a profound new identity. No longer defined by sin or separation, they are God's workmanship, created in Christ Jesus for good works prepared in advance (Ephesians 2:10). Moreover, they are entrusted with a divine calling as ambassadors for Christ, carrying the message of reconciliation to the world (2 Corinthians 5:20).

This transformation does not merely change what believers *do* but who they *are*. Their new identity causes them to function differently. As new creations they are no longer conformed to the patterns of this world but are instead transformed by the renewing of their minds, able to discern God's will (Romans 12:2).

This new life stands in stark contrast to the old, which is marked by separation, enmity, and darkness. Believers no longer belong to the world but are called out of it to live in the light of Christ, shining as His witnesses.

The difference between the old and the new is as striking as the metamorphosis of a caterpillar into a butterfly. Just as a caterpillar undergoes an irreversible change to become something new, beautiful, and free, so believers are transformed through salvation. Salvation, like the butterfly's new form, is the manifestation of God's creative and sustaining power, forever altering the believer's spiritual DNA.

Salvation is not like clothing that can be removed or lost. Eternal life is woven into the very fabric of a believer's identity as a new creation. To be made spiritually new is to have eternal life encoded in a person's spiritual DNA.

What Is Salvation?

SALVATION IS PERMANENT

The gift of salvation brings about permanent transformation. The eternal life that Jesus gives is not temporary—it is irrevocable. God gives eternal life, not a life that fades or fails. For this reason, the saved person will never perish spiritually. Eternal life cannot be lost because God's promises are unbreakable. He has sworn to save His children, and His word is utterly reliable (Hebrews 6:13-20).

Salvation, or new birth, is like a one-way switch. Once God flips you to saved, you can never be turned off again. It remains locked on, unchanging and secure, powered entirely by Christ's effort.

Assurance, however, is like a dimmer switch: it may brighten or fade based on your perspective, emotions, or understanding of God's truth. But the presence of doubt doesn't change the reality of salvation any more than a dim light changes the fact that the power is on. Assurance does not determine salvation—it only indicates how clearly a believer perceives it. Just as a dim light does not mean the power is off, faded assurance does not mean salvation has disappeared.

The believer will persevere because of her new, God-given nature. Holy Spirit is permanently present in her life, a sure sign that God will never abandon or forsake her (Hebrews 13:5; Deuteronomy 31:6). The old way of life is not only dead but irretrievable, lost forever. There is no going back to what once was. Even when struggles arise, the believer cannot spiritually return to who she was before salvation. Her identity has been permanently rewritten in Christ.

Just as biological life is alive from conception, so too is spiritual life. Whether a person is born from the womb or by the Spirit above, she cannot reverse the process to become "unborn" (John 3:6). What is born of God's imperishable seed, His enduring Word, will remain imperishable for eternity:

> **Having purified your souls by your obedience to the truth for a sincere brotherly love, love one another earnestly from a pure heart, since you have been born again, not of perishable seed but of imperishable, through the living and abiding word of God; for**

> "All flesh is like grass and all its glory like the flower of grass. The grass withers, and the flower falls, but the word of the Lord remains forever."
>
> And this word is the good news that was preached to you.
> 1 Peter 1:22-25 ESV

Our fleshly bodies will fade away, but the new spiritual life given by God's Word endures forever. Jesus vividly describes eternal life as a permanent passage from death to life. Consider the absolute terms He uses:

> I tell you the truth, those who listen to my message and believe in God who sent me have eternal life. They will never be condemned for their sins, but they have already passed from death into life.
> John 5:24 NLT

Believers:
- have eternal life (already)
- will never be condemned
- have already passed from death to life

Believers are born from above by God's will and God guards them by His power (John 1:12-13). Jesus holds us securely (1 Peter 3:5). The evil one cannot remove our salvation.

> For every child of God defeats this evil world. We know that God's children do not make a practice of sinning, for God's Son holds them securely, and the evil one cannot touch them.
> 1 John 5:4, 18 NLT

New birth is a miraculous transformation, and its permanence rests entirely on God's power. Salvation is not something we can initiate or maintain through our efforts; it is God who ensures that His children are forever safe from all spiritual harm.

SALVATION IS COMPLETE INTEGRATION WITH CHRIST

Jesus is the whole body, including its members—the true believers. After becoming a new creation, a believer is permanently joined to the body of Christ. She becomes part of Him in an inseparable union. To remove her would be like Christ mutilating His own body—a concept contrary to His love and care. Just as Christ commands husbands to love their wives as their own bodies, He tenderly cares for His church, His body (Ephesians 5:21-33).

SALVATION IS UNITY WITH JESUS

At the heart of salvation is a profound mystery: the believer's unity with Jesus. Through this union, she shares in everything He has: His life, His victory, and His eternal inheritance. At the moment of spiritual birth, Holy Spirit dwells within her, uniting her with Jesus and making her a new creation (John 1:12). This union manifests eternal life, instantly granting saving faith, a new relationship with God, and spiritual power.

To visualize this unity, imagine being wholly enveloped in Christ's embrace—a secure and unbreakable bond where His life surrounds a believer entirely. God places the believer into Christ, wrapping her in His love and victory, while Holy Spirit fills her within, illuminating her heart with truth and power (John 14:20). She has become inseparably bound to Jesus's life. Because He has conquered death, she shares in His eternal victory. Jesus lives forever and so will she.

When our hearts are aligned with His, we can live in ways that genuinely please Him. In this unity, we function not only as participants in the divine nature but also as members of the divine huddle, working in harmony with the Trinity.

Knowing God in an intimate way requires a union with Jesus. Believers' union with Christ is absolutely essential. Anyone who desires the blessings of Christ apart from a relationship with Him, will suffer disappointment. Jesus's sacrifice, complete payment for spiritual debt, and reconciliation to God only apply to those in a relationship with Him.

This miraculous union transforms the believer's nature. Although the sinful flesh persists, her spirit, united with Jesus, is like God in its essence and cannot sin (Romans 7-8). Her spirit will not abuse the freedom found in Jesus, despite the rebellion desired by her flesh. She is now controlled by the Spirit, not by sin. She is not condemned; Christ bore that condemnation, and through His death, sin's power over her has been broken.

> For God has done what the law, weakened by the flesh, could not do. By sending his own Son in the likeness of sinful flesh and for sin, he condemned sin in the flesh... You, however, are not in the flesh but in the Spirit, if in fact the Spirit of God dwells in you. Anyone who does not have the Spirit of Christ does not belong to him.
> Romans 8:3, 9 ESV

Salvation is inseparable from Jesus Himself. God does not give eternal life apart from Christ; rather, He gives His Son, and with Him, all the benefits of salvation. Simply put, if you have Christ, you have eternal life. If you don't, you don't (SB#2, Ferguson, p. 45).

Holy Spirit's presence provides faith, justification, and adoption to the believer all at once:
- **Saving Faith:** The ability to see Jesus rightly, recognize the truth of the Gospel, and trust in Him as Savior and Lord.
- **Justification:** God credits Jesus's righteousness to the believer, making her right in His sight.
- **Adoption:** The believer becomes God's child, a part of His family, and a member of the body of Christ.

With Holy Spirit's indwelling, the believer is empowered to bear spiritual fruit. She gains the ability to repent of sin, choose righteous behavior, and endure trials. These actions are evidence of her salvation, though not its cause:
- **Repentance:** Agree with God that sin is wrong, feel it to be undesirable, and confess it.

What Is Salvation?

- **Sanctification:** Holy Spirit shapes the believer's character into Christ's righteous character, in a lifelong pursuit of spiritual maturity.
- **Perseverance:** Endure trials and remain faithful until the end of earthly life, culminating in a glorified body.

God provides saving faith, justification, and adoption completely at one time, so they do not need to be pursued. Saving faith and "unbelief" are opposed to each other. Therefore, unbelief is no longer considered, measured, or possible. There can be doubt, struggle, and sin, but not unbelief that could negate faith or salvation. For example, a believer might question how a good God can let bad things happen, but won't stop believing.

> Therefore, my dear friends, as you have always obeyed—not only in my presence, but now much more in my absence—continue to work out your salvation with fear and trembling, for it is God who works in you to will and to act in order to fulfill his good purpose.
> Philippians 2:12-13 NIV

A believer's life is a work in progress, only moving forward into greater freedom and holiness, never backward into spiritual death. The "fear and trembling" reflect the awe and reverence believers feel during sanctification—the magnitude of God's operation being similar to undergoing life-saving surgery. Believers are witnesses to the extraordinary power of God as He works in them to guarantee complete sanctification. Believers should remain ever aware and amazed at God's desire to use His power to fulfill His good purposes in and through them.

SALVATION IS JESUS WITH US

God's story is a revelation of who He is, inviting us to know and understand Him. Jesus is actively working within us, and we have a "front row seat" to witness His truth and power. As responders to truth—not creators of it—we observe and testify to what God is doing both in the world and in our hearts. Through Holy Spirit, who dwells within us, God trains us to reject the desires of the flesh and live according to His Spirit.

We are empowered to live the spiritual life because God lives for us (Galatians 2:20). Holy Spirit works in us in real-time, showing us how to live and enabling us to accomplish good works. Witnessing the Spirit's active presence in our lives reminds us of God's unwavering faithfulness and power.

At the moment God unites us with Himself, He brings about a complete transformation. All of the following happen simultaneously:
- God gives Holy Spirit.
- God regenerates (revives) the spiritually dead, transferring them from darkness to light, from death to life.
- God causes spiritual birth.
- God grants eternal life.
- God gives faith to recognize and believe that Jesus is Lord and Savior.
- God gives the right to become His child.
- God adopts the believer into His family.

These changes happen all at once, securing the believer's eternal destiny in Christ. None occur before or after salvation—they are inseparable components of the moment God causes salvation. They happen together because God gives us all of Christ, including associated benefits. Our eternal security comes only from our union with Christ, not from any of our efforts.

Salvation invites a response, but emotions or human will cannot alter the spiritual transformation. Holy Spirit sustains the believer spiritually, making her alive—like a permanently built-in battery that never loses energy. The expected responses to so great a salvation are profound and simple:
- worship
- repentance
- continuous belief
- faith actions, good deeds
- obedience
- perseverance, endurance, faithfulness

Holy Spirit empowers believers to actively participate in these spiritual activities. By cooperating with the Spirit, the regenerated believer can bear fruit and accomplish good works that glorify God.

SALVATION IS RELATIONSHIP WITH JESUS

Salvation is more than a theological concept. God does not only rescue us; He invites us into deep intimacy with Him. At its heart, salvation is a personal relationship that allows us to know God intimately through Jesus—both in our hearts and minds—as we experience His love and grace. This relationship secures our place as His children in His family.

> **And this is eternal life, that they know you, the only true God, and Jesus Christ whom you have sent.**
> **John 17:3 ESV**

Knowing God is not merely an intellectual pursuit but a deeply personal experience rooted in truth. Jesus reconciled believers to God through His sacrifice, making it possible for them to call Him Father. This transformative relationship invites believers to walk with Christ, not as distant followers, but as those who fully belong to Him.

God makes this relationship a reality by sending Holy Spirit to dwell within believers. Through His Spirit, they come to understand God's love, experience His presence, and respond to Him in trust and worship. To illustrate the richness of this relationship, Scripture offers several metaphors:

- **Body:** Believers form the body of Christ, with each member joined to the other in unity and purpose.
- **Temple:** Holy Spirit dwells within believers individually and the church corporately as His sacred dwelling place.
- **Marriage:** The relationship between God and His church is even more intimate and everlasting than marriage. Just as God commands husbands not to abandon their wives, He will never forsake His Bride.

This relationship is underscored by God's standard for human marriage, which reflects His perfect care for His church: He joins man and woman together and declares that no one should separate them. Since God expects so much from human marriage, He will all the more honor His commitment to His Bride, the church.

Jesus Is The Whole Body

The closeness and belonging believers have with Jesus are poetically described by several theologians, reflecting the richness of this relationship:

> As I thought of the Vine and the Branches, what light the blessed Spirit poured directly into my soul. I saw not only that Jesus would never leave me, but that I was a member of His body, of His flesh, and of His bones. The Vine, now I see, is not merely the root, but all: root, stem, branches, leaves, flowers, fruit. Jesus is not only that: He provides the soil, sunshine, air, rain, and ten thousand times more than we have ever dreamed, wished for, or needed. Oh! the joy of seeing this truth.
> SB#28, Huegel, p. 105

Believers are members of the body of Christ, cared for with God's perfect love—a love so enduring that He will never abandon His Bride, the church. Andrew Murray captures this closeness in Jesus's parable of the vine and branches:

> The vine parable teaches us the completeness of the union. So close is the union between the vine and the branch, that each is nothing without the other, that each is wholly and only for the other.
> SB#4, Murray, p. 30

This relationship brings both glory to God and joy to His people. John Calvin emphasizes how Jesus delights in His connection with believers:

> [Ephesians 1:]23. The fulness of him that fills all in all. This is the highest honor of the Church, that, until He is united to us, the Son of God reckons himself in some measure imperfect. What consolation is it for us to learn, that, not until we are along with him, does he possess all his parts, or wish to be regarded as complete!
> SB#22, Calvin, p. 218

What Is Salvation?

Through this relationship, believers share in the fullness of salvation, as explained by Ferguson:

> [Totus Christus] goes back at least as far as Augustine. It is echoed by John Calvin when he tells us that Christ does not consider himself to be complete apart from us. It is language that stresses that all our salvation comes to us from God the Father in Jesus Christ [the Son] and through the Holy Spirit. This salvation is by grace alone, in Christ alone, through faith alone. It is Ephesians 1:3-14, Christ-centered, Trinity-honoring, eternity-rooted, redemption-providing, adoption-experiencing, holiness-producing, assurance-effecting, God-glorifying salvation.
> SB#2, Ferguson, p. 228

Through our relationship with Christ, Holy Spirit elevates believers as sons and daughters of God, heirs of His kingdom, and joint heirs with Christ (Romans 8:15-16). Because of this profound bond, believers can confidently cry out, "Abba, Father!"

FOR REFLECTION AND DISCUSSION

1. In your own words, what is salvation?
2. Why is salvation fully accomplished the moment a person is spiritually born, rather than something that develops over time?
3. What makes salvation (eternal life) an unchangeable reality rather than something temporary, losable, or uncertain?
4. How does understanding salvation as a free gift challenge the idea of earning one's way to heaven?
5. What does it mean to be a new creation in Christ, and how does this affect a believer's identity?
6. How does salvation permanently integrate believers with Christ, and why is this relationship unbreakable?
7. How does Jesus's victory over death guarantee eternal security for believers?
8. Why does the assurance of salvation fluctuate, even though salvation itself remains secure?

9. What role does Holy Spirit play in sustaining salvation, and how does His presence empower believers?
10. How do repentance, obedience, and perseverance result from salvation rather than contribute to it?
11. Why can't a person escape judgment without a personal relationship with Jesus?
12. What do the biblical metaphors of body, temple, and marriage reveal about a believer's connection with Christ?
13. How does union with Christ create a community for believers?
14. How does salvation radically redefine a believer's purpose, calling her into God's kingdom work?

PART 2

Steady Growth In Christ Confirms Salvation

While our union with Christ secures our standing before God, the steady rhythms of growth cause us to fit as living stones in His spiritual temple and give us tangible confirmation that we are truly His. By God's grace, our affections, actions, and attitudes gradually reflect Christ's likeness. This ongoing transformation doesn't earn our salvation but provides clear evidence of its reality.

CHAPTER 3

What Are The Evidences Of Salvation?

What separates a true believer from someone who merely professes faith? The answer lies in a transformed heart that results in unwavering commitment, a new identity, and enduring fruitfulness.

While many may profess faith, true believers are spiritually alive as indicated by Holy Spirit's indwelling and the evidence of transformation. Those who merely profess without this renewal remain spiritually dead and unchanged. Believers have the Spirit within them, while non-believers are without the Spirit.

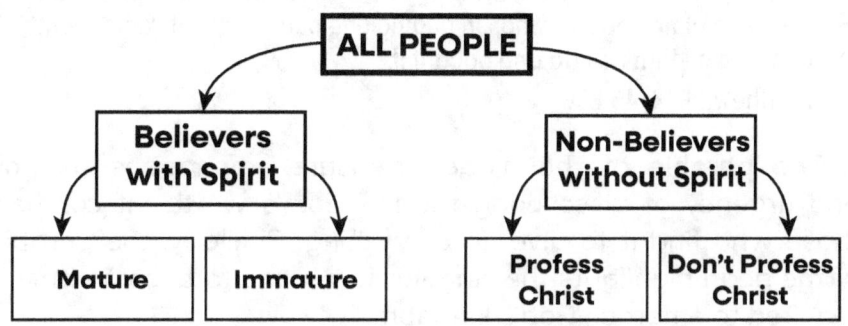

Spiritually alive people don't respond casually to the Gospel. Instead, they undergo a radical reorientation of their lives, marked by an all-in response, a new identity where God dwells within, and a connection to Jesus that bears fruit.

For those unsure of the authenticity of their faith, this chapter will either deepen their assurance of salvation—confidence in their spiritual life—or increase their awareness of their need for salvation—confidence in their spiritual death. Let's explore the first hallmark of salvation.

#1: RADICAL ALL-IN RESPONSE

A spiritually alive person responds to the Gospel with a radical, all-in commitment that reorders her priorities from earthly to heavenly. By contrast, the spiritually dead either respond casually or not at all.

For those who discover God's kingdom, nothing else compares. Jesus expects His followers to be all-in for Him, empowered by Holy Spirit's regenerating work. Christianity is not a passing fad or a short-lived New Year's resolution. Unlike human willpower, the Spirit gives believers enduring strength by transforming hearts from within.

Because God's kingdom is so rare and foreign to the spiritually dead, its discovery inspires an intense and joyful response. Jesus illustrates this with two parables:

> The kingdom of heaven is like treasure hidden in a field, which a man found and covered up. Then in his joy he goes and sells all that he has and buys that field. Again, the kingdom of heaven is like a merchant in search of fine pearls, who, on finding one pearl of great value, went and sold all that he had and bought it.
> Matthew 13:44-46 ESV

The parable of the hidden treasure emphasizes the joy and urgency of discovering the kingdom's worth—it compels those who find it to give up everything. Similarly, the parable of the pearl highlights the singular focus and total commitment required to embrace God's kingdom.

Those who cannot discern its value will hesitate to risk what they have to possess it.

> **No one who puts his hand to the plow and looks back is fit for the kingdom of God.**
> **Luke 9:62 ESV**

Recognizing the value of God's Kingdom is an essential mark of a true believer. God's kingdom is infinitely valuable, far beyond anything earthly. While the things of earth are important, they cannot be compared to the value of knowing Jesus. Those who perceive His worth quickly reorder their priorities, placing the kingdom above all else. This does not mean we become instantly perfect in all we do. Our execution will lag behind our vision of eternal life.

JESUS REQUIRES FULL COMMITMENT

Encountering truth is like tasting a dish but not fully digesting it—there's zero life improvement. But knowing truth is like consuming and internalizing it, allowing it to nourish and change you from within. True believers don't stop at tasting; the Word fuels their spiritual growth.

This difference between encountering and knowing is profound:

- **Encountering:** involves a fleeting or superficial experience, like coming across an idea or meeting a person for the first time. There's no recognition of value or deep engagement. There might even be a strong negative reaction.
- **Knowing:** goes deeper, requiring understanding, familiarity, and meaningful interaction. Study, reflection, and relationship-building satisfy spiritual hunger.

Encountering is like meeting God but feeling no spark of interest, while knowing is building a relationship with Him. Jesus makes this distinction in Matthew 7:21, emphasizing that simply addressing Him as Lord is insufficient. Only those who live by the Spirit's power can "do the will of the Father."

Jesus uses the metaphor of eating and digesting to illustrate this commitment.

> So Jesus said to them, "Truly, truly, I say to you, unless you eat the flesh of the Son of Man and drink his blood, you have no life in you. Whoever feeds on my flesh and drinks my blood has eternal life, and I will raise him up on the last day. For my flesh is true food, and my blood is true drink. Whoever feeds on my flesh and drinks my blood abides in me, and I in him."
> John 6:53-56 ESV

He is speaking of spiritual food that feeds the spirit. He says you must eat (digest) His flesh (His Word) and drink His blood (His life sacrifice) to have eternal life. To digest the Word is to understand it and apply it so that it nourishes the spirit and produces growth and fruit. To drink His sacrifice is to accept forgiveness and live under grace.

Jesus makes clear that believers are radically all-in compared to non-believers. In John 6, believers can digest God's Word, Jesus's life, while non-believers cannot. In Hebrews 6, believers can make use of the rain God sends. In Matthew 13, believers produce abundant fruit, while non-believers are barren.

Being enabled to receive and make use of God's blessings are the marks of a true believer. The spiritually dead reject blessings as useless.

God's Word nourishes the spirit and requires a serious response. The Gospel redefines and reorders a believer's identity, making her life centered on Christ. Does the soil of your heart bear fruit from the rain it receives? Does your spiritual digestive system process the Word of God, or stop at tasting? What would your life look like if you fully trusted Jesus's words? What holds you back?

#2: RADICAL CHANGE IN IDENTITY

True salvation is not simply adopting Christian beliefs—it is a complete change in nature. Without Holy Spirit's indwelling, outward actions may mimic faith, but the core identity remains unchanged.

A pig doesn't wake up one day as a sheep—yet this miraculous transformation is exactly what happens to a believer. Her fundamental nature changes at the deepest level. But even as she becomes a new creation in Christ, her unique personality remains. The primary distinction is Holy Spirit's indwelling. In contrast, the spiritually dead person remains exactly as she has always been, unchanged in nature and aligned with the desires of her flesh. She inevitably returns to her old habits:

> What the true proverb says has happened to them: "The dog returns to its own vomit, and the sow, after washing herself, returns to wallow in the mire."
> 2 Peter 2:22 ESV

H. A. Ironside explains it well:

> If that dog had ever been regenerated and become a sheep, if that sow had ever been changed and become a lamb, neither would have gone back to the filth; but you see, the dog was always a dog, and the sow was always a sow. They were just whitewashed, not washed white, they were never regenerated, and so went back to old things. But the sheep of Christ are different. "They follow me," Jesus says.
> SB#10, Ironside, p. 18

We can be sheep fully under the great Shepherds care, yet drift away. True believers may drift from God, but they are never lost eternally. For example, drifting away because of discouraging events is a temporary condition. A child remains a child—no matter where she is within all of creation. David affirms this in Psalm 139: "Where can I go from Your Spirit? Where can I flee from Your presence?" God never abandons His children.

Warnings Reveal A Person's True Identity

Biblical warnings do not threaten loss of salvation; they reveal it. Rather than creating fear in true believers, warnings expose self-deception in the lost and urge them to seek a real spiritual transformation.

Warnings distinguish between the saved and the lost. Scripture presents salvation as an absolute reality—those whom God saves, He secures. True believers persevere, not because they are strong, but because God holds them securely.

Warnings in Scripture serve three distinct purposes:
1. **To expose false assurance**—urging self-deceived individuals to examine whether they truly belong to Christ (2 Corinthians 13:5).
2. **To refine immature believers**—challenging the weak and carnal to grow in faith rather than remain stagnant. They define the right path and foster a healthy attitude toward sin.
3. **To strengthen the faithful**—affirming salvation and reinforcing perseverance in those who are secure in Christ. They remind believers that persecution is normal and that hardship is to be expected.

Stern warnings help reveal those who are Christians in name only (false believers). Some may profess faith outwardly yet lack the inward, heart transformation that true salvation brings. Though they might clean up their behavior externally, their unregenerate nature remains. True spiritual life always produces an inward, lasting change that bears real fruit.

Warnings act as diagnostic tools, surfacing contradictions within people (Hebrews 4:12). For true believers, they help ensure that God's sheep act like sheep, not dogs or pigs. They also expose immature believers who temporarily behave like dogs and false believers who only appear to be sheep. Hebrews 6 offers a perfect example of such a warning, which we'll explore in Chapter 4.

God intends warnings to boost believers' morale, giving them energy for living out their faith, not create fear of loss. Warnings facilitate cooperation between God and His children, aligning their efforts toward the same goal. Much like guardrails on a winding road or training wheels on a bicycle, they guide believers to grow efficiently while preventing catastrophic failure. God sees salvation through to completion, so warnings aren't meant to threaten believers with actual failure. Instead, they keep believers from confusion and discouragement, ensuring their success.

Some people may encounter the light of Jesus but remain untransformed. They clean the outside of their lives like whitewashed tombs, but remain aligned with the evil one (Matthew 23:27-28). True transformation is evidenced by a heart that craves God and produces lasting change, while the spiritually dead remain enslaved to sin.

Warnings in Scripture act as both guardrails for true believers and challenges to those who lack inward transformation. An immature believer (a "carnal" Christian) struggles with sin but desires to grow spiritually, seeking alignment with God. In contrast, false believers remain unrepentant and unchanged, enslaved to their sinful nature despite outward professions of faith.

Does your life reflect the inward transformation of a child of God, or are changes superficial—merely for appearances before men (Matthew 6:1, 6)?

#3: RADICAL FRUITFULNESS IN CHRIST

Fruitfulness is the natural outflow of spiritual life in Christ. A spiritually alive person, united with Jesus through Holy Spirit, produces fruit that lasts into eternity. But the spiritually dead remain barren and disconnected. They might muster the appearance of spiritual fruit through self-effort, but it will not last.

At the moment of salvation, we can do nothing to earn it. Similarly, after salvation, we can do nothing on our own to produce fruit. Instead, we abide in Christ, allowing Him to bear fruit through us.

In John 15, Jesus shares a powerful metaphor of the vine and branches to encourage His disciples and other true believers. This parable reveals both the necessity of abiding in Him and the assurance of salvation it brings:

> I am the true vine, and my Father is the vinedresser. Every branch in me that does not bear fruit he takes away, and every branch that does bear fruit he prunes, that it may bear more fruit. Already you are clean because of the word that I have spoken to you. Abide in me, and I in you. As the branch cannot bear fruit by itself, unless it abides in the vine, neither can you, unless you abide in me. I am the vine; you are the branches. Whoever abides in me and I in him, he it is that bears much fruit, for apart from me you can do nothing. If anyone does not abide in me he is thrown away like a branch and withers; and the branches are gathered, thrown into the fire, and burned.
> John 15:1-6 ESV

Like many of Jesus's parables, the vine metaphor divides people into two categories: genuine believers and non-believers. This dichotomy eliminates confusion, helping individuals recognize the evidence of spiritual life or death in their own lives.

Everyone is physically born as a "dead branch on the vine." Therefore, when considering if this parable teaches that salvation can be lost, the issue is not how did the branch die, but rather, why isn't it bearing fruit? Jesus must first cleanse the branch for it to become a live branch that will bear fruit. Jesus's purpose in sharing this parable with His disciples is to not only give them eternal life but also instructions on how to make the most of it.

> The thief comes only to steal and kill and destroy. I came that they may have life and have it abundantly.
> John 10:10 ESV

ABIDING IS LIVING

In the context of the vine parable, "abide" can be replaced with "live". For example, "Whoever lives in me and I in him, he it is that bears much fruit, for apart from me you can do nothing." Just as a branch cannot survive apart from the vine, the believer cannot thrive spiritually apart from Christ. This abiding is not static existence, but active dependence and participation in His life. This isn't superficial contact but a dynamic, intimate relationship, that allows life-giving sap to flow from vine to branch.

What Are The Evidences Of Salvation?

The flowing sap represents Holy Spirit working in the believer. Therefore, the branch that does not bear fruit cannot be alive spiritually. The parable might be paraphrased as:

> I am the only life-giving vine. I have many branches. Some are alive; they bear fruit. My Father prunes those to encourage more fruit. Some are dead; they cannot bear fruit. My Father removes those. You are the living branches because I cleansed you with my word. The branch is completely dependent on the vine. The living branches stay connected to me and they bear much fruit. The dead branches do not have a real connection with me. They are worthless, so I throw them away.

We abide in, live in, and are one with Jesus because we have Holy Spirit dwelling with us. The following translations show that these three phrases mean the same thing.

> By this we know that we abide in him and he in us, because he has given us of his Spirit.
> 1 John 4:13 ESV

> God has given us his Spirit. This is how we know we are one with him, just as he is one with us.
> 1 John 4:13 CEV

> And God has given us his Spirit as proof that we live in him and he in us.
> 1 John 4:13 NLT

Believers abide "passively" by acting according to their new nature as a new creation. Just as breathing requires no conscious effort, abiding is the natural result of Christ living within us:

> I have been crucified with Christ. It is no longer I who live, but Christ who lives in me. And the life I now live in the flesh I live by faith in the Son of God, who loved me and gave himself for me.
> Galatians 2:20 ESV

Murray affirms God's activity and our passivity in telling us to abide:

> Wandering one, as it was Jesus who drew you when he said 'Come', so it is Jesus who keeps you when he says, 'Abide.' The grace to come and the grace to abide are both from him alone. The word come, heard, meditated on, accepted, was the cord of love to draw you close; the word abide is the band with which he holds you fast and binds you to himself.
> SB#4, Murray, p. 25-26

The command to abide is necessary because we can know the truth but fail to live in it. We can have money in the bank but not spend it. We can have food on the table but not eat it. The command to abide reminds us to stay close to receive the blessings of closeness. Distance does not nullify salvation, but it does minimize blessing. We "work out our salvation" as we "remember" to abide.

How can we know that the branch in 15:2 and 15:6 is not a true believer who could possibly lose salvation?

- Branches that have Holy Spirit are alive; they bear fruit. Branches that do not are spiritually dead; they will not bear fruit.
- Jesus promises to not abandon the true believer. Jesus came to seek and save the lost; He is able to find and restore those sheep who wander away.
- Jesus says that He chose the disciples to bear fruit and that the fruit would last (15:16).
- Jesus says that He has already cleansed and pruned the disciples, implying that they are already bearing fruit (15:3). What could have been cleansed? Their sinful nature. They have been made righteous.
- Jesus says He told the disciples this so they can experience abundant, overflowing joy (15:11).

The most worshipful, thankful believer is the secure believer. Assurance leads to praise of God and joy in living.[1]

---

1. thegospelcoalition.org/essay/assurance

ABIDING IS DEPENDING

The essence of union with Christ lies in complete mutual dependence. The vine and branch can only fulfill their purpose together, so they remain wholly connected. A branch does not strive to produce fruit—it simply receives life and nourishment from the vine. Murray captures this truth:

> Without the vine the branch can do nothing. To the vine it owes its right of place in the vineyard, its life and its fruitfulness. And so the Lord says, "Without me you can do nothing." The believer can each day be pleasing to God only in that which he does through the power of Christ dwelling in him.
> SB#4, Murray, p. 30

Just as a branch relies entirely on the vine for life and fruit, believers depend on Christ's presence and power. Holy Spirit continually nourishes and sustains them, enabling spiritual growth and fruitfulness. And yet, just as believers depend on Christ, He has chosen to depend on His people to carry out His work in the world. As Murray also points out:

> Without the branch the vine can also do nothing, A vine without branches can bear no fruit. No less indispensable than the vine to the branch, is the branch to the vine.
> SB#4, Murray, p. 30

Christ, in His grace, has ordained that believers are essential to His mission. He works through them to dispense His blessings, spread His truth, and reveal His love. This profound unity means that just as believers find life in Christ, He has chosen to use them as instruments to bear spiritual fruit.

God chooses us and we respond. God blesses us and we bless him. His love always comes first, a necessary example, allowing believers to fully participate in His divine nature and plans (1 John 4:19).

ABIDING IS RELATING

Abiding is the mark of a true believer who is receiving sap (life-giving Spirit) from the vine (Jesus). Those who only profess belief, without true heart-faith, may appear attached to Him, but in reality no sap flows. Their "fruit" is tied on by self-effort and lacks the genuine, enduring quality that flows from a Spirit-filled life. Only believers who are cleansed and pruned of disease (sin) by God will produce abundant, genuine spiritual fruit.

While "abide" can mean endure, remain, or stay, it speaks most powerfully of an intimate connection (SB#12, Rosscup, p. 111). This connection distinguishes those who pretend to be in Christ from those who truly belong to Him. Jesus makes this distinction clear in Matthew 7:21–23, showing the dichotomy between those He "never knew" and those He has known since before creation.

Abiding is like breathing—it's not optional. It's the constant, life-sustaining relationship with Christ that nourishes believers and enables them to grow. To abide is to live in continual trust and dependence on Holy Spirit for strength, guidance, and fruitfulness. It means staying connected to Christ through prayer and Scripture.

Abiding is self-awareness of one's connection with Jesus and His power to keep (never cast out) the believer despite any shortcomings. It is faith, trust, and dependence focused on God's promise to completely save.

Consider how Peter's abiding relationship with Jesus is revealed in Matthew 14:22–33. When Peter looks to Jesus in faith and focuses on His voice, he accomplishes the impossible: walking on water. But when his faith gives way to doubt, Peter begins to sink. Even in failure, Jesus's presence and power hold him fast. This interaction shows that abiding in Christ is not about perfection, but about dependence. When we falter, Jesus reaches out His hand to lift us again.

The power of abiding lies in trusting Jesus through both faith and failure. "Apart from me you can do nothing." Peter's temporary struggle with fear and doubt did not jeopardize his relationship with Jesus. In his moment of weakness, Jesus saved him and restored him. Though Peter was not "fruitful" during his doubt, this moment didn't disqualify him from bearing fruit later. Peter, who struggled with fear and even denial (Matthew 26:69–75), ultimately became a bold leader of the early church. This demonstrates that because we abide in Christ, God can transform our failures into evidence of spiritual life and ongoing growth.

> **The literal branch abides by being there 'positionally'. The disciples abide by being there 'relationally'.**
> **SB#12, Rosscup, p. 165, quoting Mickelson in Interpreting the Bible**

Abiding is continually making oneself available to Jesus—maintaining close fellowship and recognizing that He is always present within us through the Spirit. While the connection is constant, its quality may vary.

> **The difference between Christians is the matter of the consistency, degree, depth, and richness of intimacy with the Lord.**
> **SB#12, Rosscup, p. 171**

Time spent in intimate connection with Jesus also plays a significant role in spiritual maturity. The more we consciously abide, the more deeply we grow in faith and fruitfulness.

ABIDING IS REPENTING

Saving faith is resilient, enduring even through moments of doubt or emotional turmoil. Psalm 51 presents David as a steadfast believer who sinned. He had faith, but he expressed emotional concern for his salvation (51:12). He confessed his sin with a repentant heart—a sign of a true believer. He knew he deserved judgment, yet he also knew God as merciful (51:1). David's lament is without pretense. His sincere concern is not evidence of fatal doubt in God but of lasting salvation.

Doubt does not mean a person lacks salvation—it is an opportunity to deepen trust in Christ's unwavering grip. Assurance comes from recognizing God's steadfast mercy, not personal perfection.

For the discouraged and doubtful, do they need to remain unsure? No, they need a quiet assurance—a steady, unmoved faith. Everyone boasts in something. The prideful boast in their own efforts, unaware of their self-deception. But a branch draws life from the vine and has no reason to boast in itself. The believer who boasts in Christ knows her place—wholly dependent, fully connected, and joyfully grateful for the gift of salvation.

David's prayer in Psalm 51:10–12 exemplifies this humility and dependence:

> Create in me a clean heart, O God, and renew a right spirit within me. Cast me not away from your presence, and take not your Holy Spirit from me. Restore to me the joy of your salvation, and uphold me with a willing spirit.
> Psalm 51:10–12 ESV

Even in his brokenness, David clings to God's mercy, pleading not only for forgiveness but for restored joy and strength. His response mirrors that of the tax collector in Luke 18:13, who simply prays, "O God, be merciful to me, for I am a sinner." Both David and the tax collector recognize their unworthiness, but rather than despair, they turn to God in faith.

This is in contrast to the other man in Luke 18, a Pharisee, who exalted his own efforts and boasted in his self-righteousness. We need to recognize the internal brokenness—the sin sickness of self-sufficiency—but rejoice that God has provided the cure.

It is not the Pharisee but the humbled man who receives God's favor because he "came clean" before Him. This demonstrates that God values self-awareness over self-righteousness. Assurance comes not through our works or flawless behavior but through dependence on God's mercy, as we humbly embrace the salvation He freely provides.

ABIDING IS RESTING

To abide is to receive what we need to accomplish God's work. When we rest in Jesus, He draws us into a fruit-producing life that nourishes others.

What Are The Evidences Of Salvation?

True fruit doesn't grow from self-effort but from how much we cooperate with God's work within us. Jesus reminds us in Matthew 11:28–30 that His yoke is easy and His burden is light, because He does the heavy lifting. Spiritual growth is about letting Christ work through us, not striving alone.

Jesus said, "Apart from me you can do nothing." But this doesn't mean believers do nothing. We are partners with Christ—His very hands and feet—to accomplish His plans. As 1 Peter 4:11 reminds us, we serve not by our own power but with the strength God provides, ensuring that all things bring glory to Him through Christ.

Fruit takes time to grow. A living tree develops gradually but surely. If you are growing, you are alive. The more you remain close to Christ, the more fruit you will produce.

Abiding means resting in Christ's finished work rather than striving to prove ourselves worthy. It's a conscious trust—leaning entirely on Jesus and believing in His ability to sustain us. He is our Sabbath rest, freeing us from the pressure to earn what He has already given. The "narrow path" is keeping our eyes fixed on Him, walking in faith rather than relying on our own effort.

True fruit is never only for personal growth—it nourishes others. Abiding leads to Christlike love, kindness, and generosity, drawing others to God's grace. This is fruit that lasts.

If you are uncertain about your salvation, remember that salvation is entirely God's internal work—He calls, transforms, and nourishes for His purposes. Instead of striving for assurance, seek Him. Trust that He alone brings life to those who abide in Him. Jesus does not ask you to carry the weight yourself; He invites you to rest in Him. Ask Him for faith, for strength to persevere, and for dependence that produces fruitfulness that lasts.

CONCLUSION

True believers abide in Christ, recognizing He is both their foundation and sustainer. Spiritual growth happens because of His power at work within them. He nourishes, prunes, and shapes His people, ensuring they bear lasting fruit.

Abiding leads to assurance—not a life free of struggle, but the deep confidence that Christ holds His children securely. Just as He reached out to lift Peter from the water, He lifts every believer who falters. Salvation rests on God's perfect work, not human perfection. If you belong to Him, He will never cast you out.

If you are His, live in the truth of your abiding relationship with Him. Salvation is not just believing a set of doctrines—it is a radical all-in response to Christ and a new identity shaped by His presence within you. Open His Word, reflect on His promises, and trust in His unchanging love. He will draw you deeper into the joy of knowing Him. As you abide, He will bear fruit through you to bless others and bring glory to God.

FOR REFLECTION AND DISCUSSION

1. What distinguishes a true believer ("washed white") from someone who merely professes faith ("a whitewashed tomb")?
2. Why does Jesus compare salvation to discovering hidden treasure or a priceless pearl?
3. Why does a radical all-in response to salvation demonstrate true spiritual life?
4. In what ways does salvation change a believer's identity, making her a new creation?
5. How does the vine and branches metaphor illustrate the cooperative relationship believers have with Christ?
6. What does it mean to abide in Christ, and how can believers know they are truly abiding?
7. How do warnings in Scripture have distinct purposes for believers (with true faith) and non-believers (including those who might have false assurance)?
8. Why does abiding in Christ lead to assurance, rather than fear of losing salvation?
9. How does the story of Peter walking on water illustrate abiding as dependence rather than perfection?

10. What role does pruning play in a believer's growth, and how should it be understood in spiritual life?
11. Why can believers do nothing apart from Christ, and how does this shape their understanding of fruitfulness?
12. How does abiding involve relationship rather than mere obedience or duty?
13. What does Jesus mean when He says His yoke is easy and His burden is light?
14. How have you responded to the Gospel? What evidences do you see?

CHAPTER 4

How Does A Fertile Heart Reveal True Salvation?

The state of the heart determines the authenticity of salvation. Scripture does not present salvation as ambiguous—it is either rooted in fertile soil or lost in barren ground. Jesus taught in the Parable of the Sower that a heart's condition determines its receptivity to God's truth.

Except for Christ securing salvation through His sacrifice and His eventual second coming, nothing is more eagerly anticipated—nothing carries more weight or glorifies God more—than the unveiling of who will be saved and who will be condemned (Romans 8:18–19). Life is like a funnel, wide at the start but narrowing as time runs out. It presses each person toward judgment day, where only two outcomes remain: mercy or condemnation, until one final verdict is revealed based on one's relationship with Christ.

Salvation is never lost—it is proven as either genuine or false. Even the smallest amount of true faith is sufficient for eternal life, while even the greatest display of false faith is spiritually worthless. For believers, the proving process strengthens faith.

For non-believers, it exposes their lack of true faith rather than strengthening false assurance.

Salvation can never be lost for the one who is regenerated and indwelled by Holy Spirit. But those who profess Christ without Holy Spirit can lose their in-name-only status, which would be a positive step forward because they would be more likely to see their clear need for Jesus.

GOD SORTS PEOPLE BY THEIR RELATIONSHIP WITH HIM

The Bible calls believers to remain steadfast in their hope, but calls non-believers to become disillusioned with their emptiness without Christ. Salvation is not dependent on human performance but on endurance. **Performance is motivated by fear of failure, whereas endurance is about holding onto truth.** The difference is profound. Performance is human-based but endurance is God-based. God is intimately bound to those He has saved but will condemn those who reject Him. Therefore, knowing for certain that you are saved is of utmost importance.

Because salvation is all-or-nothing, the gap between being lost and being saved is immeasurably wide. This reflects a high view of salvation—one that honors the magnitude of what only God can accomplish. In contrast, believing that humans can contribute anything of value to closing the gap reflects a low view—as if salvation required human will or effort. But human effort can neither secure salvation nor undo it. Only God's resurrection power can bridge the chasm.

THE BIBLE'S FOCUS ON SORTING AND SEPARATION

One way to understand the Bible is through its ability to divide humanity into two distinct groups:
1. **Those who are God's children**—called, saved, and eternally secure.
2. **Those who are not**—the wicked who belong to the devil.

God favored His children in the Old Testament. He speaks of the two distinct categories:

> "On the day when I act," says the Lord Almighty, "they will be my treasured possession. I will spare them, just as a father has compassion and spares his son who serves him. And you will again see the distinction between the righteous and the wicked, between those who serve God and those who do not.
> Malachi 3:17-18 NIV

To accomplish this separation, Scripture emphasizes two core truths:
1. The identity of Jesus Christ as the one and only true God.
2. Humanity's need for Jesus Christ as Lord and Savior.

Those who are true believers wholeheartedly believe these truths. The Bible assures them that they are permanently saved. But it also shouts out to non-believers, convicting and urging them toward salvation as God allows. The Bible's purpose is twofold:
1. To strengthen true believers in their assurance.
2. To convict non-believers, including false believers, revealing their lack of genuine faith.

JESUS'S FOCUS ON SORTING AND SEPARATION

Throughout the New Testament, Jesus's teachings emphasize the division between those who are for Him and those who are against Him. The absolute, categorical nature of salvation is reinforced through Jesus's parables that distinguish between:
- **Sheep and goats** (Matthew 25:31–46)—revealing the separation of believers and non-believers.
- **Believers and non-believers** (John 3:18)—believers are not condemned (will be in heaven) and non-believers are condemned (will be in hell).
- **Wheat and weeds** (Matthew 13:24–30)—illustrating the distinction between God's children and the devil's children.

A person is either saved or not. Both believers and non-believers may sin, but there is a critical distinction:
- **Believers:** Sin no longer dominates their lives. Through Jesus's sacrifice, the eternal consequences of sin are absorbed, allowing believers to refocus on acting from the Spirit within them.
- **Non-believers:** Sin dominates their lives completely, leaving them enslaved to destructive desires and unable to crave God. Their future is hopeless apart from Christ.

A person cannot be partially saved, partially a child of God, just as a woman cannot be partially pregnant. Jesus describes this all-or-nothing reality in the parable of the weeds and wheat:

> The field is the world, and the good seed is the sons of the kingdom. The weeds are the sons of the evil one.
> Matthew 13:38 ESV

The Bible presents salvation as a clear, definitive reality. People either live for self or for God:
- Those living for self may do "good works" or make "positive contributions," but this does **not** save them.
- Those living for God may stumble or sin, but this does **not** unsave them.

True salvation results in abiding in Christ, and those who are in Him remain secure. The Bible does not describe salvation as a fluctuating state, but as an eternal reality rooted in God's sovereign power and choice (John 10:28-29).

THE PARABLE OF THE SOWER'S SORTING

God is the great gardener who is responsible for ensuring salvation is robust (John 15:1-2). Likewise, the Parable of the Sower illustrates the sovereign work of God in cultivating hearts for salvation. It highlights three false salvations before revealing the characteristics of true, fruitful faith. The contrast is vivid:

> Listen! A farmer went out to plant some seeds. As he scattered them across his field, some seeds fell on a footpath, and the birds came

and ate them. Other seeds fell on shallow soil with underlying rock. The seeds sprouted quickly because the soil was shallow. But the plants soon wilted under the hot sun, and since they didn't have deep roots, they died. Other seeds fell among thorns that grew up and choked out the tender plants. Still other seeds fell on fertile soil, and they produced a crop that was thirty, sixty, and even a hundred times as much as had been planted!
Matthew 13:3-8 NLT

The first three examples describe circumstances that are insufficient for salvation:
1. **The Path:** Hardness of heart that blocks out the message.
2. **The Rock:** Seeking of benefits without desiring a relationship with Jesus.
3. **The Thorns:** Holding more tightly to worldly concerns than heavenly priorities.

Each of these examples reflects a self-reliant mindset that resists surrender to God. These hearts, unwilling to depend on His grace, remain unfit for His kingdom and unable to embrace true salvation (Luke 9:62).

Many have professed Christ and even engaged in ministry, yet have never truly been born again. The person who does not persevere was a Christian in name only.

The evidence of true salvation is perseverance—not perfection. When believers doubt, stumble, or even sin, God remains their sustainer, ensuring their endurance to the end. Those born again as new creations persevere because they are upheld by His power. Though they may falter, God's Spirit lifts them, strengthens them, and keeps them on the right path (Proverbs 24:16; Isaiah 41:10; Psalm 37:24; 1 Peter 5:10, Colossians 1:11).

As God preserves us with perfect love, He also matures us, leading us from fear to deeply rooted faith. Thus, while the Parable of the Sower exposes the pitfalls of shallow, self-reliant interest, it also beckons us to thank God for a heart that is deeply rooted in God's grace—a fertile soil where His Word can flourish and sustain us through every trial.

The Believer: Roots Grow In Fertile Soil

Being healthily rooted means commitment to one's faith from the depths of one's heart. It goes beyond surface-level belief and involves an authentic personal relationship with God. A person with deep roots has a solid understanding of her faith, built on foundational principles and truths. She is not easily swayed by doubts or external influences. Deep roots provide stability in times of adversity. Just as a tree with deep roots stands firm during a storm, a deeply rooted person remains steadfast in her beliefs through life's challenges.

The deeply rooted person continually seeks to grow and mature in faith. This involves regular study, reflection, prayer, and application of spiritual teachings. A deeply rooted faith helps a person resist temptations. She is less likely to stumble because her connection to her faith is resilient. Just as deep roots allow a tree to bear fruit, a mature believer exhibits the fruits of her faith through her actions, character, and relationships. This includes qualities like love, kindness, patience, and integrity.

Overall, being deeply rooted in faith means having a robust internalized belief system that goes beyond superficial knowledge. The enduring connection with Jesus withstands life's trials and remains fruitful over time. The believer benefits from and appreciates her God-given faith, through which spiritual truth is not only grasped intellectually, but also emotionally and spiritually lived out from the heart.

The Non-Believer: Roots Can't Grow In Infertile Soil

Some people profess faith, but their actions and lack of endurance reveal the absence of true transformation. Though they claim belief, their lack of spiritual fruit shows that they have not been born of God. Their connection to Christ is superficial, not rooted in the life-giving relationship required for enduring faith.

The Parable of the Sower vividly illustrates this reality. The person who fails to grow is illustrated by a seed in rocky soil. Jesus explains that the rocky ground represents those who initially receive the idea of salvation with joy, but because they have no room for roots, they quickly fall away when trouble or persecution arises. Their initial enthusiasm cannot endure hardships because it has room for the benefits of salvation but no room for the giver of salvation. Without a firm foundation, their joy fades, and they fall away, proving their faith was never established.

This shallow faith is like a sugar high—an initial burst of energy and excitement that quickly fades due to a lack of essential nourishment. Just as a sugar high cannot sustain the body through a marathon, the fleeting joy of rocky-ground faith lacks the enduring power of true transformation. The energy goes above ground rather than into roots. When challenges come, their faith withers because it was not grounded in a real relationship with Christ.

This same reasoning can be repeated for the "hard" and the "thorns" soil. Like the rocky soil, they do not have room for the spiritual life to grow. Superficial false-believers desire the benefits of salvation without embracing its calling, cost of discipleship, or relationship with God. They are drawn to the idea of escaping hell but resist surrendering to Jesus and following Him in His passionate suffering.

> Then Jesus said to his disciples, "If any of you wants to be my follower, you must give up your own way, take up your cross, and follow me. If you try to hang on to your life, you will lose it. But if you give up your life for my sake, you will save it. And what do you benefit if you gain the whole world but lose your own soul? Is anything worth more than your soul? For the Son of Man will come with his angels in the glory of his Father and will judge all people according to their deeds."
> Matthew 16:24-27 NLT

Shallow, self-centered motivation seeks lazy comfort rather than transformation and commitment. In contrast, the true disciple will suffer to the point of death, if necessary. True salvation produces lasting roots, grounded in a relationship with Jesus, enabling believers to endure trials and bear fruit.

GOD CALLS IMMATURE BELIEVERS TO SPIRITUAL GROWTH

Hebrews 6 calls for a deeper spiritual maturity in the faith, warns non-believers of the perils of abandoning it, and reassures believers of the reliability of God's promises. The author exhorts believers to grow toward maturity, leaving behind spiritual stagnation and producing a life marked by discernment and fruitful engagement with God's truth.

> 1 Therefore let us leave the elementary doctrine of Christ and go on to maturity, not laying again a foundation of repentance from dead works and of faith toward God, and of instruction about washings, the laying on of hands, the resurrection of the dead, and eternal judgment. And this we will do if God permits.
> 4 For it is impossible, in the case of those who have once been enlightened, who have tasted the heavenly gift, and have shared in the Holy Spirit, and have tasted the goodness of the word of God and the powers of the age to come, and then have fallen away, to restore them again to repentance, since they are crucifying once again the Son of God to their own harm and holding him up to contempt.
> 7 For land that has drunk the rain that often falls on it, and produces a crop useful to those for whose sake it is cultivated, receives a blessing from God. But if it bears thorns and thistles, it is worthless and near to being cursed, and its end is to be burned. Though we speak in this way, yet in your case, beloved, we feel sure of better things—things that belong to salvation. For God is not unjust so as to overlook your work and the love that you have shown for his name in serving the saints, as you still do. And we desire each one of you to show the same earnestness to have the full assurance of hope until the end, so that you may not be sluggish, but imitators of those who through faith and patience inherit the promises.
> Hebrews 6:1-12 ESV

FIVE INTERPRETATIONS OF HEBREWS 6:4-6

Hebrews 6 presents one of the most debated passages regarding salvation and apostasy. Understanding its context is crucial to discerning its meaning. The following five views summarize how people attempt to understand it. I briefly explain all five interpretations before I provide my view along with a detailed analysis and conclusion.

1. The Loss Of Salvation View (invalid)

This interpretation suggests that the passage warns true believers about the possibility of falling away and losing their salvation. It emphasizes the seriousness of apostasy and the irreversible consequences of abandoning the faith after receiving the truth.

This interpretation is incorrect because it misses the major biblical teaching about a person's heart. The immediate context of Hebrews 6 shows this warning is meant to divide people into "fertile" and "infertile." True believers have fertile hearts—they endure. The author affirms that immature believers have a genuine faith (6:9) and will endure (Hebrews 10:39). Those who believe this view cannot provide a specific sin that disqualifies believers. They only propose a general abandonment.

2. The Loss Of Rewards View (invalid)

In this interpretation, the passage is not about losing salvation but about losing rewards. It warns believers that falling away results in a loss of rewards and blessings in this life and in eternity, but not in the loss of salvation itself.

Given the serious tone of Hebrews and surrounding context of Hebrews 6, the rest of Hebrews, and the Bible in general, this interpretation has little if any support.

3. The False Believer View (valid)

According to this perspective, the individuals described in the passage are not true believers but those who have only superficially experienced the Christian faith. They have tasted the heavenly gift but have not digested it. They have had the abundant rain of God's blessings, but produce nothing of value. Their falling away demonstrates that they were never genuinely saved. This view is also labeled "profession only" or "Christian in name only." The rocky soil illustrates it well.

4. The Jewish Context View (valid)

Some scholars argue that the passage is limited in scope to addressing Jewish Christians who were considering returning to Judaism. The warning is about the futility and danger of abandoning the new covenant in Christ to return to the old covenant practices. The author goes through great lengths to encourage maturity instead of returning to the incomplete, insufficient, shadow Old Covenant system.

This corrects bad theology. Christ is the only way. When you already have Christ securely, don't reject the real deal only to return to the old, inferior way.

Jewish people had a difficult time letting go of the Old Covenant. The transition to the new covenant was confusing. The book of Hebrews helps them complete the transition by clearly articulating the New Covenant as the only option for a true relationship with God.

Jewish professors were at a crossroads. They should not return to the former ways and risk falling away from the new covenant. Returning to the previous system, even a dual system, tarnishes the name of Christ, publicly humiliating Him. It is a horrible witness. It displays a lack of faith and would be unbelief in the sufficiency of Jesus.

The warnings against returning to the Old Covenant highlight its insufficiency for salvation. Hebrews repeatedly underscores that Christ's New Covenant alone secures eternal life—providing assurance for those tempted by old traditions.

The mature believer trusts that Jesus's sacrifice is complete—she counts on it absolutely. There is no benefit from returning to the old covenant sacrificial system. It never was able to take away sins. It only pointed forward to Jesus's sacrifice.

The original audience is Jewish Christians and their only hope is Christ. But scripture is for teaching everyone—the principles it expounds are generalizable to all people to (a) help believers grow in confidence in the faith or (b) help non-believers see that rejecting Christ is a spiritual death sentence.

5. The Hypothetical Warning View (mixed)

This view proposes that the passage presents a hypothetical scenario to emphasize the importance of perseverance in faith. It serves as a strong warning to believers about the dire consequences of apostasy, even though the author knows that true believers will not actually fall away.

The people who support this view believe that "tasting" spiritual blessings is sufficient for salvation. So if believers then reject Christ and fall away, they cannot be restored to repentance and therefore have lost salvation. It's hypothetical because a genuine believer would never reject Christ.

This interpretation is invalid because it wrongly determines that "taste" means fully consume and convert to Christianity. But it is valid because it upholds the integrity of a secure salvation. The author effectively uses a warning to catch immature believers in their ignorance, causing them to feel the foolishness of considering options other than relying on Christ.

TASTE MEANS SUPERFICIAL ENCOUNTER

Considering verses 7 and 8, there are only two outcomes:
1. Eternal life (verse 7)
2. Eternal death (verse 8)

Given these two extreme options, the key to understanding Hebrews 6 is found in whether the tasting in verse 5 is sufficient to define a true conversion experience, or it is not sufficient, indicating only a superficial encounter.

If we assume "taste" indicates "true believer", it would be impossible for the true believer to fall away because:
- it would mean Christ failed to save all true believers (John 10)
- the true believer is the good, fertile soil that bears fruit and will be saved (6:7, 6:9, Matthew 13:3-8)
- Christ only needed to die once; He won't die again (6:6, 9:28, 10:10)

In Chapter 3, we learned that Jesus requires believers to be fully committed to eating His Word, not merely tasting it. Jesus

calls His disciples into a deep relationship—one that goes beyond momentary exposure to the truth. Therefore, we can conclude that "taste" indicates non-believer. Anyone who rejects Christ will not be saved because:
- without Christ, sin continues without a sacrificial payment (6:8, 9:22, 10:26-31)
- all other soils (hard, rocky, thorny) do not produce fruit (Matthew 13:18-23)

This reinforces that verses 4 through 8 present a clear warning for believers but a threat only for non-believers.

HOW SORTING CLARIFIES HEBREWS 6:4-6

God does not sort randomly. He does so intentionally, sovereignly, according to His perfect will. His sorting is absolute—you are either in or out, for Jesus or against Jesus, saved or not saved (Matthew 12:30; Luke 9:50). Since this is a dominant theme in Scripture, it should guide our interpretation of passages like Hebrews 6:4-6.

Hebrews 6:4-6 teaches that those who have tasted the heavenly gift, and then fallen away, cannot be restored again to repentance; it is impossible. Without the sorting principle, this passage could be misread as proof that salvation can be lost. However, sorting into absolute categories—saved or unsaved—clarifies the meaning.

The saved are permanently secure because salvation is rooted in God's sovereign choice. The unsaved may have been exposed to God's truth but were never transformed. Their rejection reveals that they were never among the elect.

> They went out from us, but they were not of us; for if they had been of us, they would have continued with us. But they went out, that it might become plain that they all are not of us.
> 1 John 2:19 ESV

Hebrews 6 is not warning believers about losing salvation; rather, it is separating those who merely experienced the external blessings of Christianity from those who truly belong to Christ.

This aligns with Jesus's statement in Matthew 7:21-23—many will claim to have followed Him, yet He will declare, "I never knew you." The warning of Hebrews 6:4-6 serves to expose false assurance and reinforce the separation between true believers and those who fall away.

By applying the biblical sorting principle, Hebrews 6:4-6 is not a passage about believers drifting too far, but about revealing who was never truly saved in the first place.

This is why it is so important for believers to make their calling and election sure. The more sure a believer is of her faith, the more effective she is for fulfilling Christ's purposes. But we must be clear that spiritual growth does not save a person, it proves a person is saved. A living tree grows but a dead tree does not. A spiritually alive person will grow. Peter encourages believers to work in cooperation with the spiritual powers given to believers, and not be ignorant of this (2 Peter 1:1-11).

THE FERTILE, INFERTILE VIEW

After careful study, Hebrews 6 is best interpreted by whether a person has a fertile or an infertile heart. This view is compatible with the False Believer view, Jewish Context view, and to some degree the Hypothetical Warning view.

To highlight the importance of spiritual growth, the author contrasts immature believers, mature believers, and non-believers.

- **Immature believers**, though at risk of stagnation, remain part of God's family and are capable of growth. Their faith, while genuine, may lack the discernment and fruitfulness that come with spiritual maturity.
- **Mature believers** demonstrate growth through perseverance, understanding, and the ability to bear abundant, lasting spiritual fruit as evidence of their connection to Christ.
- **Non-believers**—including those who superficially engage with the Gospel—do not possess true faith. Their hearts

remain untransformed, and their lives are ultimately barren, unable to produce the fruit that stems from a relationship with God.

Expanding on this distinction, immature believers have fertile hearts but lack the intimacy with God required to produce abundant fruit. Maturity develops through regular engagement with Christ, as believers seek a deeper understanding of the truth found in Scripture. In contrast, apostate non-believers are spiritually infertile, completely devoid of genuine intimacy with Christ. They are limited to intellectual facts about Christ.

A Fertile Heart All believers have a new spiritual heart capable of receiving God's word.		**An Infertile Heart** All non-believers have the old hardened heart, incapable of understanding God's word.
Mature Believer Has mastered the basics of the Christian faith and continues to grow in understanding the deeper truths.	**Immature Believer** Is stuck because of a lack of understanding of foundational truths about the Christian faith.	**Apostate** Has experienced spiritual blessings, but cannot accept them. Anyone who continues to reject Christ's sacrifice is "near to being cursed."
Abundant Fruit Intimate knowing of Christ and fellowship with Holy Spirit produce much fruit.	**Minimal Fruit** Limited effort and understanding of the truth weaken the connection and limit fruit.	**No Fruit** Barrenness and a lack of connection with Christ make fruit impossible.
	Author's Message You are immature believers. Grow up! Only non-believers give up.	

Building on this contrast, non-believers illustrate the sobering reality of infertility despite encountering God. While God's seed is inherently potent, their hearts are infertile, unable to receive and respond to His truth. Despite God providing enlightenment, a taste of heaven, an experience of Holy Spirit, and a basic understanding of Scripture, these individuals remain spiritually barren. This highlights a sobering reality: God has fully communicated who He is, yet the heart must change to receive Him. Without transformation, His blessings cannot take root and bear fruit.

This infertility reaches its fullest expression in apostates, who decisively reject God's transformative work. Apostates exemplify barrenness as they are "dead in the womb," unable to produce spiritual fruit. Though they may momentarily "see" who God is, their rejection forfeits the only way to true spiritual life. By rejecting Jesus's sacrifice, they imply that He must do more—even to the point of sacrificing Himself again—for them to understand. Yet the issue does not lie with God but with their own hardened hearts. God's Word is potent and produces fruit without fail where it is received, but the spiritually dead remain unwilling and ultimately fruitless. To taste the truth but outright reject it, all but finally condemns them. To be ignorant of the truth would be better (2 Peter 2:20-22).

The phrase "fallen away" in Hebrews 6:6 refers to a deliberate and decisive rejection of Christ after having been exposed to the truth of the Gospel. It describes individuals who have experienced significant spiritual blessings but ultimately turn away from God. This falling away is not a momentary lapse or struggle in faith but a hardened, willful abandonment of the truth they once encountered. If they become acquainted with Christ and reject Him, there is nothing else that can be done to further persuade them, beyond what they already know.

This is similar to the story of Lazarus (Luke 16:19–31). In the parable, the rich man, now in torment, pleads with Abraham to send Lazarus to warn his brothers so they might avoid his fate. Abraham responds that they already have "Moses and the Prophets" (the Scriptures), and if they do not listen to them, they will not be convinced even if someone rises from the dead. This underscores the sufficiency of God's revelation and the hardness of heart that leads to rejection of His truth.

Similarly, Hebrews 6 describes individuals who have been exposed to God's truth—yet fall away. Their eyes-wide-open rejection of God's salvation through Jesus leaves no further means of repentance. Like the rich man's brothers, they have been given all they need to conceive, to take in the truth, but their hardened hearts prevent them from doing so.

Both passages emphasize human responsibility in responding to God's revelation. The apostate and the rich man's brothers illustrate the tragic reality of rejecting God's truth despite having ample opportunity to embrace it. These warnings serve as sobering reminders of the importance of a genuine, transformative response to God's Word.

In stark contrast to the apostate, spiritually alive believers thrive through their connection to God's Spirit, producing fruit that endures. True believers, transformed by God's grace, can grow toward maturity, bearing fruit as evidence of spiritual life. Maturity is not instantaneous; it is a continual process that requires perseverance, learning, and abiding in Christ. Believers' growth reflects the potent work of God's Word in their fertile hearts, allowing His blessings to flourish and sustain them as they endure trials and produce lasting fruit.

Regardless of which valid interpretation resonates most with you, the core message remains: salvation is real, and God is faithful to His promises.

SALVATION IS REAL—GOD IS TRUSTWORTHY

No interpretation can change that a person is either a believer or she is not. If she is, then she has enduring faith. A believer does not shrink back, but has faith that endures (Hebrews 10:39). She shouldn't become "psyched out" of her confidence in God's promises.

> When God made his promise to Abraham, since there was no one greater for him to swear by, he swore by himself, saying, "I will surely bless you and give you many descendants." And so after waiting patiently, Abraham received what was promised. People swear by someone greater than themselves, and the oath confirms what is said and puts an end to all argument. Because God wanted to make the unchanging nature of his purpose very clear to the heirs of what was promised, he confirmed it with an oath. God did this so that, by

two unchangeable things in which it is impossible for God to lie, we who have fled to take hold of the hope set before us may be greatly encouraged. We have this hope as an anchor for the soul, firm and secure. It enters the inner sanctuary behind the curtain, where our forerunner, Jesus, has entered on our behalf. He has become a high priest forever, in the order of Melchizedek.
Hebrews 6:13-20 NIV

Just as God's promise to Abraham was unwavering, so is His promise to save those who believe in Christ. This unshakable hope anchors the soul, giving believers confidence to endure. Their patient perseverance is worth the wait.

The following is my verse-by-verse interpretation and commentary of Hebrews 6:

Hebrews 6:1-2

Don't remain an infant in the faith. Stop questioning (being anxious about, equivocating about, being wishy-washy about) the basic teachings of the faith. Accept the truth and move beyond it. Build on the foundation, the Gospel.

Hebrews 6:3

But realize that God is in control of whether a person can move on to maturity. God chooses who He will enlighten with understanding (1 Corinthians 3:6).

Hebrews 6:4-6

The person who gives up on Jesus's sacrifice and the Spirit's workings has no other options for salvation. Whoever trashes the Son of God has no hope of ever being saved. Those who reject Jesus publicly declare that His sacrificial death was not sufficient.

Hebrews 6:4-8

Those who encounter God, but reject Him (give up on Him, turn away from Him) are like land that encounters necessary rain but produces only weeds. The problem is not with the rain, but with the soil. God has blessed with rain, but has not blessed the soil. Those who hear the message but fail to grow have only a superficial understanding. If nothing of value is growing, then faith is not authentic.

Christ's sacrifice was sufficient; it does not need repeating. To understand it but reject it leaves no other options for salvation. Christ's one sacrifice is enough, therefore, one true repentance is enough. To declare Christ's sacrifice as insufficient or invalid, and then leave the faith, would require Christ to sacrifice a second time and a second repentance. Therefore, a person has only two options (1) to accept Christ's one and only sacrifice as sufficient and continue to mature in the faith, or (2) to reject Christ's one and only sacrifice thereby condemning herself to hell. Which will it be? You don't have an unbelieving heart, do you?

Hebrews 6:7-8

A person who bears fruit has been blessed by God. God causes the fruit to grow. Apart from God, the person can do nothing. In contrast, the person who does not bear fruit, does not have a life-giving connection with God (John 15:1-6). Such a person is of no use; she will perish. Just as land that receives rain and produces useful crops has been blessed, so too are true believers who bear fruit, demonstrating the authenticity of their faith. Those who fail to grow reveal a superficial faith, lacking the true connection with God that secures eternal salvation.

The rain represents God's blessings and truth, while the soil represents the heart's receptiveness. A fruitful response demonstrates authentic faith, while barrenness points to spiritual rejection.

Bearing fruit is evidence of God's working in the believer, not evidence of the believer's self-effort working. The branch connected to the vine passively (effortlessly) bears fruit.

Hebrews 6:9

When we mention people who are barren (unfruitful, unproductive), we are not thinking about you. You are meant to produce the fruit of your salvation. True believers, having genuinely embraced the Son of God, have their salvation secured permanently by God's unchanging promise.

Hebrews 6:10-12

You have already demonstrated fruit by loving and caring for other believers. As long as you produce some fruit, your hope is alive because no one can bear fruit without God's favor. This will keep you encouraged—making it easier to faithfully endure like Abraham.

Hebrews 6:13-14

God promised Abraham that He would bless him, make him abundantly fruitful.

Hebrews 6:15

Abraham believed God, waited patiently, and received the promised fruit. You can too. Just as Abraham's patience led to fulfillment of God's promise, believers today are called to endure with unwavering hope, knowing salvation is secure through Christ.

Hebrews 6:16-20

God promises He will bless you and save you. Jesus has gone ahead and paid the debt, clearing the way for you. The way is already prepared. Given God's promise and oath, taking God at His word, your salvation is as guaranteed as if you fully had it already. God cannot change or fail in His promise. God's unchanging nature guarantees the permanence of salvation. God promises salvation and it cannot be revoked. God does not change His mind about His promises. Those who trust in God have great assurance, confidence, and hope, a strong and trustworthy anchor for their souls.

CONCLUSION

The book of Hebrews dismantles the old system, revealing its inability to provide salvation. Christ's perfect sacrifice is not an option among many—it is the exclusive way to a true relationship with God.

The author of Hebrews challenges immature believers to grow, urging them to wake up from spiritual dullness (Hebrews 5:11). He presents a stark contrast to jolt them from their complacency. They need to grow up, not give up on Jesus. The author contrasts an unbelieving, infertile heart that cannot digest God's truth with a fertile heart that leans into faith with confidence. He affirms their salvation and exhorts them to live as those who truly believe, trusting fully in Christ's sufficiency.

Enduring faith is authentic faith, and confident faith reflects spiritual maturity (Hebrews 6:19). Thorns and thistles represent an unbelieving heart that makes obedience impossible, while a fertile heart responds to God's truth. Salvation is secure, and through faith and patience, believers inherit God's promises (Hebrews 6:12). Understanding this security allows them to grow without fear, trusting fully in Christ.

Faith fully trusts in the sufficiency of Christ alone. To declare Christ insufficient is an insult to His powerful sacrifice—exposing an insufficient faith incapable of salvation. A true believer will not waver between belief and unbelief. True salvation is permanent—it does not waver or fade. Those who are truly saved will endure, while those who deny Christ reveal their professions were empty of genuine faith.

Salvation is always open to those who will believe. Yet, without a fertile heart, even those who have been exposed to Christ can only reject His sacrifice and be condemned. There is no need to crucify Jesus again—His sacrifice was fully sufficient for all time.

Salvation is revealed through the fruit it produces—but the fertile heart does not come from human effort. God alone prepares the soil, making the heart receptive to His truth and producing lasting life, faith, and spiritual maturity (more will be said about this in Chapter 8). Salvation is secure for those He regenerates, ensuring they persevere and reveal His work.

FOR REFLECTION AND DISCUSSION

1. How does God's Word function as a sorting mechanism? Why does Scripture emphasize this division?
2. How does sorting help us understand that Hebrews 6:4-6 does not teach that salvation can be lost?

How Does A Fertile Heart Reveal True Salvation?

3. How do the four responses in the Parable of the Sower expose the falseness of an unregenerated heart compared to the genuineness of the believer's fertile heart?
4. What makes rocky soil incapable of real faith, despite its initial enthusiasm? How does this reveal the essential elements of true salvation?
5. What does it mean to have deep spiritual roots, and how do they enable growth and endurance?
6. How does Hebrews 6:4-6 warn non-believers, but serve as encouragement for believers to pursue maturity?
7. Why is it impossible to bring back to repentance those who reject Christ after encountering Him?
8. How does the imagery of fertile and infertile soil clarify the difference between real salvation and superficial profession of faith?
9. What distinguishes immature believers, mature believers, and non-believers in terms of intimacy with Christ?
10. How does God's promise to Abraham in Hebrews 6:13-15 reinforce the certainty and endurance of salvation?
11. What does it mean for salvation to be an "anchor for the soul," and how does this shape a believer's confidence?
12. Why is perseverance a natural result of a fertile heart and how does enduring faith produce spiritual maturity?

CHAPTER 5

How Sure of Salvation Can Believers Be?

The security that the Gospel provides is the certainty that Jesus will finish the saving work He started. Assurance is for our comfort like a child's assurance of her mother's or father's love. God wants believers to be fully confident in their salvation—His goal is to strengthen assurance. He wants believers to trust Him and experience the joy of fully resting in His unwavering parental love.

Trusting and resting in God lie at the heart of salvation. Isaiah 30:15 powerfully illustrates this truth, showing that salvation is found in "returning and rest"—turning away from self-reliance and placing full confidence in God's provision.

> This is what the Sovereign Lord, the Holy One of Israel, says: "In repentance and rest is your salvation, in quietness and trust is your strength, but you would have none of it."
> Isaiah 30:15 NIV

This rest is not passive; it is an active surrender. It calls us to abandon the exhausting pursuit of security through human effort and, instead, fulfill God's will by relying on His strength and promises. True peace is found when we quiet our hearts, trusting that He is our refuge and our strength—the One who holds our salvation securely in His hands (Psalm 46:1, 91:2; Proverbs 18:10).

Quietness and trust replace fear and uncertainty, allowing us to experience the fullness of His kindness. Scripture reminds us that while human strategies may fail, God's faithfulness endures. His gift of salvation is complete and unconditional, providing believers rest and confidence not only for eternity but for today as well.

When we anchor our assurance in God's character and His promises, we experience the freedom to live securely in His love, knowing that He has done all the work to bring us into His family. This assurance is a gift meant to strengthen us and fill us with joy and peace as we take up our cross to follow Him.

THE GOOD NEWS IS THE ASSURANCE OF SALVATION

Assurance of eternal life is related to the enjoyment of salvation. Love without assurance is no longer love. Love and certainty are woven together in God's character—when He chooses and saves, He does so without "take-backs."

Without the security that salvation is guaranteed, the Good News would not be good at all—it could not produce lasting comfort and therefore could not produce a peace that surpasses understanding. The "good news" would be worthless because it would leave the completion of salvation in imperfect human hands.

Only the perfect hands of Jesus can save. We can enjoy salvation because it is outrageously good news—because it is beyond our wildest dreams. Nothing can separate the believer from God's love. Not even guilt and shame—the robbers of the joy of salvation. Jesus died to remove all obstacles between Him and His children (Romans 8).

Herman Bavinck described this essential need for assurance when he wrote:

How Sure of Salvation Can Believers Be?

> In order to live comforted and die happily, we need certainty about the invisible and eternal things above. We must know [who] we are and where we are going. We must know that our personhood is more that a ripple in the ocean, that the moral battle stands far above the natural order, and that the highest and purest ideals of the soul are not illusions but reality. We must know how we can be liberated from the accusations of our conscience and from the weight of sin. We must know that God is, and that He is our God. We must be sure we are reconciled to Him and can therefore approach death and judgement without terror. In all this, our greatest need is for certainty. It is the deepest, although often unconscious, need of the human soul.
> SB#27, Bavinck, p. 12-13

Believers can know that they are saved. It's not only possible, but desirable that they experience full assurance of their salvation. I am as sure of my salvation as much as I trust that Jesus Christ accomplished what He said He accomplished. Taking Him at His word, I am 100% secure in my salvation.

Assurance is inseparable from salvation. Just as wetness cannot exist without water, and breathing cannot exist without a living body, salvation and confidence in Christ's saving work go together. This certainty is not an extra feature of faith but an essential reality. Assurance is always at least somewhat present, while the underlying reality of salvation is all-or-nothing. Salvation, once given, cannot be separated from the assurance that follows because true faith naturally produces confidence in Christ's sufficiency (SB#1, Gilmore, p. 102).

At the moment of spiritual birth, assurance naturally follows, growing as believers trust in His promises. People who are spiritually alive will know it, just as people are aware of their physical existence. To lack assurance may indicate the absence of spiritual life altogether. Genuine faith, given by Holy Spirit, awakens confidence that salvation is real and unshakable. It produces joy, trust, and perseverance, shaping the believer's walk with Christ as she grows in the certainty of her redemption (SB#1, Gilmore, p. 154).

FACT AND FAITH TOGETHER PRODUCE ASSURANCE

Assurance stems from knowing the facts of the Gospel and possessing God-given faith to trust His truth above all distractions of life. While faith itself is unshakable, its clarity can sometimes be obscured—like a masterpiece hidden beneath a layer of darkness. Yet, even in such moments, the truth of faith remains steadfast, awaiting the light of Holy Spirit to unveil its beauty.

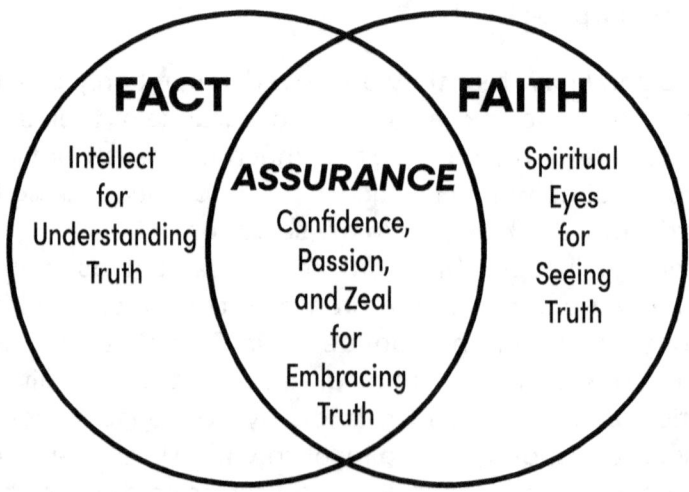

Intellect grasps Gospel facts. Spiritual eyes perceive eternal realities. Their union births assurance—fueling confidence, passion, and zeal.

WHAT IS FACT?

Facts are the words, ideas, and historical events that objectively define the Gospel as described in the Bible. They are true or false. Jesus died and rose again or He did not. A person is a genuine believer or a non-believer.

WHAT IS FAITH?

Faith is God-given, Spirit-enabled spiritual sight that allows believers to perceive God and His kingdom and then engage with their eternal reality. Acting as the spiritual eye, faith is the primary indicator of spiritual life, as essential to the spirit as a heartbeat and breathing are to the body. It enables three vital spiritual activities: belief in God, trust in His truth, and assurance of salvation.

Faith is neither an objective fact nor a subjective feeling. Rather, it enables believers to experience the absolute truth of spiritual life in a deeply personal and unique journey. Through faith, believers see God with certainty, even as the world remains spiritually blind.

To the worldly person, the visible appears solid and reliable, while the spiritual seems suspect and uncertain (2 Corinthians 4:18). Yet God grants spiritual sight, healing blindness so that discerning believers understand that the unseen holds eternal stability, while the visible proves fleeting and temporary. This clarity and conviction grounds and assures believers so they can act with "trusting faith"—far removed from the "blind faith" of the world (SB#1, Gilmore, p. 95).

With respect to salvation, faith is all or nothing. The smallest measure of faith is as effective as the largest amount. It's not that faith needs to increase as much as faith needs to be exercised. Any amount of faith is evidence of salvation because all faith comes from God.

THE SYNERGY OF FACT AND FAITH

When the fact of salvation is true, faith will inevitably be present, not as a product of human effort but as a supernatural gift from God. The facts are simple enough that a child can understand them and the faith can be as small as a mustard seed, but both are required. Getting the facts right means having a correct theology. Getting faith right means having a correct focus on Jesus, not self, circumstances, or Satan. For example, a believer might have this brief testimony:

1. **Fact:** *Jesus lived a perfect life, died, and rose again, replacing my sin with His righteousness.*
2. **Faith:** *I set the eyes of my heart on Jesus. I believe in my heart that I am saved.*

The fact and assurance of salvation reveal four different realities:

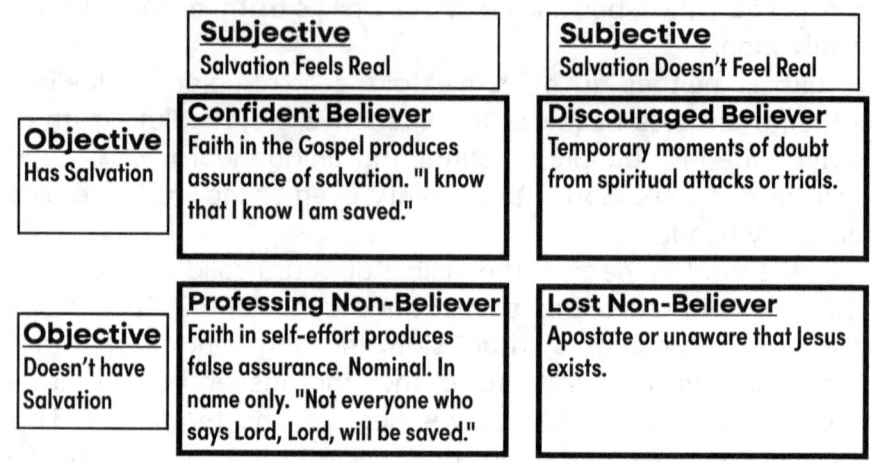

FAITH PRODUCES ASSURANCE

Can someone say she really has faith if she is not assured of her salvation? Faith is not complete or genuine if it does not produce assurance.

A believer can, and must, be confident in knowing she is truly saved. If she is an authentic believer, she will be with Jesus for eternity. The stakes are high, therefore, uncertainty is not a valid endpoint. To doubt the authenticity of her faith means that she either (a) lacks the understanding of her faith, which means she is misinterpreting the Gospel's message in practice (at best) or (b) she isn't a believer (at worst).

Genuine assurance comes from authentic faith, while false assurance comes from misplaced confidence—whether in works, emotions, or external signs rather than in Christ's finished work. There are no maybes in God's kingdom, only believers with faith. This doesn't mean that true believers don't sin or don't doubt, but in spite of these, their core faith in God is resolute. A believer's faith will speak louder than sin or doubt.

Faith brings assurance of what we hope for because it allows us to see God's promises as if they were fulfilled already. Faith is confidence in what believers hope for—the spiritual, heavenly reality as nothing less than a certain future. We have eternal life today but we must also wait patiently for its complete fulfillment. We could not wait without faith. Furthermore, to wait with an expectation of possible failure would no longer be waiting in faith, but, instead, uncertainty.

Review these four different versions of Hebrews 11:1 until you are convinced that faith and assurance go together.

> Now faith is confidence in what we hope for and assurance about what we do not see. NIV
>
> Now faith is the assurance of things hoped for, the conviction of things not seen. ESV
>
> Faith shows the reality of what we hope for; it is the evidence of things we cannot see. NLT
>
> Faith makes us sure of what we hope for and gives us proof of what we cannot see. CEV

Where we put our attention is of utmost importance. Where we place our confidence is of supreme significance. To be encouraged in faith, we only need to put our attention on Jesus's saving work. Faith comes by hearing, reading, and meditating on the Gospel (Romans 10:17).

WHAT DECREASES ASSURANCE?

Before we explore in detail what increases assurance, let's be clear on what decreases it. The enemy seeks to use any methods at his disposal to decrease faith's effectiveness—the result being increased doubt. All of the following weaknesses can give him opportunity to work:
- sin and resulting guilt or self-condemnation
- negative experiences (abuse, neglect)
- the itch to be in control like God
- self-sufficiency (pride)
- lack of relationship, encouragement, support
- lack of theological understanding (false teaching)
- believing lies and falsehoods

- lack of seeing God clearly
- lack of correct application

Can Christians have absolute assurance? Yes, but our feelings and worldly experiences will interfere with it. We know there is no condemnation for those in Jesus (Romans 8:1). But emotions can be volatile. Devastating experiences can convince us to doubt God's goodness.

Feelings are valuable to discern errors in belief, but they are not reliable confirmers of truth. When a person feels depressed, it does not mean she is worthless. Feelings are true in the sense that feeling bad means she is believing a lie. Knowing she is feeling bad can help her correct the beliefs in her heart. She can change from believing "I am worthless" to "I am loved." This is the healing and sanctification process.

Some trials disrupt assurance. Much like a car in the shop, or a person in the ICU, they interrupt normal function and introduce uncertainty. Growth often demands painful "surgery" that may temporarily heighten doubt. Yet, the ultimate goal is to confront doubt—to step into the battle and refuse to let evil take hold. The pursuit of truth can be a bumpy ride, but it is worth the momentary discomfort.

Weakened assurance does not indicate absence of salvation. Being angry at God, disappointed in God, or any of the other weaknesses listed above do not have to reduce assurance of salvation, although, they often do. We might not be seeing God clearly; we might be overwhelmed with doubt temporarily, but doubt or emotions cannot eliminate saving faith.

Being in relationship with Jesus is all that is required for salvation (as described in Chapter 2). A person can be saved, but not feel happy about her life. She can be saved, but not yet fully grasp the depths of God's love for her. She can know God personally, but misunderstand scripture at times. Objective truth and saving faith prevail over human emotions and imperfections.

Doubt will thrive in people who shift their focus from Christ to self. Whether they believe they are too unworthy or too worthy, their focus is off-target. Doubt grows when we value our negative experiences more than we value our God experiences.

Assurance grows the more we know God for who the Bible says He is.

Deviation from the truth is possible when we sin, take our eyes off Jesus, and put our trust in worldly philosophies or treasures. When we are in the flesh, we are once again expressing our distaste for God.

FALSE ASSURANCE IS POSSIBLE

Saying the words "I believe" or responding to an altar-call, by themselves, should not create assurance. Words in a "prayer" hold no power without the Spirit's activity. Assurance arises from the profound richness of truly believing in Christ—a depth that goes beyond mere words and reflects the fullness of genuine faith. Where true faith exists, that richness will naturally follow. However, merely professing belief does not guarantee authentic faith.

Suggesting that simply "opening the gift" makes someone a Christian is misleading. Faith cannot be manufactured; God initiates salvation by giving faith. If someone believes she has accepted salvation but experiences no true change, she may come to distrust God, wondering why she feels empty. Trusting God's timing to present the gift is better than forcing a "decision."

Likewise, works without faith contribute nothing to salvation and should not create assurance. Works motivated by the flesh will not survive into the next life. But works motivated from genuine faith and the Spirit's activity will survive. Only by cooperating with the Spirit can believers produce the fruit Jesus desires.

Sincere evangelism requires patience, creating space for a genuine response to God's work in the heart. Emotional appeals can result in false conversions—momentary decisions that lack spiritual transformation. Reducing the Gospel, for example, by using a scripted prayer or promising health and wealth, is like handing someone a faulty parachute—a false security that will fail when it matters most. True assurance begins with God's transforming work, which naturally produces a response in the believer:

1. God transforms the heart through the hearing of the true and complete Gospel.
2. The person recognizes an internal, spiritual change.
3. The person desires to testify publicly to God's work in her heart.

The only fatal doubt is unbelief—a rejection of God's reality and love—which is impossible for a true believer. To overcome all other doubt, return to the Gospel message to stir the power of faith. This renewed faith will naturally bear the fruit of good works, strengthening assurance over time.

WHAT INCREASES ASSURANCE?

God's truth appeals not only to the intellect but also the heart—it heals, inspires, and satisfies both—uniting them in purpose. The Spirit makes truth alive in both intellect and inner-self—deepening spiritual conviction that strengthens and sustains the believer.

FOCUSING ON JESUS

If faith produces assurance, then doubt obscures it. A person's spirit knows faith but the flesh knows doubt. The presence of doubt doesn't eliminate genuine faith; it walks alongside it and clouds its clarity. Faith remains ever-present in the believer, but doubt dampens its ability to function. Every believer wrestles with doubt at some point. Doubt is like a fog that can obscure the light of faith, but the light remains present, shining steadily beneath the haze. The light shines, but the darkness cannot overcome it (John 1).

The story of Peter walking on water, found in Matthew 14:22-33, clearly illustrates both (a) the interplay between faith and doubt and (b) how believers can find assurance in Jesus. Peter steps out of the boat with great faith, trusting Jesus's call to him. His faith allows him to walk on the water—a miraculous moment that reflects the clarity and confidence faith brings when focused on Christ. However, when Peter notices the wind and waves, doubt creeps in, and he begins to sink. This demonstrates that faith and doubt can coexist; Peter's faith remains intact (he cries out to Jesus for help), but doubt weakens its effectiveness.

Just as Peter's focus on Jesus sustained his faith on the water, believers must fix their hearts and minds on God to experience true assurance. Peter depends on Jesus—the sole source of light and faith—to overcome his doubt and fear. When Peter calls out to Jesus, the "light" of his faith dispels the "darkness" of doubt. Doubt can challenge faith, but it cannot eliminate it. Jesus's immediate response demonstrates that salvation does not hinge on our perfection, but on His affection. This is the anchor of assurance: that even when doubt challenges faith, Jesus hears our cries and secures our relationship with Him.

But is spiritual awareness (faith) enough to produce confidence sufficient to extinguish all worry about whether a person will be saved? Yes, but knowing this complete assurance is only possible when a person remains steadfastly focused on God with complete trust. Believers must lean into God with all they have, to know Him intimately and feel secure in Christ (SB#1, Gilmore, p. 153). *I can relax. I know God is trustworthy. God, You said I am safe, so I am. I trust You to not abandon me. I praise You for Your extravagant love.*

> **You will keep in perfect peace those whose minds are steadfast, because they trust in you.**
> Isaiah 26:3 NIV

> I keep my eyes always on the Lord. With him at my right hand, I will not be shaken.
> Psalm 16:8 NIV

HOLY SPIRIT

God and Jesus communicate to the world in a way that only Holy Spirit can make believers understand. Holy Spirit translates the words written in the Bible into the spiritual reality of God's truth—the language of the heart. The believer is able to understand God's truth through faith. Physical sight is not helpful (2 Corinthians 5:7).

Holy Spirit provides assurance by His presence, but we can still be persuaded by our lie-infected feelings that seem to scream louder than His voice. This is what it means to continue to live in the flesh. This is our ongoing struggle as we live in both worlds. Satan can still whisper lies to us that stir our fleshly thinking. Who we look to makes all the difference (SB#1, Gilmore, p. 103).

Holy Spirit brings peace and assurance by teaching and reminding believers of God's truth.

> But the Advocate, the Holy Spirit, whom the Father will send in my name, will teach you all things and will remind you of everything I have said to you. Peace I leave with you; my peace I give you. I do not give to you as the world gives. Do not let your hearts be troubled and do not be afraid.
> John 14:26-27 NIV

> The Spirit himself testifies with our spirit that we are God's children.
> Romans 8:16 NIV

> Now it is God who makes both us and you stand firm in Christ. He anointed us, set his seal of ownership on us, and put his Spirit in our hearts as a deposit, guaranteeing what is to come.
> 2 Corinthians 1:21-22 NIV

KNOWING GOD'S HEART

God is always for us. God perseveres with His saints. He will not cast out the believer. He is tender, compassionate, slow to anger, and abounding in love (Psalm 103:8, 13). He wants us to feel secure in our relationship with Him. He is not looking for reasons to disqualify us from the spiritual race we are running.

God provides faith so that believers can spiritually connect with Him through trust and dependence. Our struggles are not signs of God's rejection, they are opportunities for confirming His love. To believe with saving faith is to believe Christ is telling the truth, that He cares, saves, and wants us to be assured—not that He lies or changes His mind about us. The devil wants us to doubt our worthiness or be prideful of our ability, our faith, or our works—as if we had contributed something to sway Christ to make the decision to save us.

To know the truth we must read the Bible and communicate with God about our doubts and imperfections. God's truth grows our understanding of His spiritual reality (SB#1, Gilmore, p. 88).

The more certain we are of our salvation, the more freely we take faithful risks. The more we forsake worldly gains, the more we have to invest in God's great kingdom. God is on our side—He wants us to finish the race. He is the author and perfecter of our faith. To be a winner, all He asks is that we cooperate with Him.

Winning, however, looks different in God's kingdom. The world's race glorifies self at the expense of others. The godly race glorifies God, as every accomplishment advances His kingdom. When God wins, we win.

God is cheering us on. Assurance grows as we truly know His character and heart. Without His encouragement and acceptance, we risk running toward the wrong finish line—one of self-righteousness. The goal is not to outrun others—it is to run in step with Christ, knowing that He ensures we endure to the end.

God is completely for believers. He will not lose one of His children. This truth fuels the heart for the race, motivating us to good works—not to prove ourselves worthy, but from the overflow of the joy of God's grace and mercy.

TRIALS

Since God is sovereign over all things, trials serve a refining purpose in the lives of believers. Though they vary in duration and intensity, all trials—whether short-term or long-term—are designed to deepen faith and cultivate reliance on Him. Some trials are brief, offering quick resolution that strengthens faith and energizes believers for immediate action. Others extend over months, years, or even a lifetime, cultivating dependence, producing endurance, and shaping faith in ways that short-term resolution cannot.

Trials teach us to trust God—whether in an acute event or over a lifetime of perseverance. Trusting God is far better than seeking to eliminate suffering by short-sighted solutions. Suffering may not always be resolved this side of heaven, but God redeems it by using it to deepen assurance, perseverance, and trust in His eternal purposes rather than earthly health, wealth, or rewards.

True believers have eternal security, and their perseverance through intense trials reveals the authenticity of their faith. Though genuine faith cannot be lost, it is refined through testing. Such faith inevitably bears spiritual fruit—manifesting in works and deeds.

God has no need to prove His character to us, but we need assurance that our character is grounded in truth. As we persevere, we grow in confidence—not only in who we are, but in whose we are. Because faith is a journey of trust, certainty matters. And through trials, that certainty is refined, revealing the genuineness of our faith.

Fake faith falls away; real faith perseveres. The person who suffers under hardship either grows more confident in her salvation or realizes with greater certainty that she is not saved. Both outcomes move her away from complacency, creating the potential to pursue deeper truth.

Trials build perseverance and spiritual maturity, whether caused by a fallen world, spiritual opposition, or God's refining purpose. They deepen faith, teaching reliance on Him rather than on circumstances.

Short-Term Trials: Immediate Growth

Short-term trials function as tests of faith that call for immediate reliance on God. These may be temporary hardships, moments of doubt, or challenges designed to refine trust in His wisdom. Rather than being draining, these trials often lead to strengthened assurance, renewed energy, and increased spiritual maturity, preparing believers for greater use in God's kingdom.

Scripture offers vivid examples of short-term trials: Abraham preparing to sacrifice Isaac, Peter sinking in doubt, and Jesus facing temptation in the wilderness. In each case, the testing demanded an active response—choosing to trust God in the moment. Once the trial passed, the individual emerged strengthened in faith, assured of God's presence, and equipped for greater works.

> In all this you greatly rejoice, though now for a little while you may have had to suffer grief in all kinds of trials. These have come so that the proven genuineness of your faith—of greater worth than gold, which perishes even though refined by fire—may result in praise, glory and honor when Jesus Christ is revealed.
> 1 Peter 1:6-7 NIV

Peter reminds us that trials are temporary but they allow faith to be proven genuine. He fully expects believers to persevere because their faith is real. Gold will perish, but faith endures. Remember: faith is not fueled by human willpower, but by God's Spirit.

Long-Term Trials: Endurance

Unlike short-term trials, long-term trials persist beyond a single moment or situation. Long-term suffering is not always a clearly defined test. These hardships—whether chronic illness, prolonged persecution, or ongoing grief—often drain energy for a season but ultimately cultivate a deeper, more resilient faith. While believers may struggle to endure, God uses these trials to produce unwavering confidence in His sovereignty.

Examples include Paul's thorn in the flesh, Job's ongoing suffering, and the faithful believers who endured persecution throughout history. Though relief did not always come in their lifetime, God redeemed their hardship by strengthening their perseverance and assurance in eternal promises.

> Dear brothers and sisters, when troubles of any kind come your way, consider it an opportunity for great joy. For you know that when your faith is tested, your endurance has a chance to grow. So let it grow, for when your endurance is fully developed, you will be perfect and complete, needing nothing.
> James 1:2-4 NLT

Trusting God Through All Trials

Regardless of duration, all trials serve the same purpose—to refine faith, deepen reliance on God, and shift focus away from self-effort toward His sovereignty. While short-term trials provide strength for immediate spiritual growth, long-term trials forge lasting endurance, ensuring faith is unshaken even when hardship lingers.

Believers are not meant to simply endure trials, but to trust that God is working through them. Whether a trial lasts days or decades, the call remains the same: trust God, surrender human understanding, and rely on His wisdom over temporary resolution.

Even when we are assured of our salvation we may experience moments of spiritual uncertainty, yet God remains faithful in deepening our trust. God will not boot us out of heaven when we are struggling to see Him clearly. Instead, He is working to help us see Him and trust Him.

Faith in God can be solidly grounded in the truth, but some events can temporarily shout louder than the voice of assurance. Believers struggling to maintain assurance have not abandoned their faith. Rather, it is a test that will strengthen faith. In those moments we must decide what we believe, where we stand. Jesus in His moments of temptation stood on the solid ground of the Scriptures. He did not give in to the lies (SB#1, Gilmore, p. 100).

God intends trials to increase confidence rather than discouragement. As believers trust God through hardship, their assurance grows, preparing them for greater challenges. Trials teach believers to trust God in the moment, and suffering teaches believers to trust God for a lifetime.

Embrace Suffering Now For Rewards Later

God uses suffering to move believers into alignment with His truth and larger-than-life plans. While He forgives our sins, He also calls us to share in Jesus's suffering as He straightens what is bent within us. The ability to repent—to humbly acknowledge our crookedness—is a gift of the Spirit which enables agreement with God. Therefore, the cross-bearing believer embraces both God's grace and His parental discipline.

Suffering has a profound purpose: realization that believers are one with God and nothing can divide or take away that oneness. People who feel their inherent sinfulness often try to compensate by performing good works. However, true salvation is found in trusting Christ alone, not in personal efforts. Aligning with God can feel painful, as it requires abandoning pride and self-reliance, yet this surrender increases assurance of authentic spiritual life.

Relying on good works for acceptance adopts a mindset focused on human achievement rather than divine grace. True faith calls believers to embrace a theology of the cross—a willingness to face the pain of abandoning everything for the sake of knowing Christ's redeeming power—rather than a theology of glory, which uses personal effort to feel acceptance (SB#1, Gilmore, p. 16).

Though suffering is difficult, believers should not lose heart because suffering points to future glory and strengthens reliance on God, inspiring perseverance rather than sad withdrawal from life (2 Corinthians 4:16–18).

God's people throughout history have demonstrated steadfast faith, living as though the rewards of their faith were already in hand. Though their faith was strong, they did not receive in their lifetimes all that God had promised. God's plan is to unite all His people at the end of time and finally reward them together with perfection (Hebrews 11:39–40).

As we reflect on their example, we are reminded that Jesus, who ignites and perfects our faith, empowers us to strip away distractions and sin that hinder us, so we can run with endurance. Our strength comes from keeping our eyes on Him—the victor who endured the cross with joy, secured our salvation, and now reigns in glory, having paved the way for us to follow (Hebrews 12:1–2).

CONCLUSION

Suffering strengthens assurance. Spiritual growth does not come by avoiding hardship, but by embracing God's Holy alignment process. The full rewards of faith await us in the next life, challenging us to prioritize eternal pleasures over fleeting, worldly ones.

Assurance of salvation is a gift from God, rooted in faith and nurtured through trials, surrender, and reliance on the Spirit. True assurance transcends fleeting emotions and is grounded in the unchanging truth of God's character and promises. While doubt and suffering may challenge assurance, they ultimately refine faith, deepen conviction, and align believers' hearts with God's heart.

Genuine faith produces spiritual fruit and perseveres through trials, proving its authenticity and strengthening confidence in God's saving work. To cultivate assurance, believers must focus on Christ, depend on the Spirit, and embrace the sanctification process, knowing that eternal rewards far surpass any present struggles. Assurance thrives where God's love empowers believers to live boldly for His kingdom, enduring trials with confidence.

FOR REFLECTION AND DISCUSSION

Read the following prayer of accepting a theology of suffering. Then answer the discussion questions.

Prayer

I know I have been selfish and desperately want freedom from this. God, help me. I cannot produce love on my own; You must supply it and fulfill the law within me. Even with Your help, I realize I have a long way to go. Though I cannot love the world as You do, I trust You to use me to share Your love and truth, building others up for Your kingdom. While fear might motivate me at times, Your presence, care, and love are my greatest motivators.

Accepting the pain of abandoning my pride and self-reliance feels like agony at times—like bearing a cross—but I know it is necessary. You ask me to lay down my illusions of control, and though it feels like defeat, You assure me it brings true spiritual life. This surrender is not misery for its own sake; it is a transformation of my heart, a realignment to Your will. In letting go of my will, I find a freedom and peace that only You can give.

God, teach me to embrace this higher calling of oneness with You, shaped by Your love and purpose. When Your light shines on me, in me, and through me, I cannot help but be different and see differently.

Your Spirit fuels the works You've prepared for me and brings fulfillment as I follow Your lead. My deepest desire is for a relationship where I am valued, not simply as a tool to accomplish tasks, but as someone loved and appreciated by You. When our hearts align, obedience becomes joyful, flowing from oneness with You. I long for this higher calling—a heart transformed by Your kindness, mercy, and light, reshaping my life and perspective.

Questions

1. Can salvation exist without assurance? Why or why not?
2. How does assurance of salvation shape the way believers experience their faith?
3. Is it possible to enjoy the Christian life with a consistently low assurance of salvation? Why or why not?
4. How does trusting in God's character strengthen our confidence in salvation?
5. Why does Isaiah 30:15 link salvation with rest and quietness rather than striving?
6. How can guilt and shame rob believers of their assurance?
7. How can we recognize the difference between faith and false assurance?
8. What role does repentance play in strengthening assurance?
9. How do trials and suffering strengthen faith and deepen assurance, instead of weakening them?
10. How does the story of Peter walking on water illustrate the relationship between faith, doubt, and assurance?

11. Why is it misleading to tell a non-believer that she can simply "open the gift" of salvation? How could this unintentionally lead to false assurance?
12. How does Holy Spirit confirm our assurance and guide us through doubt?
13. How does running the spiritual race require confidence in God's love rather than fear of failure?
14. How does focusing on Christ rather than personal effort help strengthen assurance?
15. How does considering eternal rewards help believers persevere through hardship?

CHAPTER 6

Can Believers Ever Lose Salvation?

Do you ever fear losing your salvation? God desires His children to live with confidence, fully assured of His love. Yet many Christians wrestle with spiritual insecurity, fearing they have done something to break their relationship with Him. Despite the Bible's repeated affirmations that God will not abandon His children, some believers feel as though their weaknesses will separate them from Him. However, God's heart is to correct and restore, not to abandon.

Faith keeps believers spiritually secure. So what causes insecurity to take hold and overshadow faith, despite God's firm reassurance? What imagined threats or failures make people question His unchanging love? Insecurity arises from misplaced focus—fear looks inward, dwelling on human imperfection, while faith looks to Christ and His sufficiency. True assurance is found in placing confidence in the Spirit, not in the flesh.

FEAR IS THE PRIMARY MENTAL HEALTH ISSUE

Fearing God's rejection distorts the nature of His love. If God were eager to cast away His children rather than embrace them, then worry would be justified. However, those who fear rejection are often the ones who care about God's opinion, meaning they likely have genuine faith from Him and in Him. Those who are indifferent to God are the ones who should be concerned.

This raises a crucial question: What is the nature of God's acceptance, accomplished through Christ's sacrifice? What is required to gain God's favor? Once a person has been welcomed into His family, can that acceptance ever be lost? Could any sin be so great that it disqualifies a believer?

Trying to hedge one's bets on salvation is both costly and unnecessary. Jesus's sacrifice covers all believers' sin, or no one is truly saved. Believing that salvation can be lost diminishes the power of God's work, choking the strength out of the Gospel message. It turns salvation into an unstable, uncertain state rather than the secure rescue that Scripture describes.

Believing that salvation is temporary misunderstands God's heart. It undermines the very foundation of faith and weakens the full power of His grace. At best, it reduces love to something conditional. At worst, it introduces a false gospel that compromises the ability to fully trust God. If fear is a mental health struggle, then the only true remedy is resting in God's unwavering faithfulness. Peace of mind is only possible through complete reliance on Christ.

WHAT'S AT STAKE?

Believing that salvation is fragile opens the door to a false Gospel. If salvation could be lost, then it is not true salvation at all—it would be an uncertain probationary status dependent on human effort. Instead of simply raising awareness of spiritual realities, the Gospel provides the complete and final solution to sin. It eliminates fear and uncertainty for those who belong to Christ. Hebrews 10:14 powerfully affirms this truth:

Can Believers Ever Lose Salvation?

> For by a single offering he has perfected for all time those who are being sanctified.
> Hebrews 10:14 ESV

> By his one sacrifice he has forever set free from sin the people he brings to God.
> Hebrews 10:14 CEV

Those who are truly saved no longer live in fear or need to manipulate their way into God's favor. A true believer cannot ultimately betray God or do anything that would cause expulsion from His kingdom. God's rescue is not precarious or conditional. There is no such thing as an authentic but complacent Christian. Only a false believer shrinks back from her profession of faith.

Every person who is genuinely saved has been transformed into a new creation. If salvation were merely a process dependent on human effort or will, it would leave its final outcome uncertain. Promoting the idea that people can choose God also supports the idea that believers can reject salvation—but this is impossible.

Those who rely on their own ability to maintain salvation are following a different gospel—one that does not save. Trusting in self rather than in Christ creates false assurance for non-believers or false insecurity for believers. Paul addresses this issue in Galatians 1:6-8:

> I am astonished that you are so quickly deserting the one who called you to live in the grace of Christ and are turning to a different gospel—which is really no gospel at all. Evidently some people are throwing you into confusion and are trying to pervert the gospel of Christ. But even if we or an angel from heaven should preach a gospel other than the one we preached to you, let them be under God's curse!
> Galatians 1:6-8 NIV

Other passages also warn against false teachings:
- **2 Corinthians 11:4** — Paul rebukes those who accept a different Jesus or a different gospel.
- **2 Timothy 4:3-4** — Warns that people will turn away from truth and follow myths.

- **1 John 4:1-3** — Encourages believers to test spirits to discern truth from deception.
- **Jude 1:4** — Warns of abusing grace by sinful indulgence.

Paul's warning in Galatians directly confronts those who distort grace by adding human effort as a requirement for salvation. Specifically, he refutes the Judaizers, a group insisting that Gentile believers must follow Jewish law, including circumcision and adherence to Mosaic regulations.

Paul forcefully rejects this view, emphasizing that salvation comes solely through faith in Christ, not through religious customs or human effort. Throughout Galatians, he contrasts grace and legalism, teaching that righteousness is found in Christ alone.

A false gospel enslaves people to rules rather than freeing them in Christ. The Galatians, instead of living by the Spirit, were being led back into legalistic practices that undermined the sufficiency of Christ's sacrifice. Paul refutes this, insisting that faith—not law—justifies and brings true freedom (Galatians 2:16, 5:1).

GOD AND HIS CHILDREN SHARE SIGNIFICANT ATTRIBUTES

God cannot die, nor can He act against His nature. He would not kill himself if He could, nor can anyone else kill Him. Salvation transforms believers to be like Him, shaping their desires and identity. A believer filled with Holy Spirit, fully aware of God's love, would never want to be separated from Him through spiritual death. Nothing can separate those in Christ from God, as Romans 8 assures.

SPIRITUAL MURDER IS IMPOSSIBLE

God promises never to abandon His children. Once saved, a person is fully secure in His love—nothing can sever her bond with Him.

> Keep your life free from love of money, and be content with what you have, for he has said, "I will never leave you nor forsake you." So we can confidently say, "The Lord is my helper; I will not fear; what can man do to me?"
> Hebrews 13:5-6 ESV

A believer is permanently included in God's family, making separation not only unnecessary but impossible. Her identity and purpose are fulfilled in Him, and her place in His body is an unchangeable reality. Instead of those in Christ requiring space to exist independently from Him, they find security in His unwavering presence and delight in their God-given identities.

Abusing God's Grace Is Impossible

Once God saves a person, she is fully justified before Him. Good works and spiritual fruit inevitably follow salvation—they are its result, not its cause. Works do not secure salvation and believers do not lack works, because God empowers them to produce the fruit of salvation.

Could someone abuse this truth? If salvation is truly free and irrevocable, what prevents a person from receiving it and then returning to a life of complete sin? That would require divided allegiance—living for both God and self—but Scripture teaches that such a division is impossible.

> No one can serve two masters. For you will hate one and love the other; you will be devoted to one and despise the other. You cannot serve God and be enslaved to money.
> Matthew 6:24 NLT

True believers serve God as their master, even though they can yet sin. They love Him more than anything else, including wealth. Non-believers, however, remain enslaved to sin and love money in a way that prevents them from loving God. Money itself is not the issue—it is the love of money that hardens hearts, as 1 Timothy 6:10 warns. Believers may possess wealth, but they do not elevate it above God.

These scriptures do not establish conditions for keeping salvation. Rather, they guide believers in living in harmony with the Spirit who dwells within them. True believers are compelled to turn away from sin, not exploit grace. As 1 John 3:6-9 teaches, those who belong to Christ do not continue in sin.

SPIRITUAL SUICIDE IS IMPOSSIBLE

God will never abandon His children—but could a believer choose to abandon God? No. It's impossible. And, this does not violate the human will.

While humans have a will, a new creation in Christ never desires to leave God. In contrast, the spiritually dead have a will, but they never desire Him. Only Holy Spirit can create the desire to seek God.

Just as it is impossible for God to destroy Himself, spiritual suicide is impossible for a believer. God's omnipotence never requires Him to act against His holy nature, and the same is true for His children. If God cannot destroy Himself, then neither can any of His children separate themselves from Him spiritually. The very thought of leaving God does not arise in a regenerated believer. If such doubt occurs, it stems from the rebellion of the flesh, not wisdom. Salvation is not a casual decision, like choosing between two outfits, but a matter of life and death. Choosing death is undesirable and, therefore, impossible for God and His children.

God acts not out of external motivation but according to His perfect, just nature. As children of God, believers grow to reflect His character (1 John 3:2). Because God cannot reject His goodness, neither can His children.

A believer cannot leave God once He has chosen her. He is the best possible reality, and salvation is more than a passive gift—it is an intentional act of grace given personally to each believer. Eternal life cannot be stolen, revoked, or discarded.

Insecurity comes from misunderstanding God's commitment as a parent—a commitment far greater than any human parental bond.

GOD ACCEPTS RESPONSIBILITY FOR HIS CHILDREN

In legal adoption, a parent assumes full responsibility for the child for better or worse. What loving parent would feel positive about abandoning her child? Would we expect to be more faithful in loving our children than God is in loving His own? As a perfect Father, God would never abandon His children by returning them to spiritual death.

Human parental love, though imperfect, is idealized as sacrificial. If even flawed human parents strive to love sacrificially, how much greater is God's perfect love? His love prevails against every enemy, including sin and the forces of hell, as Paul writes in Romans 8:

> And I am convinced that nothing can ever separate us from God's love. Neither death nor life, neither angels nor demons, neither our fears for today nor our worries about tomorrow—not even the powers of hell can separate us from God's love. No power in the sky above or in the earth below—indeed, nothing in all creation will ever be able to separate us from the love of God that is revealed in Christ Jesus our Lord.
> Romans 8:38-39 NLT

We know we are God's children because He adopted us:

> So you have not received a spirit that makes you fearful slaves. Instead, you received God's Spirit when he adopted you as his own children. Now we call him, "Abba, Father."
> Romans 8:15 NLT

Adoption forms an unbreakable bond because God chooses His children. Every person He entrusts to Jesus is saved, and Jesus never fails to accomplish this purpose:

> For I have come down from heaven to do the will of God who sent me, not to do my own will. And this is the will of God, that I should not lose even one of all those he has given me, but that I should raise them up at the last day.
> John 6:38-39 NLT

SECURE IN CHRIST

God's sheep follow Jesus. They do not run away. Even when they wander, He finds and protects them:

> My sheep listen to my voice; I know them, and they follow me. I give them eternal life, and they will never perish. No one can snatch them away from me, for my Father has given them to me, and he is more powerful than anyone else. No one can snatch them from the Father's hand.
> John 10:27-29 NLT

Revoking eternal life is not a corrective parenting tool that God ever considers. Our status as His children removes any need for condemnation, as Romans 8:1 states. He responds to wrong behavior with loving correction—not the loss of eternal life. The threat of not obtaining eternal life is necessary only for the spiritually dead. They need to realize that their heart is dead and requires reviving.

Can you see that the threat of losing eternal life for the child of God, who knows God as love, is never helpful, motivating, or necessary? It would be against God's character to condemn His children. How could He give His very life, conquer death itself, bring us to a place of health and safety, only to take it all back? It would require that He do even more than abandon His children. To condemn would mean reversing the new birth. He would need to "uncreate" the new creation. Removing His Spirit, after we have been justified, would be murder!

But only people are capable of evil. God does not destroy—He gives life. God is so motivated for good, He never abandons His children.

> "Ask, and it will be given to you; seek, and you will find; knock, and it will be opened to you. For everyone who asks receives, and the one who seeks finds, and to the one who knocks it will be opened. Or which one of you, if his son asks him for bread, will give him a stone? Or if he asks for a fish, will give him a serpent? If you then, who are evil, know how to give good gifts to your children, how much more will your Father who is in heaven give good things to those who ask him!"
> Matthew 7:7-11 ESV

Can Believers Ever Lose Salvation?

God's best gift is Holy Spirit, who seals believers, guaranteeing their salvation. This seal is unbreakable. If salvation could be lost and regained repeatedly, the seal would be useless and salvation would hold no meaning. Holy Spirit's seal ensures the fulfillment of God's unchanging promise—believers will inherit eternal life:

> In him you also, when you heard the word of truth, the gospel of your salvation, and believed in him, were sealed with the promised Holy Spirit, who is the guarantee of our inheritance until we acquire possession of it, to the praise of his glory.
> Ephesians 1:13-14 ESV

God does not change His mind about His promise. He is not playing games. He is trustworthy. He will do what He says He will do. Do you trust Him to fulfill His promise to completely save you?

GOD MOTIVATES HIS CHILDREN BY LOVE, NOT FEAR

God is fully committed to parenting by love not fear. Jesus's act of sacrificial love demonstrates that He will never give up on those who belong to Him. Permanently removing His presence, reversing regeneration, would be the severest of punishments, contradicting His nature. Instead, His correction heals, restores, and strengthens. His love is unwavering and more than sufficient—it cannot fail (1 Corinthians 13:4-8).

Fear arises when someone has not yet grasped the depth of God's love. But God is not a quitter—His promise of eternal life through Christ is irrevocable. He cannot lie or cancel His promises (Hebrews 6:18). His discipline and training are fully capable of completing the work He begins in every believer (Hebrews 12:1-2).

One of the greatest blessings of salvation is freedom from the fear of catastrophic punishment. Fear and God's perfect love cannot coexist, as His love guarantees forgiveness and eternal security.

> There is no fear in love, but perfect love casts out fear. For fear has to do with punishment, and whoever fears has not been perfected in love.
> 1 John 4:18 ESV

The phrase "perfected in love" highlights the maturity that comes when believers deepen their understanding and trust in God's unfailing love. This assurance allows them to focus on learning, serving, and growing—without anxiety over eternal consequences.

Jesus changes believers as faith produces a shift from self-reliance to dependence on Him. As children of God, believers are invited into spiritual cooperation with Him, where growth is nurtured by His presence. Only God has the power to heal and cleanse hearts, but this transformation will only unfold as believers learn to trust Him more fully. Experiencing God's care strengthens believers confidence in His goodness; their growing trust opens them to His healing work. Through this ongoing relationship of love and trust, believers grow to reflect Christ more fully.

Rather than fearing God as if He were harsh or unstable, we are invited to focus on His purpose—to perfect us in love. His intent is always positive, shaping us for endurance, maturity, and joy. He will never abandon us, nor will He forsake His plans. God is on our side; even if we let go, He holds on.

FULLY DEPEND ON CHRIST'S RIGHTEOUSNESS

The Gospel transforms lives when believers fully rest in Christ's finished work, leaving no room for self-reliance. Any mixture of faith in Christ and trust in personal effort exposes lingering fear and doubt. If a person does not fully rely on Christ's sacrifice, she must not be confident in its sufficiency.

Can Believers Ever Lose Salvation?

The belief that salvation depends on performance distorts the Gospel. Some mistakenly view salvation as fragile—dependent on achieving enough obedience to maintain it. They see salvation as a football that must be carried securely across the goal line—fearful that a single fumble could lose it forever. If salvation depended on human effort, it would inevitably be lost, just as a football carried by a clumsy player would be fumbled before reaching the goal.

A focus on "fragile" fuels reliance on self-effort, which directly opposes grace. But Scripture is clear—the only way to please God is by faith (Hebrews 11:6). Salvation is not an object that can be lost; it is an irreversible transformation into new life. Believers cannot "fumble" salvation because God carries it for them—He is our salvation.

If someone filled with God's Spirit can struggle with sin, how could someone entirely enslaved to sin ever achieve perfection on her own? Romans 7 makes clear that righteousness cannot be earned by human effort. Martin Luther, a champion of the Reformation, proclaimed salvation by faith and grace alone:

> God has surely promised His grace to the humbled: that is, to those who mourn over and despair of themselves. But a man cannot be thoroughly humbled till he realizes that his salvation is utterly beyond his own powers, counsels, efforts, will and works, and depends absolutely on the will, counsel, pleasure and work of Another—God alone. As long as he is persuaded that he can make even the smallest contribution to his salvation, he remains self-confident and does not utterly despair of himself, and so is not humbled before God; but plans out for himself (or at least hopes and longs for) a position, an occasion, a work, which shall bring him final salvation. But he who [has no] doubt that his destiny depends entirely on the will of God despairs entirely of himself, chooses nothing for himself, but waits for God to work in him; and such a man is very near to grace for his salvation.
>
> These truths are published for the sake of the elect, that they may be humbled and brought down to nothing, and so saved.
> SB#9, Luther, p. 100

His point is clear—no one is saved by placing even the smallest hope in their own efforts. People either humbly receive the Gospel, recognizing their complete dependence on God, or their prideful self-reliance blocks the Gospel from their hearts. Only in humility can self-reliance die, allowing hope in God's unfailing love to flourish.

A HOPE THAT DOES NOT DISAPPOINT

God's love gives believers hopeful assurance, even in the midst of trials and persecution. Trusting in Him is never wasted effort because God will certainly reward His people in the afterlife.

> Not only that, but we rejoice in our sufferings, knowing that suffering produces endurance, and endurance produces character, and character produces hope, and hope does not put us to shame, because God's love has been poured into our hearts through the Holy Spirit who has been given to us.
> Romans 5:3-5 ESV

The phrase "not put us to shame" is a profound declaration of the reliability of the hope believers have in Christ. Human hope can often lead to disappointment when placed in unreliable sources. But the hope described in Romans 5 is rooted in God's unwavering character, ensuring that it will never fail or leave believers feeling ashamed for trusting Him.

This assurance is crucial to salvation, reinforcing the truth that those who trust in God can be fully confident in His promises—including eternal life and fellowship with Him. Their hope is not in their ability to remain faithful, but in God's unchanging faithfulness.

Vindication Despite Trials

Trials can sometimes bring doubt, making believers question whether they are truly secure in their salvation. The phrase "not put us to shame" serves as a reminder that God is actively at work even in suffering, turning difficulties into opportunities for growth (Romans 5:3-4). Endurance, character, and hope developed through trials serve as evidence of salvation's reality. Far from being ashamed of their hope, believers can stand confident, knowing their suffering has purpose and affirms their connection to God.

Job's story illustrates this truth powerfully. Though he endured immense suffering and faced accusations from his friends, he never abandoned his trust in God. In the end, Job was vindicated—not by being declared innocent of wrongdoing, but by having his faith confirmed as genuine. His steadfast hope was not misplaced, and God honored him by restoring what had been lost and rebuking those who doubted him (Job 42:7-10). Similarly, believers can take heart in their trials, knowing their perseverance affirms the authenticity of their faith and strengthens their assurance of salvation.

God's Love As The Anchor

Salvation's assurance is ultimately grounded in God's outpouring of love through Holy Spirit. This love is not fleeting; it is permanently given and testifies to the believer's secure place in God's family. The presence of Holy Spirit seals believers, giving them confidence that the hope they cling to will be fulfilled (2 Corinthians 1:21-22).

In this way, "not put us to shame" is a powerful statement about the permanence and reliability of salvation. God's love ensures that believers can confidently endure trials, grow in hope, and remain secure, knowing their salvation will not end in disappointment.

SECURITY DESPITE NEEDING RENOVATION

While the assurance of salvation is a foundational truth, it does not mean believers stop growing or cooperating with God's work in their lives. Salvation does not eliminate the need for transformation—it guarantees it.

A believer can be permanently saved by Christ's work while also needing to engage in the ongoing process of spiritual renewal. Imagine God gifting you a house, fully paid for, with unlimited resources for restoration. You live securely in it while He works with you to improve it—without any risk of eviction or loss.

God's gifts and His calling are irrevocable, yet during the remainder of this life, believers remain in constant need of renovation. The born-again believer is a new creation, spiritually aligned with God. Jesus's crucifixion eliminated the hostility that once existed due to sin, leaving a spirit that only desires fellowship with Him. Nothing can separate believers from God's love, and He continues His refining work for the remainder of their lives. The security believers have in Christ is entirely independent of their imperfections—just as home ownership is not invalidated by the ongoing need for repairs.

However, even with these glorious truths, Christians can experience debilitating anxiety. Does God really love me? Will He truly save me? If life feels overwhelming now, how can I be sure? Some continue to fear that imperfections in their lives could cause God to abandon them, but Scripture assures that He remains a faithful and loving owner, committed to restoration rather than rejection.

Salvation is irreversible because believers are united with Jesus. Just as He cannot be separated from life, neither can those who belong to Him. Their destiny is permanently bound to His. What happens to Him happens to them. They have crossed over from death to life. Because He conquered death and lives forever, they too will live eternally, guaranteed.

Salvation is given by God, not taken away by Him (Hebrews 13:5). Jesus paid the full price for believers' redemption. God owns His people, and He preserves what belongs to Him for all time. His power and desire to enable believers to persevere until the end are unwavering. We can trust that He will complete the good work He started.

FOR REFLECTION AND DISCUSSION

1. Under what conditions can salvation be lost?

Can Believers Ever Lose Salvation?

2. How are immature believers susceptible to believing salvation can be lost?
3. What does it mean to be spiritually insecure, and how does faith counteract it?
4. How does the concept of adoption deepen our understanding of God's commitment to believers?
5. Would loving parents ever discipline their children by using murder?
6. How does Hebrews 13:5 reinforce the idea that salvation is permanent?
7. How does Hebrews 10:14 explain the sufficiency of Christ's sacrifice?
8. What does it mean that God's gifts and calling are irrevocable, and how does this reinforce eternal security?
9. How does the fact that believers are spiritually aligned with God after salvation affect their desires and relationship with Him?
10. How do the promises of Scripture reassure believers who fear abandonment by God?
11. Why is abusing God's grace impossible?
12. Why is spiritual suicide impossible?
13. How does God's role as Savior and Sustainer clarify salvation's permanence while allowing for spiritual growth?
14. How does God's ongoing renovation of believers, like the house analogy, reinforce salvation's permanence?
15. What is the significance of Jesus paying the full price for believers' redemption?

CHAPTER 7

How Does Spiritual Growth Strengthen Assurance of Salvation?

God parents His children, guiding them toward spiritual maturity rather than fear, frustration, or condemnation. His heart does not demand immediate perfection but rather steady progress—a journey of learning, embracing truth, and following Christ's example. This growth strengthens a believer's assurance of salvation, serving as visible evidence of the transformative power of Holy Spirit at work.

God is patient as believers unlearn fleshly habits and learn to live to please the Spirit. Even though immature Christians must grow beyond struggles with sin, their identity as God's children remains secure (1 Corinthians 3:1-2).

Even the smallest steps of spiritual growth demonstrate living faith, providing hope and strengthening assurance of salvation. God does not impose a rigid timeline for growth—He works patiently and faithfully, sanctifying believers according to His perfect plan.

TRUST GOD'S DISCIPLINE

God's discipline is an expression of His love, designed to shape His children into His likeness. Like a wise and loving parent, He corrects not to condemn, but to lead toward righteousness. His discipline instills hope, confirming His absolute commitment to salvation. Through His presence within believers, He reveals Himself as both the way and the guide.

In contrast, judgment brings condemnation—a penalty without hope of restoration, reserved for those whose hearts remain hardened against Him. But for His children, discipline affirms their place in His family; it refines and restores, confirming salvation:

> And have you forgotten the encouraging words God spoke to you as his children? He said, "My child, don't make light of the Lord's discipline, and don't give up when he corrects you. For the Lord disciplines those he loves, and he punishes each one he accepts as his child." As you endure this divine discipline, remember that God is treating you as his own children. Who ever heard of a child who is never disciplined by its father? If God doesn't discipline you as he does all of his children, it means that you are illegitimate and are not really his children at all. Since we respected our earthly fathers who disciplined us, shouldn't we submit even more to the discipline of the Father of our spirits, and live forever? For our earthly fathers disciplined us for a few years, doing the best they knew how. But God's discipline is always good for us, so that we might share in his holiness. No discipline is enjoyable while it is happening—it's painful! But afterward there will be a peaceful harvest of right living for those who are trained in this way.
> Hebrews 12:5-11 NLT

Discipline is whatever God ordains to prepare His people for the good works He designed for them—training and correction that deepen spiritual life and increase understanding.

GOD CREATED EMOTIONAL GROWTH

Our physical developmental process can help us understand our spiritual developmental process. Every child starts out as

How Does Spiritual Growth Strengthen Assurance of Salvation?

a baby in her mother's womb. From the moment of conception babies grow toward independence. It's not very long before they are speaking, going to school, and leaving home.

Healthy emotional growth moves individuals through distinct stages—dependency as children, independence as adults, and interdependence as mature adults. Dependency focuses on receiving care and survival. Independence seeks to develop individuality and appropriate self-sufficiency. Interdependence transcends independence by fostering collaboration and sacrificial love for others.

Young children need clear boundaries—what is healthy behavior and what is not. Then they can develop a healthy respect for rules (the "law"). Learning that actions have consequences helps instill wisdom and responsibility, so that future attitudes and behaviors are less likely to be harmful.

All children have unique personalities and mature at different paces. They require a balance of discipline and compassion, truth and grace, to navigate life's complexities. Trusting a loving parent or mentor to set boundaries is crucial for emotional health.

Of course, emotional development isn't always smooth. Sometimes, growth is disrupted—a child may become stuck in dependence or rebellion, unable to reach her full potential. Helping a child develop requires patience, wisdom, and an approach tailored to her specific needs.

While healthy children eventually outgrow dependence on their parents, God's children remain eternally dependent on Him. Though we grow in wisdom and capability according to His purposes, we will always and forever rely on His Spirit for life and right behavior from a pure heart. He customizes the perfect strategy to shape attitudes, correct behaviors, and foster growth.

GOD CREATED SPIRITUAL GROWTH

The emotional development process produces emotionally intelligent adults fit for earthly works, but spiritual growth transforms believers into the people God created them to be, fit for eternal works.

For the non-believer, the law remains external, functioning only as a restraint against destructive behavior. The law is good, but it cannot change the rebellious heart. Those led by the sinful nature do not want to do right; they obey only out of fear of earthly consequences, not eternal consequences.

When God creates a new heart in the new believer, she forever has a transformed relationship with the law. Internal motivations inspired by Holy Spirit supersede the external restraints. Instead of following commands out of obligation, believers joyfully obey because the Spirit produces love, purity, and holiness within them.

> For this is the covenant that I will make with the house of Israel after those days, declares the Lord: I will put my laws into their minds, and write them on their hearts, and I will be their God, and they shall be my people.
> Hebrews 8:10 ESV

Genuine obedience flows not from fear of punishment, but from a transformed heart motivated by love. God's Spirit softens the believer's heart, creating a desire for righteousness. Those who long to do right but struggle must be disciplined with compassion. But, for those who reject truth entirely, God reserves judgment because their hearts' motive is to only avoid consequences.

As God's children, we have been given new life and a new heart. He desires that we cultivate internal motivation to love. He freed us from the law, which only proved our inability to measure up. Without the requirements of the law standing in the way, believers experience true freedom. When they act in love, they can be confident their motivation is genuine—not driven by obligation, fear of punishment, or the shame of falling short, but by the joy of honoring God.

Though God still disciplines, believers no longer carry the shame of failure. His love flows from His perfect nature; He cannot fail. Similarly, as believers live in the freedom of their new identity, their love matures, becoming a genuine reflection of God's character. They love because they want to, not because they "have to" or because "it's the right thing to do."

Spiritual life continues for eternity, therefore, so will spiritual growth. The depth and uniqueness of believers' identities reflect God's creative image. Each person provides a unique perspective into His nature, ensuring eternal relationships remain fresh. God's creativity is inexhaustible, forever inviting new discoveries and new lessons. Even greater is His unending, perfect love—so vast and limitless that His children will continue learning and growing in it for eternity.

USE THE LAW CORRECTLY

Immature believers often misunderstand the purpose of God's law. Some are **carnal**, failing to take sin seriously, while others are **weak**, relying to some degree on the law for security. Despite both of their struggles with favoring the flesh, their salvation remains secure.

Carnal believers tend to overlook the seriousness of sin. They:
- rely on grace without prioritizing growth.
- give in to temptation more easily.
- struggle to delay gratification.
- view suffering as purposeless and avoid it.

Though their understanding is flawed, carnal believers are saved. Judging them as unsaved discounts the transformative grace of God. They need encouragement to embrace spiritual maturity as both necessary and natural for the believer.

Weak believers, on the other hand, often seek security in meeting the requirements of the law (SB#25, Kendall, p. 125). They:
- place confidence in personal effort rather than faith in Christ.
- emphasize legalistic adherence over developing their love relationship with God.

- weaken the Gospel's power by emphasizing works over grace.
- believe suffering can be avoided if behavior is good enough.

Though weak believers struggle with legalism, they are fully accepted by God (Romans 14). They need to understand that justification does not come through the law but through faith, and spiritual growth happens through Holy Spirit working in their lives.

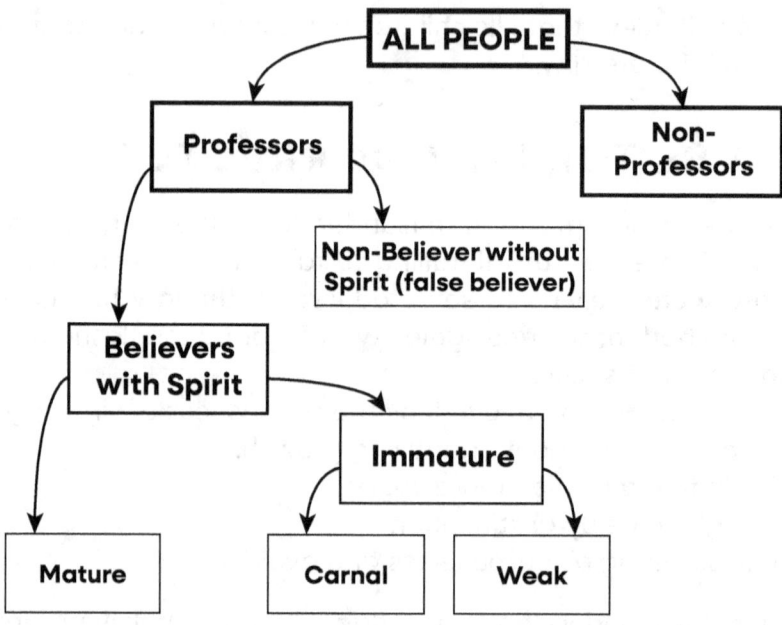

Spiritual immaturity is different than not being spiritually alive. Just as a newborn is fully human despite not being able to care for herself, an immature believer is fully alive in Christ, even while needing guidance and support.

DEAD TO THE LAW, ALIVE IN CHRIST

The law brings condemnation, but God, in His mercy, frees believers from its impossible demands. Trying to achieve righteousness through law-keeping denies Christ's sacrifice (Romans 3:20).

How Does Spiritual Growth Strengthen Assurance of Salvation?

> You were dead because of your sins and because your sinful nature was not yet cut away. Then God made you alive with Christ, for he forgave all our sins. He canceled the record of the charges against us and took it away by nailing it to the cross.
> Colossians 2:13-14 NLT

The law exposes sin and restrains destructive behavior. When it leads non-believers to conviction of sinfulness, it serves a valuable purpose. But for believers, while the law does not provide justification, it remains a guide for righteous living. Only Holy Spirit can produce the fruit of righteousness and fulfillment of the law (SB#2, Ferguson, p. 114).

> We know that the law is good when used correctly. For the law was not intended for people who do what is right. It is for people who are lawless and rebellious, who are ungodly and sinful, who consider nothing sacred and defile what is holy, who kill their father or mother or commit other murders.
> 1 Timothy 1:8-9 NLT

Apart from God, the law is harsh, but with God it becomes kind. Because God is love, we see that the law without love is harsh, while the law with love is kind. Recognizing the kindness of His mercy leads to worship. God teaches us that truth needs love and love needs truth to be helpful (Ephesians 4:15).

Ferguson warns against the peril of divorcing God's law from His love, as Eve did when she perceived the law as deprivation rather than wisdom from a loving Father. This distortion fosters legalism and undermines trust in God's grace and generosity. The devil was able to turn her affections away from God.

> God thus became to her "He-whose-favor-has-to-be-earned." ... Legalism is simply separating the law of God from the person of God.
> SB#2, Ferguson, p. 82-83

The law is good when used correctly but it cannot save—it brings condemnation. For non-believers, it reveals sin. For believers, the Spirit enables them to fulfill the law's intent: to love and live righteously (2 Corinthians 3:6, Romans 7:5).

> He has made us competent as ministers of a new covenant—not of the letter but of the Spirit; for the letter kills, but the Spirit gives life.
> 2 Corinthians 3:6 NIV

Believers grieve the Spirit when choosing fleshly desires even while acknowledging their sin. Non-believers reject God's authority entirely, creating their own standards. The believer, though imperfect, agrees with God's absolute truth, whereas the non-believer justifies wrongdoing. This distinction underscores the believer's reliance on grace for salvation.

Concerning sin, the believer thinks, "I know this is wrong, but I want to do it anyway." She acknowledges sin because the Spirit lives within her. The non-believer thinks, "I want to do this, therefore it isn't wrong." Rejecting God's law, she creates her own morality, for which she will face condemnation.

The law is good as an absolute standard but is not a "loving parent" like Holy Spirit. Believers are free from condemnation, regardless of their struggles with sin, because they live under grace. The Spirit convicts them inwardly, modeling grief over sin and leading them toward holiness. Unlike external law, which condemns, God's discipline guides them in love. Through His Spirit, He enables them to fulfill the law in love, following Jesus's example. They love because He first loved them.

OBEY THE LAW BY MEANS OF THE SPIRIT

Obedience through the Spirit is superior to legalistic compliance. God works within believers, aligning their hearts with His, so they desire to do what is right out of love, not obligation. Christ's grace liberates them from a rule-driven approach to holiness and fosters genuine love.

> For if you live according to the flesh you will die, but if by the Spirit you put to death the deeds of the body, you will live.
> Romans 8:13 ESV

Only non-believers can live according to the flesh so only they will die. Only believers can live by the Spirit so they will put to death the misdeeds of the body and live.

How Does Spiritual Growth Strengthen Assurance of Salvation?

I want to do right. I want to please God. I agree that the absolute standards for living that God has decreed are perfect and wonderful. I want God to work in me so that I want to do what is good. I want to feel the desire to do good from the motives of a pure heart rather than having to obey out of obligation or because it is the right thing to do.

Through Christ's obedience, believers are made righteous apart from their own effort (Romans 5:19). Spirit-led living naturally fulfills God's law, as believers love others through His transformative work. This freedom allows them to fully express their unique God-given personalities while reflecting His love to the world.

LIVE TO PLEASE THE SPIRIT

Spiritual maturity brings the understanding that God's kingdom matters far more than immediate pleasure or comfort. Living to please the Spirit honors the freedom He gives through His presence, and in return, believers will reap eternal blessings.

> For you were called to freedom, brothers. Only do not use your freedom as an opportunity for the flesh, but through love serve one another.
> Galatians 5:13 ESV

> Those who live only to satisfy their own sinful nature will harvest decay and death from that sinful nature. But those who live to please the Spirit will harvest everlasting life from the Spirit. So let's not get tired of doing what is good. At just the right time we will reap a harvest of blessing if we don't give up.
> Galatians 6:8-9 NLT

Only believers can truly please the Spirit because only they have faith to see God as good.

> And without faith it is impossible to please God, because anyone who comes to him must believe that he exists and that he rewards those who earnestly seek him.
> Hebrews 11:6 NIV

Non-believers, lacking faith, live to satisfy their sinful nature. However, God's gift of faith, His preserving presence, and the righteousness He credits ensure that believers are free from harvesting decay and death. They are dead to the law, and their sin has been crucified with Christ (Galatians 2:19-20).

Jesus calls believers to prioritize God's kingdom and righteousness above all else, trusting in His provision for their needs (Matthew 6:33). Those who genuinely recognize their place in God's plan will find motivation to advance His mission.

Mature believers have learned to favor the Spirit over the flesh. Through God's training, they gain a greater ability to walk by the Spirit and deny the cravings of the flesh and the world. Spiritual growth happens as God teaches His children to desire Him more than worldly distractions.

> But I say, walk by the Spirit, and you will not gratify the desires of the flesh. For the desires of the flesh are against the Spirit, and the desires of the Spirit are against the flesh, for these are opposed to each other, to keep you from doing the things you want to do.
> Galatians 5:16-17 ESV

Spiritual growth moves believers from instability in the flesh to peace and stability in the Spirit. A mature believer harvests the fruit of walking by the Spirit—a peaceful and purposeful life (Romans 8:5-6).

Romans 7 explores the believer's ongoing struggle with sin, showing that while faith in Christ sets a person free from sin's dominion, its presence still lingers. Paul describes his internal conflict, affirming that although he desires righteousness, his flesh remains interested in sin. Romans 6 clarifies that believers are no longer slaves to sin but are now slaves to righteousness through Christ. The tension in Romans 7 highlights that, though sin remains, it no longer defines the believer's identity. Romans 8 ultimately provides resolution, affirming that those in Christ live by the Spirit, not the flesh. While believers battle sin's presence, their true status is secured in righteousness.

When Christians refer to themselves as "sinners," they often do so humbly, acknowledging their ongoing struggle with sin.

How Does Spiritual Growth Strengthen Assurance of Salvation?

But we should not confuse that humility with a return to our former identity. We are no longer dead in sin—we are alive in Christ (Ephesians 2:5), adopted into God's family, and driven by a new nature. To continue labeling ourselves primarily as "sinners" can slowly erode the assurance of salvation. It frames sin as our core identity, rather than a defeated enemy we still contend with. Over time this could lead us to believe we are not really saved—undermining the confidence and joy God intends for us as His children. We are not sinners who occasionally act like saints; we are saints who, by grace, are learning to overcome sin.

DESIRING GOD'S WILL

Believers are transformed by God's Spirit, gaining a new heart that desires to align with His will. Although they may still sin, their motives reflect agreement with God's standards and trust in His grace. They no longer want to sin or experience separation from God because Holy Spirit teaches them to desire what God desires.

Spiritual maturity shifts a believer's motivation from external to internal. The more a believer understands God's unconditional love, the more she wants to please Him with righteous living. This new way of being motivated by love is truly a work of the Spirit. This positive motivation is far superior to any negative motivation.

God sees the complete picture—He's not concerned with how much grace is required because He knows His love will ultimately produce the desired behavior (Romans 5:20).

In contrast, an immature person wants only to avoid "getting caught." She may return to sinful behavior once the threat of consequences is removed. Rules are necessary to keep her out of trouble and guide her toward growth. Though immature believers do not respond as readily to internal motivation, they remain saved, as God works patiently to train and refine them.

Even in moments of failure, believers desire alignment with God's will. They do not rely on fear of losing salvation to motivate righteousness, for their security is rooted in God Himself.

Moral striving in the flesh has always failed and will continue to fail, but God changes hearts, inspiring agreement with His truth. Genuine transformation is sustained by God's constant revelation of His goodness in the believer's life.

God and His goodness are inseparable. Goodness does not exist apart from God. "No one is good but God alone" (Mark 10:18 ESV). Goodness is not a human construct or independent force. Therefore, we can only be "good" because of God's presence, which enables us to be good.

EVERYONE IS ACCOUNTABLE TO GOD

Even though salvation is secure, the believer's choices still matter in God's plan. Salvation cannot be earned through self-effort, and no amount of effort—whether righteous or sinful—can disqualify a believer from salvation. However, this security does not grant permission for reckless behavior without consequences.

Persistent sin that takes grace for granted may indicate a lack of genuine salvation. For believers, God corrects sinful desires through loving discipline, while non-believers ultimately face judgment and destruction. For those in Christ, freedom from condemnation does not mean freedom from responsibility. Sin is harmful, so, God disciplines His children to prevent spiritual decay and guide them into His plan. Those who belong to Him accept and appreciate His correction.

The key distinction between a believer and a non-believer is the presence of Holy Spirit—not necessarily immediate outward right behavior. Transformation in Christ is not about appearances but reflects a new, cooperative way of relating to our Creator.

Believers do not belong to themselves. Jesus purchased them for God through His sacrifice, granting freedom from sin and calling them to glorify Him. God's plans for His children far exceed what self-indulgence offers. A believer who focuses on the Spirit will honor God in all aspects of life.

How Does Spiritual Growth Strengthen Assurance of Salvation?

> Or do you not know that your body is a temple of the Holy Spirit within you, whom you have from God? You are not your own, for you were bought with a price. So glorify God in your body.
> 1 Corinthians 6:19-20 ESV

Scripture reminds us that everyone is accountable to God—"You will always harvest what you plant" (Galatians 6:7). Some will be saved, but only as through fire (1 Corinthians 3:15). Rewards reflect the decisions believers make in this life. When they fail to surrender to God's ways, He disciplines them in love, reshaping their desires toward His will for ultimate good. Pursuing spiritual maturity brings blessing.

Believers are united with Christ, one in spirit with Him (1 Corinthians 6:17). Scripture provides no condition that triggers God's removal of Holy Spirit's indwelling presence. However, grace is never a license to sin (Romans 6:1-2). God's kindness includes loving discipline. His actions work for the ultimate good of His children, even when they are confused or hurt by how history unfolds.

Warnings in Scripture address those who might exploit grace or lack genuine faith. When faced with consequences, a person who only professes Christ may abandon belief, but the person with a regenerated heart continues to love God and seek growth. This is why assurance of salvation is so critical—believers must understand the stark contrast between life with Christ and life without Him.

The God who restores His children does not abandon them. If a genuine believer struggles with seasons of doubt like Peter who denied Jesus three times, she has not lost her salvation—only the time spent at a distance. When she returns, God does not scold or condemn but patiently continues revealing His kingdom, one gentle truth at a time.

Trials test and strengthen faith, deepening the believer's experience of salvation. Assurance of salvation fosters confidence and joy in relationship with God. This certainty of His presence increases resilience and endurance, shaping a believer's heart to remain steadfast.

Jesus's sacrifice is sufficient once for all time. Believers are holy, cleansed by His blood, and called to live as God's children. Though salvation cannot be lost, God continually aligns believers with His purposes, moving them toward maturity. Open rebellion marks the nature of non-believers—not God's children. While salvation is rooted in Christ's sacrifice, believers must approach their faith with reverence, recognizing that their relationship with God is of incomparable worth. Faith of great value should not be treated casually.

SURRENDER TO THE SPIRIT

Living without fear of losing salvation changes everything. It frees believers to rely on the Spirit rather than self-effort that so often ends in shameful failure. Paul contrasts this Spirit-led life with the old way—life under the law versus life under grace.

> But now we are released from the law, having died to that which held us captive, so that we serve in the new way of the Spirit and not in the old way of the written code.
> Romans 7:6 ESV

Believers can make mistakes yet trust God to guide them. Righteousness cannot be attained through attempts to meet the behavioral requirements of the law (Romans 3:20). True maturity means accepting and trusting God's help. The saved person witnesses God's power working within her, experiencing a completely different life from the one without Him. While she can still remember the old life, God declares it gone, having seated her in the heavenlies with Christ.

The light of the law reveals sin, bringing only condemnation. The light of the Gospel through the Spirit reveals salvation—Jesus as the true solution to the problem of sin.

The law identifies sin, but the human will, by itself, does not know the difference between sin and not sin. The law provides the measure of right and wrong, but it does not empower the will to act righteously—it merely exposes the need for grace.

How Does Spiritual Growth Strengthen Assurance of Salvation?

Though living is difficult in a world filled with evil, temptations of the flesh, and distractions, Paul urges believers to set their minds on what is true, holy, and good (Philippians 4:8).

The Christian life centers on abiding—believers presenting themselves to God and trusting Him to work through them. Salvation is not merely "fire insurance" but a journey of transformation, surrender, and reliance on His power. When believers fail, His loving discipline shapes their desires to align with His will, correcting them for their ultimate good. Through the Spirit, believers reflect their new nature, pursuing God's will in all aspects of life.

The Spirit's leadership is essential for any spiritual growth. This is the life to which God calls His children—not striving for self-righteousness but trusting the One who loved them before the foundation of the world. Works produced through the Spirit glorify God and fulfill His purposes, reflecting the lives He planned for His people to live.

Growth takes time, but as believers surrender to Him, they experience the depth of His love. It takes time to be able to love like God. We love because He first loved us.

FOR REFLECTION AND DISCUSSION

1. Reflect on the difference between spiritual immaturity and spiritual maturity. In what ways do you see both at work in your spiritual walk?
2. In what ways have you seen evidence of God's transformation in your heart and desires?
3. What does assurance of salvation mean to you, and how does experiencing spiritual growth strengthen it?
4. Why do you think God allows believers to grow at different paces rather than imposing a strict timeline for maturity?
5. Can you recall a time when you experienced God's discipline? How does recognizing God's discipline as confirmation of salvation change the way you respond to challenges and correction?

6. What does it look like to walk by the Spirit in practical ways, and how does that shift us away from relying on external rules?
7. What is the purpose of the law compared to the purpose of grace?
8. How does setting your mind on spiritual things help you navigate struggles with fleshly desires?
9. How can we avoid misusing the freedom we have in Christ while still living in the grace God provides?
10. What makes surrendering to the Spirit a different kind of relationship than striving through self-effort, and how does this shape your view of yourself and God?
11. How does understanding that we are "bought with a price" affect the way we live and serve God?
12. How has your understanding of spiritual growth changed after reading this chapter?

PART 3

God's Groundwork Secures Salvation

Before God laid a single stone, His initiating love and unstoppable purpose set the foundation for our salvation. He predestined us as His beloved children, designed us in His image, and planned for Christ's sacrifice to free us from the bondage of sin. Through the Spirit's power, He summons us into existence and sustains our faith so we can stand firm. Because He began this work, we can trust He will carry it to completion.

CHAPTER 8

Who Causes Salvation?

Salvation begins with God. Long before creation, He loved His people, choosing them not based on merit but on mercy. This chapter explores how God causes salvation from start to finish: how He foreloves, summons, and recreates believers. Through Scripture, we'll see that salvation is not earned but gifted—born in His sovereign grace, shaped by His delight, and sustained by His power.

GOD INITIATES SALVATION MAKING IT A STUMBLING BLOCK

To understand how salvation happens, we must begin with God as the initiator. He loved His people before time, reveals Christ to them in time, and secures them for eternity. Through Christ, God has taken the worry of condemnation off the table. Even if we sin, He no longer "sees" our imperfections. That's the true Gospel.

> Even before he made the world, God loved us and chose us in Christ to be holy and without fault in his eyes.
> Ephesians 1:4 NLT

Believers respond to God's gift of salvation, which is caused entirely by His sovereign will. They do not initiate or choose salvation but are drawn by His grace to believe and confess Him as Lord. Believers cannot claim credit for their faith or redemption (Ephesians 2:8-9).

Monergism, meaning "work by one," emphasizes that salvation is entirely God's sovereign work, without any contributions from the individual. He alone initiates, grants, and sustains salvation, while the believer passively receives this gift. Now we can confidently answer "Who causes salvation?" with "God is fully responsible." We can also address, "Why must God cause salvation?"

ONLY GOD IS GOOD

God alone holds ultimate dominion over earth and heaven, and Scripture makes it clear that there is only one God. All existence has room for only one supreme being—all-loving, all-powerful, and all-perfect—and Jesus Christ alone qualifies.

There is only one true option for worship. We can worship Jesus, who is good, or we can worship something lesser—whether Satan, a human, self, or another created thing. There are not multiple good gods to choose from. Therefore, the only two options are life, which is God, and death, which is separation from Him. Since only one good, rational option exists, to say a choice exists is misleading. The so-called freedom to reject God is a false freedom because those who reject Him are deceived, living in darkness as children of the devil.

SALVATION'S SIMPLICITY

Many struggle to accept the simplicity of salvation, finding it difficult to let go of human pride and the desire to earn favor. Yet God's grace allows believers to see salvation as His perfect and merciful plan. For those who believe, the beauty of the Gospel

Who Causes Salvation?

lies in its simplicity—unconditional acceptance into God's family. For those who reject it, the Gospel becomes a stumbling block, exposing the divide between belief and unbelief (1 Corinthians 1:18–25, Romans 9). The Gospel holds immeasurable value—but only those who believe it can benefit from its worth.

Salvation requires nothing more than looking to Jesus and recognizing Him as Lord.[1]

> And as Moses lifted up the serpent in the wilderness, so must the Son of Man be lifted up, that whoever believes in him may have eternal life.
> John 3:14-15 ESV

Belief does not cause salvation but reveals the work of God's Spirit within us. God must provide the faith to enable belief, underscoring that salvation is not earned or performance-based but entirely love-based. God created all believers in love because He wants to spend eternity with them.

The Gospel is the key that opens human hearts, but only Jesus can unlock them (Romans 10:17; Ephesians 1:13). Through His grace, the way to salvation is radical, amazing, merciful, and wonderful. The Gospel is unimaginably good news—scandalous to some, unbelievable to others, yet made real by God's grace, enabling believers to see Jesus as Lord and Savior.

The believing thief on the cross is the ultimate example of salvation's simplicity. His attitude stands in contrast to the belligerent thief beside him. His receptiveness to belief can only come from God's merciful work in his heart. To be able to recognize Christ as the Son of God requires supernatural spiritual intervention.

> Jesus told them, "This is the only work God wants from you: Believe in the one he has sent."
>
> "I tell you the truth, anyone who believes has eternal life."
>
> "The Spirit alone gives eternal life. Human effort accomplishes nothing. And the very words I have spoken to you are spirit and life."
> John 6:29, 47, 63 NLT

---

1. bibleref.com/John/3/John-3-15.html

Jesus empowers belief—the first evidence of new life. Salvation cannot be earned, but it produces fruit in believers' lives. While Scripture teaches that true believers will bear fruit, it does not provide a specific amount or timeframe. Believers who live longer than the thief eventually show evidence of salvation through good works, but these evidences do not cause salvation—salvation causes them.

Scripture teaches that salvation is verified by two events:
1. **Internal:** Believing in your heart that God raised Jesus from the dead.
2. **External:** Confessing with your mouth that Jesus is Lord.

> If you confess with your mouth that Jesus is Lord and believe in your heart that God raised him from the dead, you will be saved. For with the heart one believes and is justified, and with the mouth one confesses and is saved.
> Romans 10:9-10 ESV

The thief confessed aloud, "Remember me when You come into Your kingdom." Jesus, seeing the belief in his heart—something only God can do—responded with, "Today you will be with me in paradise" (Luke 23:39-43).

Many resist the truth that so little is required—not because salvation is difficult, but because simplicity itself can be unsettling. People are suspicious of "free"; they naturally seek control or effort in spiritual matters, making the Gospel a stumbling block. They assume something so valuable must require human effort. But, salvation remains God's merciful gift—freely given, yet misunderstood by those who seek to control grace rather than receive it.

The simplicity of the Gospel reveals both the mercy and sovereignty of God. Without God-given faith, pride thrives like a weed, crowding out the Gospel's message. Salvation requires no work from humans, yet not everyone will receive it.

Why do so many reject this priceless gift? The answer lies in God's sovereign choice to reveal Himself. Before anyone can choose to look to Him, He must first draw them, allowing them to see Him as He truly is (John 6:44).

GOD'S LOVE IS IRRESISTIBLE

God does not override the human will when He chooses His children. Yet, neither does He ask permission to save them. He aligns their nature with His own, revealing Himself so compellingly that they freely follow. Saul's dramatic conversion into Paul (Acts 9) is a clear example of God's infinitely persuasive grace—a revelation so powerful that it alters a person's entire life-direction. God didn't force Saul into His service; He awakened him to the reality of who He is.

Grace is irresistible not because it overpowers, but because it fulfills. God is loving, good, and sovereign. He initiates a relationship with His people who are in desperate need, and there is no other good option. Since He created humans with deep longings for love, His perfect fulfillment of those desires cannot be rejected.

Picture this: *A woman lives in a cave, surrounded by echoes of her own voice. She's never heard another. One day, a song enters—not her own—and it doesn't echo. It's pure, clear, and alive. She follows it to the mouth of the cave. Realizing her heart will never be alone again, she leaves behind the cave, never to return.*

GOD OPENS SPIRITUAL EYES

God created us with a need for spiritual light, but we are born blind to it, in darkness. We are dependent upon God for everything. When we are hungry and food is provided, we eat. When we need light, and God provides it, we see.

God authored Scripture, and only He can unlock its meaning. He speaks intentionally through parables and spiritual truths that require faith to understand—faith He gives to those He chooses. True believers receive understanding from Holy Spirit, who guides them into all truth (Matthew 11:25-27; Mark 4:10-12; John 3:27).

God alone provides spiritual illumination, causing believers to see His truth. Once revealed, salvation transforms reality forever—what has been seen cannot be unseen. God's plan for His people is increasing clarity, never a return to blindness.

The "eyes to see" and the "ears to hear" are supernaturally provided by the Spirit. Without faith, even the most learned person cannot comprehend Scripture's meaning. But the humblest child, with the Spirit, can know Jesus personally. Human effort based on factual knowledge cannot produce faith. Holy Spirit produces the faith that even a child without elaborate knowledge can receive.

The only way to be chosen by God is through His revelation of Himself in Jesus Christ (John 6:44-47, 60-69). In John 6, Jesus asks Peter if he wants to walk away, as many others had done. Peter's response defines saving faith, the faith that secures every true believer:

> Simon Peter answered him, "Lord, to whom shall we go? You have the words of eternal life, and we have believed, and have come to know, that you are the Holy One of God."
> John 6:68-69 ESV

Where else can we go? We have received the greatest gift and are no longer enemies of God. There is no logical reason to leave Him. The new nature causes believers to desire Christ, never to escape Him. Fear leads people to flee, but God's perfect love drives out fear and keeps His children secure.

Eternal Life As A Priceless Pearl

Once a person has received eternal life, any status change would leave her worse off. Why would anyone trade an infinitely better reality for an infinitely worse one?[2]

Suppose that free will choice exists. Imagine a contest offering a priceless pearl as the grand prize. After days of competition, you win the pearl. Now, you have the option to cash out or continue playing. If you continue, you must forfeit the

---
2. bibleref.com/Romans/6/Romans-6-12.html

pearl—though you might win something else, nothing could match its value.

If the pearl represents eternal life with God, no one who understands its worth would risk losing it. Only someone blind to its value would trade it for something lesser. This person may hold eternal life in her hand but not in her heart—never understanding its value, never having truly received Christ as her own, and never having truly consumed Christ's flesh and blood, as referenced in John 6.[3]

Jesus Heals Spiritual Blindness

Without God's intervention, people remain spiritually blind, unable to grasp the truth of eternal life. God delights in revealing Himself to those He has foreknown and chosen. Only God can open spiritual eyes and ears, allowing people to see Christ and receive faith as a gift.

> For by grace you have been saved through faith. And this is not your own doing; it is the gift of God, not a result of works, so that no one may boast.
> Ephesians 2:8-9 ESV

Motivated by love, God causes eternal life by gifting faith. Therefore, "saved through faith" means "saved only by God's spiritual power." It does not mean "saved through human generated faith." Faith is the evidence of this new life, not the cause. God is the sole source of the faith, but once given, the believer exercises it. Faith enables her to recognize the truth of Christ. This is illustrated in Scripture:

> Simon Peter replied, "You are the Christ, the Son of the living God." And Jesus answered him, "Blessed are you, Simon Bar-Jonah! For flesh and blood has not revealed this to you, but my Father who is in heaven."
> Matthew 16:16-17 ESV

Peter did not recognize Christ's identity through human ability. Furthermore, God's revelation is not limited to Peter—it

---

[3]. gotquestions.org/Jesus-eat-flesh-drink-blood.html

reflects how He works in the heart of every believer, shaping not just their eternity, but their present reality and identity.

GOD FORELOVES BELIEVERS

God's initiation of salvation begins with His forelove—a sovereign love that motivated Him to create His children and set His plan for redemption into motion. Forelove means that God chose to love His people before they even existed, demonstrating His purposeful and deliberate grace.

Because God foreloved us, His love precedes and enables our response to Him. We do not initiate love toward God; rather, His love initiates salvation, shaping our identity as His chosen people. We can only truly love and value ourselves because God's love shows us how. Without His forelove, we remain spiritually blind and unable to enter His kingdom. We are wholly dependent on God's mercy; we cannot love ourselves into His eternal family.

This forelove is not a passive sentiment but an active, sovereign decision to set His people apart and guarantee their salvation through His grace. This truth affirms our identity—we are not random, forgotten, or overlooked. God's love is neither arbitrary nor earned; instead, it reflects His sovereign will and unshakable purpose, as seen in Romans 8:

> For those whom he foreknew he also predestined to be conformed to the image of his Son, in order that he might be the firstborn among many brothers. And those whom he predestined he also called, and those whom he called he also justified, and those whom he justified he also glorified.
> Romans 8:29-30 ESV

Paul's words show that God's foreknowledge is not merely an awareness of future events—it is His active decision to love and predestine His people for salvation. Each person's existence reflects God's affectionate love. God is not cold toward you—He is excited about you.

God's love is not neutral—it is the opposite of random, careless, or indifferent. Flowing from His sovereign will, it delights in purposeful relationship. This love is the special favor of choosing a bride for Jesus, predestining individuals to be part of His eternal kingdom. Love is love because it is exclusive; it magnifies the depth of God's care and intention.

> In the words of the Scriptures, "I loved Jacob, but I rejected Esau."
> Romans 9:13 NLT

God is sovereign. He is under no obligation to produce "one size fits all" love; He does not love everyone the same. His love is not defined by human standards of fairness, equal access, or unbiased interest—it is the deliberate, purposeful favor of calling and saving His people. God's forelove is the foundation of salvation. It underscores that salvation is caused entirely by Him, defining the believer's reality and identity in Christ.

Eternal life is much more than endless existence. Without God, life would be eternally miserable. God's forelove elevates living forever into eternal life: abundant, joy-filled fellowship with Him.

GOD SUMMONS BELIEVERS

Because of His forelove, God summons His children into His kingdom, ensuring His plan unfolds as He intends. He not only calls them into existence but places them precisely in time and history as part of His greater story (Acts 17:26).

We are not asked to be brought into the physical world or God's spiritual kingdom—we are summoned by God Himself. Our testimonies proclaim our summoning as made possible by God's mercy. He loves, chooses, and transforms individuals—not because they have anything to offer Him that He lacks, but simply because He delights to show mercy.

God Causes Spiritual Birth

Every person is born spiritually dead and in need of new life in Him. There is no possible escape from spiritual death (hell) apart from being born again into spiritual life.

Physical birth is a passive experience—no one chooses it or earns it. Likewise, spiritual birth is entirely God's doing. Just as we don't take credit for being physically born, we cannot claim credit for being born again. Both are purely acts of God's will, accomplished by His power alone.

> Blessed be the God and Father of our Lord Jesus Christ! According to his great mercy, he has caused us to be born again to a living hope through the resurrection of Jesus Christ from the dead, to an inheritance that is imperishable, undefiled, and unfading, kept in heaven for you, who by God's power are being guarded through faith for a salvation ready to be revealed in the last time.
> 1 Peter 1:3-5 ESV

The person who believes God's message in her heart has eternal life. Belief does not cause eternal life; rather, it is evidence that God has already recreated the person. Holy Spirit causes eternal life, guarantees it, and is evidence of it (Ephesians 1:14). He makes specific individuals able to believe the Gospel.

In John 3, Jesus tells Nicodemus that he must be born again. Without this new birth, no one can see or enter the kingdom of God. Holy Spirit, like the wind, moves wherever and however He pleases to bring about new birth.

> Jesus replied, "I assure you, no one can enter the Kingdom of God without being born of water and the Spirit. Humans can reproduce only human life, but the Holy Spirit gives birth to spiritual life. So don't be surprised when I say, 'You must be born again.' The wind blows wherever it wants. Just as you can hear the wind but can't tell where it comes from or where it is going, so you can't explain how people are born of the Spirit."
> John 3:5-9 NLT

Spiritual birth is not by bloodline, the self-righteous effort of the flesh to fulfill the law, nor by the discipline of any person. Free will has no part in it; it is entirely God's doing (SB#9, Luther, p. 303).

> But to all who did receive him, who believed in his name, he gave the right to become children of God, who were born, not of blood nor of the will of the flesh nor of the will of man, but of God.
> John 1:12-13 ESV

Who Causes Salvation?

To be summoned is to be called by God. He predestines people, not simply future events. The kingdom of God is not a democracy where each person has a vote, but one of revelation of spiritual truths, which God controls. God created us primarily to respond to the light of His truth which is infinitely persuasive.

God's sovereignty ensures that everything He creates remains under His control. If anything were beyond His authority, He would cease to be God, and therefore not be worthy of worship. Just as the sun shines in some places but not others, God can shine or withhold His light wherever He chooses.

He is God. He is creating His world. He has chosen His rulers, friends, and co-heirs for all eternity. He doesn't leave it to random chance. You—being saved—how would it feel if God hadn't chosen you, but left your destiny to chance instead? Could that ever feel like personal love?

Scripture makes it clear: some will be saved, and others will not. While God's act of predestining His people may seem unfair to human eyes, it flows from His infinite love, wisdom, and authority. We are called to respond not with pride or protest, but with humility and compassion—for His perfect plan lies beyond our full understanding. Only God can bear the weight of knowing whom He has predestined.

If salvation depended on human decision to accept or reject it, Christ's efforts would not secure salvation for anyone. He would be powerless to save. Humans, left to themselves, never choose salvation. Christ did not merely pay a debt. He personally credited His sacrifice to specific individuals—releasing them from spiritual bondage and opening their eyes to God's wonder.

Life isn't a battle for control—or if it is, God always wins. He is free to do as He pleases. He can show favor to whom He chooses. Humans should not presume control over their destiny while diminishing God's control. Ultimately, the difference between the saved and the unsaved is God's choosing. Salvation is caused entirely by His will, His love, and His power to accomplish what He has planned from the beginning of time (Romans 9).

God Recreates Believers

At the moment of summoning, God recreates the believer's heart, causing not only belief, but also obedience.

> And I will give you a new heart, and a new spirit I will put within you. And I will remove the heart of stone from your flesh and give you a heart of flesh. And I will put my Spirit within you, and cause you to walk in my statutes and be careful to obey my rules.
> Ezekiel 36:26-27 ESV

The true believer, a new creation, desires to follow Jesus above all else (Matthew 13:44-46, 16:25). This "newness" is more than an outward change—it is a fundamental transformation of the heart and mind, made possible only by God's Spirit. It enables a way of being and thinking that was previously impossible. This radical renewal shifts the believer's entire perspective, allowing her to see life and others through God's eyes.

> So we have stopped evaluating others from a human point of view. At one time we thought of Christ merely from a human point of view. How differently we know him now! This means that anyone who belongs to Christ has become a new person. The old life is gone; a new life has begun!
> 2 Corinthians 5:16-17 NLT

The mature Christian does not want to sin. The new nature, with Holy Spirit's training in doing right and love's motivation, leads to righteous living. Sanctification, the process of spiritual growth in righteous living, reflects God's continued work in His people. The Spirit's guidance allows believers to bear fruit and accomplish good works, testifying to the salvation caused entirely by God's grace.

SECURE AND ACCOUNTABLE

God causes believers' spiritual birth, yet this does not eliminate their accountability to Him. He defines the rules of life, setting the framework in which we exist.

BELIEVERS CANNOT KEEP SINNING

Sin is always possible, but it resides in the flesh, not in the new spirit that is reborn in Christ (Romans 7:17). Those born of God cannot sin in their spirit as a new creation, nor do they continue sinning indefinitely. God's presence prevents this.

> No one who abides in him keeps on sinning; no one who keeps on sinning has either seen him or known him. Little children, let no one deceive you. Whoever practices righteousness is righteous, as he is righteous. Whoever makes a practice of sinning is of the devil, for the devil has been sinning from the beginning. The reason the Son of God appeared was to destroy the works of the devil. No one born of God makes a practice of sinning, for God's seed abides in him; and he cannot keep on sinning, because he has been born of God.
> 1 John 3:6-9 ESV

Scripture does not specify a timeframe for how quickly transformation must take place. We are free, under grace, but also commanded to reject fleshly desires and embrace the Spirit—choosing love over sin (Galatians 5:13). Those who belong to God are transformed into His image, and their new nature cannot choose evil (SB#8, Strombeck, p. 69, 132). Therefore, part of being a new creation is having Holy Spirit who makes continuing to sin impossible. Free will cannot prevent sin.

BELIEVERS STRUGGLE
NON-BELIEVERS REBEL

Believers can resist the sinful nature, but how do we "sin yet not sin" and remain secure in our salvation? The answer lies in distinguishing between willful rebellion and the ongoing struggle against sin. Rebellion is a deliberate, persistent rejection of God's authority, whereas struggling with sin is a normal aspect of the believer's journey.

God brings about the fulfillment of His will in His timing and wisdom. He hardens the hearts of people destined for destruction (Exodus 4:21, 7:3, 10:1, 14:17; Isaiah 6:10; Romans 9:18). Soon to be believers like Saul (Paul) who persist in rebellion will face divine correction to bring about a conversion experience (Acts 9). Believers who struggle with sin will experience God's discipline. His patience, compassion, and chosen consequences work to conform their wills to His. All must give an account for everything done in the body (2 Corinthians 5:10). Yet, God is for believers, not against them, so judgement day will never include loss of salvation.

A true believer possesses a transformed nature that cannot remain in total rebellion against God. While the sinful nature within continues to resist Him, the renewed spirit remains united with Him. This tension does not mean a believer is lost—it reveals the ongoing sanctifying work of God. Instead of leaving His children trapped in their sin, He actively rescues them, leading them toward holiness.

Faith is essential because it confirms that salvation is a gift of grace, not a reward for human effort. It creates a distinction between those who belong to God and those who do not. The presence of genuine faith changes how a believer responds to life's difficulties, proving that salvation is not about perfection but about perseverance in the face of trials.

GOD-INSURED OR SELF-INSURED

Every person exists in one of two spiritual states: either "God-Insured," covered by His grace, or "Self-Insured," carrying the full weight of spiritual independence. Those who belong to God are "God-Insured": under His protection and care, secured by His love and sovereignty. Jesus sacrificed Himself to make His children righteous, ensuring they would not die under the weight of their sins. He defines their identity, protects them, and directs their paths according to His will.

However, without a relationship with God, a person is "Self-Insured", left to bear the full weight of her own existence. Without Him, she has no spiritual parent—she is an orphan, helpless and unable to provide true meaning or fulfillment for herself. Even if she cries out, *It is unfair to hold me responsible when I had no say in the matter*, she remains powerless to save herself. Unless she accepts God's care, she will remain spiritually dead.

Who Causes Salvation?

God is a responsible and loving parent, and as His children, we desperately need His care and guidance. It's a perfect relationship—He is completely able, and we are humbly in need. God alone is the source of holiness, goodness, justice, and love.

Responsibility does not come simply from having choices—those separated from Him are Self-Insured, bearing the full burden of their condition. Reality must be faced, no matter how hopeless one's situation may seem. Every person is born spiritually blind, living in darkness and rebellion against God. Those who refuse God's headship take full responsibility for their own existence, and without Him, they cannot provide true meaning or fulfillment for themselves.

God's absolute standard of perfection applies to believers and non-believers alike, proving that no one escapes His authority. Rejecting responsibility does not negate reality—it leads to deeper suffering. A person may justify wrongdoing, saying, *I steal—that's just who I am. I couldn't help myself. I can't help it if God made me this way.* Yet dismissing sin as inevitable does not change the consequences. Without God, people are left to themselves, facing the harsh realities of living in a fallen world.

CONCLUSION

God delights in revealing Himself to His people, bringing joy and purpose to those He calls and ensuring their place in His eternal kingdom. Isn't it wonderful when God reveals Himself? Can you see the joy on Jesus's face, the twinkle in His eye, when He tells Peter that God revealed Jesus's identity to him (Matthew 16:16-17)?

No one deserves salvation or anything from God. He alone holds the reasons for choosing whom He will save. From a human perspective, predestination may seem unfair, but God, who existed before creation, governs all things according to His perfect wisdom. He is under no obligation to save anyone. He saves because of His love and mercy:

> For he says to Moses, "I will have mercy on whom I have mercy, and I will have compassion on whom I have compassion."
> Romans 9:15 ESV

This truth makes salvation infinitely more valuable because it is not for everyone. Those who have it can be especially thankful—not for their own efforts but because they see how much God has done for them.

We are born spiritually blind, unable to see Christ. Without Him, there is no life. But once regenerated and brought to life, the goodness of who we are as God's masterpieces (Ephesians 2:10) is fully awakened. Through Him, believers can:
- Receive God's love
- Value themselves as His creation
- Experience joy and comfort
- Trust fully in God for spiritual life, light, power, truth, illumination, and vitality

God is the light. He shines the light so we can see. We see, we enjoy, and we live because of Him (John 1:4-5; 8:12; Isaiah 9:2; Ephesians 5:8-14).

Salvation is entirely God's work—from forelove to summoning, from spiritual birth to final perseverance. Its success does not depend on what we do but on what God has done, revealing His glory through His sovereign love that saves and secures.

FOR REFLECTION AND DISCUSSION

1. How does God's role in salvation differ from a human's role, and why is this distinction important?
2. Salvation is more than intellectual understanding—it requires spiritual illumination. Why must God provide this for people to truly grasp the Gospel?
3. How does the thief on the cross demonstrate both the simplicity of salvation and God's sovereign choice?

Who Causes Salvation?

4. How does God's revelation of Himself secure a believer's salvation—and why is this so often misunderstood as "free will"?
5. How does God's forelove shape both a believer's perseverance and her identity—and what does this reveal about assurance of salvation?
6. Why do some people completely resist becoming saved? What are the dangers of believing that salvation is a human decision?
7. Why do some people struggle to accept that salvation is entirely caused by God through His irresistible forelove? What does this reveal about the human heart and the nature of divine grace?
8. How does God summoning believers into salvation, rather than merely inviting them, shape a believer's faith journey?
9. Why is it impossible for believers to keep sinning?
10. What is the difference between struggling with sin and rebellion, and how does this affect a believer's relationship with God?
11. How does the analogy of being God-Insured vs. Self-Insured help illustrate human dependence on God?
12. If belief is evidence of salvation rather than its cause, how does this challenge common views of faith and works?
13. How does understanding God's sovereign role in salvation change the way believers approach worship and gratitude?

CHAPTER 9

Who Chooses Salvation?

Choice is power—whoever holds it determines how life unfolds into eternity. When it comes to salvation, the central question is: Who ultimately controls human destiny? Does God decide who will be in heaven, or do people determine this for themselves? Who is driving and who is the passenger? The answer carries profound implications—leading either to peace or perpetual anxiety.

Would you prefer a reality where you chose God while He remained indifferent, or one where God chose you even while you were indifferent? The true Gospel is the latter—only better. God chooses sinners even when they despise Him, because He sees beyond their sin to who they truly are.

We do not have the freedom to choose God before He chooses us:

> You did not choose me, but I chose you and appointed you that you should go and bear fruit and that your fruit should abide...
> John 15:16 ESV

We do not say, "I choose You, God. I believe. Now give me the salvation you promised!" Instead we say, "I believe. Thank you for salvation. Thank you for choosing me for this gift."

While the Gospel is available to all, the real question is not about its accessibility but about who is capable of answering its call. A human-centered Gospel emphasizes fairness—insisting that all people have an equal opportunity to reach heaven **on their own terms.** But a God-centered Gospel prioritizes His sovereign choice—ensuring that those whom God wants to be with Him forever, have eternal life.

Some see God lingering at the margins of salvation—expectant but uninvolved. Others see Him as near and active—training, guiding, choosing. Which portrayal fits the God of Scripture?

IS GOD A CHEERLEADER OR A COACH?

If God is a cheerleader, He stands on the sidelines, eagerly watching to see who will "earn" their place on the team for passage into heaven. In this view, the outcome rests in the hands of the players, outside His control. He can cheer for players to succeed, but His influence is limited to wishful, uncertain hoping.

This perspective reduces salvation to an achievement- or merit-based system, reliant on human effort or chance. From God's perspective, it resembles a lottery—arbitrary as to who will ultimately gain salvation. God must be indifferent—"closing His eyes" while creating people, then "opening His eyes" to foresee who will believe or not believe. Before creation He might think, "I wonder with whom I will be spending eternity." As a cheerleader He does not determine the outcome, therefore, the results must be random (outside of His control).

Alternatively, if God is a coach, then He is actively involved with "eyes wide open" when determining who joins His team for passage into heaven. The outcome rests in His hands rather than in the players'. As coach, He decides who will be on the team, selecting each person with purpose and intention. He assigns roles to His team members and provides training, guidance, and support to help them fulfill their roles.

This view portrays salvation as God's sovereign and intentional plan, where He actively works to accomplish His purposes. It is not a lottery but an act of divine choice. The Creator of the universe has the authority, right, ability, and responsibility to choose who He wants to be with Him (John 1:12-13). Just as He chose His disciples for their roles, He is purposeful in whom He calls to salvation (John 15:16).

God sees and knows every individual completely, having crafted each person intentionally. How, then, can God be uncertain, indifferent, or passive regarding who will be in heaven?

IF GOD WAS ONLY A CHEERLEADER

Cheerleaders have no direct power to alter the outcome of a game. Their attempts to influence the crowd cannot guarantee a win for their team. God, as only a cheerleader, handicaps His wisdom and forfeits the game before it begins.

A human-centered Gospel puts the power of choice in human hands. This worldview is relativistic, believing the illusion that individuals can determine their destiny. Secular culture often views God through this lens, limiting His power to uphold humanity's supposed necessity to choose. In this view, to be human is to possess the power to accept or reject salvation. But in reality, to be God is to possess the power to accept or reject people.

If salvation were truly random—like a lottery—then, perhaps, half of humanity might become Christian. But, who would want to leave this life-altering decision to chance? Moreover, what mechanism would allow a created being to choose or refuse God? If God creates the mechanism, He still controls the outcome.

The possibility of human choice introduces uncertainty, an undesirable position for anyone. If you had to place a bet, would you prefer a guaranteed outcome or one with only a chance of success?

If human choice determined salvation, it would lead to several consequences that diminish God's sovereign role. Forced equality would require God to love all people identically, disregarding His intentional design. Idolatry would elevate human autonomy above divine authority, reshaping God into a passive figure. Rebellion would fuel self-rule, leading people to reject submission to God. Failure would be inevitable, as spiritually dead individuals would always refuse salvation, proving that human choice cannot lead to eternal life. If God were merely a cheerleader—powerless to intervene—salvation would be left to chance, unraveling His redemptive plan.

HUMAN CHOICE LEADS TO FORCED EQUALITY

A common misconception is that God's love is uniform and without distinction—that He must love every creature exactly the same way, without variation or intentionality. But this assumption applies worldly reasoning to God's way of loving. As a result, many have come to believe that human free will—the ability to choose or reject God—is necessary for love to be genuine.

However, Scripture reveals that God **does** show favoritism—not in judgment or discipline, for everyone reaps what they sow—but according to His eternal plan. He is intentional in His purposes, implementing creative solutions rather than treating all people identically. God did not create everyone with equal opportunities, abilities, or callings (Romans 9).

Even among His children, God assigns unique roles. Jesus promised that His twelve disciples would sit on twelve thrones to judge Israel (Matthew 19:28), an honor not extended to all believers. This is a testament to His sovereignty—not a question of fairness, but of divine purpose.

Forced equality assumes that fairness requires sameness. But in reality, true fairness is found in God's intentional design, where He distributes His favor according to His wisdom, love, and purpose rather than human expectations of uniformity.

The necessity of free will arises from a misguided pursuit of fairness—a human-centered, worldly concept that deviates from biblical truth. Fairness places judgment in human hands, while justice entrusts judgment to a perfectly righteous God.

Fairness is a poor substitute for justice because fairness requires immediate equality in this life while God promises He will make all things right in the next life. It elevates personal autonomy while disregarding God's higher purposes, which often transcend human understanding. True justice does not originate from human ideals but flows from God's wisdom. This requires trusting God's timing and good judgement.

HUMAN CHOICE LEADS TO IDOLATRY

God would not be able to achieve His purposes if humans were the ultimate deciders of their fate. How can created beings claim the right to choose while denying God the same right? How can humans reserve the power to love or reject God while insisting that He must love everyone equally?

This attitude elevates human autonomy above divine sovereignty, redefining fairness by human standards rather than God's authority. It imposes human ideas of governance onto God's rule—as if He operates under human limitations. While people need such systems to prevent corruption, a perfectly just God does not. Prioritizing human independence over divine authority reshapes God into a false image, crafted by pride and inadequate human reasoning.

Does God create individuals knowing their eternal destiny? Is it possible that He creates individuals He never intends to save? Could He plan for individuals to be with Him for eternity, create them, and ensure their salvation?

To answer "no" to these questions suggests a belief that all humans could be saved or that none could be saved, stripping away the certainty of salvation. It would mean that even Jesus's disciples could have refused His call, making divine purpose subject to human decision rather than God's sovereign election (Romans 9).

Could God create someone He loves completely, longing to spend eternity with her, but be required to wait and see if she will believe? Would He risk eternal separation from someone He deeply cherishes? Would He plan a specific role, only to leave open the possibility that she may decline it?

No. There is a fundamental difference between the spiritually alive, born-again child of God and the spiritually dead person. God's relationship with His children is intimate and personal, like that of a parent knowing her child. Conversely, God does not intimately know the spiritually dead in the same way—they remain outside His covenant relationship, their hearts unchanged.

Jesus acknowledged this distinction during His earthly ministry. He grieved for those lost in darkness, yet He understood that God had not given them to Him (Luke 23:34). His sorrow was real, but it was not eternal—He does not remain in mourning over those whom God has not chosen.

HUMAN CHOICE LEADS TO REBELLION

God's sovereign will stands above human self-determination. Just as He calls His people to Himself, He also allows others to remain in their rebellion—not out of indifference, but because His mercy and justice work together in perfect harmony.

Does the devil want God to have more power or less? Both the devil and fallen humanity crave control. They seek autonomy—the essence of sin—desiring to rule themselves, be their own gods, and dictate their own destinies.

This spirit of rebellion fuels attitudes such as "My body, my choice" and "My soul, my choice," which prioritize self-rule above submission to God. This anti-Christ spirit—marked by proud independence and resistance to divine authority—rejects the sovereignty of our Creator-God, Jesus Christ.

In this context, the attitude "I don't want anyone to tell me what to do" reflects a spiritually dead heart. It is rooted in defiance, a mindset incompatible with God's rule, for it denies His rightful sovereignty.

HUMAN CHOICE LEADS TO FAILURE

Without God's intervention, everyone with the freedom to choose would not want to choose God. Left in sin, no one willingly submits to God—their natural inclination is rebellion, not faith.

Would you rather have freedom from sin or the freedom to choose? It is far better to be saved through God's grace than to merely have the possibility of salvation.

Friendship with God always makes sense—for the spiritually alive. If everyone could see salvation clearly and had the power to choose, everyone would possess eternal life. For fallen people who are spiritually dead, blind and broken, being enemies of God always makes sense. Sin has altered desire and perception: spiritually dead people do not want God nor can they see His goodness. Without divine intervention, no one turns to God (Romans 3:11).

Human choice guarantees uncertainty at best—and failure at worst—while God's sovereign choice secures His perfect outcome. When God reveals paradise to His chosen, nothing is more desirable. God enables them to recognize and embrace Him. But someone still trapped in the darkness of sin remains incapable of seeing the truth. Human choice fails to save even one person—but God's initiative makes the heart alive to what is truly good.

BECAUSE GOD IS A COACH

A God-centered Gospel places the power of choice in God's hands. This worldview is absolute, exposing the severe limitations of human decision-making.

THE POWER TO CHOOSE BELONGS TO GOD

Does God care who is in heaven? Did He plan who will be in heaven? The answers are clear when we consider the truth revealed in Scripture. In the previous chapter, we learned that

Holy Spirit determines, according to His will, who will be born again.

Here are several verses that demonstrate God's power to choose for His purposes:
- God is in control, doing whatever He pleases (Proverbs 16:33, 19:21, 20:24, 21:1; Psalm 115:3).
- God causes both well-being and calamity and uses them (Isaiah 45:7).
- God keeps true believers safe, ensuring their eventual completed salvation (John 6:37, 10:28; Romans 8:38-39; Philippians 1:6; 1 Peter 1:5; 1 John 5:18; 2 Timothy 1:12; Hebrews 7:25).

How could humanity choose against God's choosing? People cannot override God's will. Who, then, chooses who will be in heaven? The answer is unmistakable: God retains this power. He does not delegate it to humans. As the all-powerful Creator, God alone determines who will enter heaven. Humans, being subject to God, cannot come to Christ without His divine intervention (John 6:44, Romans 9:16, Ephesians 1:4-5, 2 Timothy 1:9).

Knowing that you are chosen by God is a priceless truth. It communicates love in a way no human achievement or performance ever could. Being chosen isn't about merit—it's about being the masterpiece that God Himself designed.

> But God is so rich in mercy, and he loved us so much, that even though we were dead because of our sins, he gave us life when he raised Christ from the dead. (It is only by God's grace that you have been saved!)
>
> God saved you by his grace when you believed. And you can't take credit for this; it is a gift from God. Salvation is not a reward for the good things we have done, so none of us can boast about it. For we are God's masterpiece. He has created us anew in Christ Jesus, so we can do the good things he planned for us long ago.
> Ephesians 2:4-5, 8-10 NLT

God's mercy and grace are evident in His choice to save us. Salvation is entirely a gift from God, springing from His eternal love.

Who Chooses Salvation?

Should We Try If God Controls Everything?

If God chooses people for salvation, does it matter what we do? Absolutely—it makes every difference. Believers are called to grow in faith, becoming more like their true selves in Christ by cooperating with God rather than resisting Him. Though salvation is entirely His work, He commands His children to participate in spreading His Gospel.

Some may question whether sharing the Gospel is necessary if God has already chosen His people. Yet we do not know who will ultimately be in heaven. This uncertainty calls us to treat every person impartially, trusting God to accomplish His saving work according to His sovereign plan. Believers should do their part to proclaim the Gospel while relying on God's leading and power, and leave the results up to God's sovereign will.

Salvation comes from God's call, not human persuasion. Evangelism does not create faith—it reduces human barriers to disbelief, making the Gospel clearer to those who hear it. But only God determines who will receive saving faith. If He does not choose to reveal Christ to people, they remain incapable of belief. Only God can make the Gospel come alive in the human heart.

Because we do not know whom God will save, we are responsible for faithfully proclaiming His truth to all. Salvation belongs to Him alone—while we may plant and water, only He causes the growth (1 Corinthians 3:6). Our role is not to determine who will believe, but to clearly present the Gospel and trust that He will keep His promise to save those He planned to save.

God grants believers the security of knowing they are chosen, yet they remain unaware of who else will believe. This brings the best of everything: security in salvation coupled with motivation to share the Gospel.

GOD'S COMPASSION AND WISDOM WORK TOGETHER

God desires that every person be saved. But does this mean everyone will? Will hell be empty, or will at least one person not

be saved? How can the following two seemingly contradictory truths be reconciled?
1. God desires that everyone be saved (1 Timothy 2:4; 2 Peter 3:9).
2. Not everyone will be saved (Matthew 7:21-23).

To harmonize these teachings, it is essential to understand that God's identity is significantly more complex than humans'. God possesses many attributes, including being loving, just, and sovereign. These characteristics never weaken one another—100% of them are engaged, 100% of the time. God is never divided against Himself. In contrast, humans, corrupted by sin, are often divided and confused. We are not always loving or just, and we certainly lack control over outcomes.

God's Desire And God's Will Are Different

While God desires that every person be saved, this does not mean it is His will. Whatever God desires might come to pass, but whatever He ordains will be accomplished. If God wills something, it will happen. His plans cannot be thwarted by anyone, nor does He answer to anyone for His actions or purposes. Any ability we have to make decisions is only possible because God allows it.

God has the compassion to desire all people to be saved, yet His sovereign will achieves a higher purpose. This leads to two possible interpretations of 1 Timothy 2:4:
1. "All" refers only to the elect, allowing "desire" and "will" to be essentially the same.
2. "Desire" reflects God's longing but not His final and wise decision.

Because the simplest definition of "all" is "all", option 2 is reality. God can desire all to be saved, but simultaneously choose some for salvation while not choosing others (John 6:44; Romans 9:15-18). If God willed that everyone would be saved, then they would be, but since everyone won't be saved, this must mean He is selective in choosing who is saved.

Who Chooses Salvation?

John Piper explains the tension in Scripture between God's desire for all to be saved and the reality that not all will be saved. He argues that this is not a contradiction but rather a reflection of the complexity of God's will. The Bible reveals that God has multiple levels of willing—He desires all to be saved, yet His greater commitment to His sovereign purposes takes precedence. Using biblical examples, he illustrates that God simultaneously forbids actions (e.g., murder) while ordaining them for His ultimate plan (e.g., Christ's crucifixion). This dual reality reflects God's justice and mercy working in perfect harmony, not conflict. Like George Washington's reluctant but necessary decision to execute a traitor, God's sovereign choices do not negate His compassion, but rather demonstrate His wisdom in carrying out His purposes. Ultimately, salvation is granted according to God's will, not human determination.[1]

Just like us, God makes practical decisions—but unlike us, His priorities are perfect. Though He could execute all His ideas simultaneously, He doesn't. Instead, He created a world with limitations, making each decision meaningful. Without priorities, nothing would get done.

When a couple must make a decision, how they prioritize their values determines the outcome. They must find agreement or allow one person's values to influence the decision. This happens all the time with the household budget and tithing. Many ministries may be deserving of gifts, but there is limited funds, so a couple chooses the ministry that most closely aligns with their values.

The Wisdom Of God's Decision To Save

God's use of His prerogative to choose produces a superior outcome for His purposes. Put another way, God is better at choosing who will be with Him for eternity than each individual would be.

> Jesus said, "For many are called, but few are chosen."
> Matthew 22:14 ESV

---

1. desiringgod.org/interviews/if-god-desires-all-to-be-saved-why-arent-they

God's call goes out to everyone, yet only a small subset responds (Romans 9:27). God chooses believers as "firstfruits"—meaning they are set apart as a special portion of His harvest (2 Thessalonians 2:13).

The Bible says, "Whosoever believes in Him shall not perish but have eternal life" (John 3:16). However, this does not mean that everyone will—or can—be saved.

If I say "whosoever" can run a mile in under four minutes will win a prize, I hold everyone to the same standard, but many will be disqualified. I offer the prize to everyone, but it is conditional. If I call out in a graveyard "whosoever" raises their hand will win a prize, who can answer? Only the living people who happen to be visiting the cemetery. The same can be said for the living people God predestines.

Salvation is offered to all but conditioned upon recognizing Jesus as Lord. Only the chosen—those whom God reveals Himself to can meet this condition (Matthew 16:17; John 6:44).[2] His Word goes out and will not return void, but at the same time He passes over some (Isaiah 55:11, Matthew 13:18-23, John 12:39-40, Romans 9:18, 2 Corinthians 2:14-17).

Human Decision Making Is Flawed

Knowing that not everyone will be saved, one might ask: if salvation is as simple as believing, why would anyone refuse a God who is love? What kind of a person would reject God? Answer: only a person that does not want to be with Him—a spiritually dead person. Therefore, the difference between a saved person and an unsaved person is not effort, merit, or worth—it is God's sovereign will.

It has to be this way because there is no logical reason to reject God's love when everyone has an equal opportunity to choose Him. Either (a) all people naturally reject God without His intervention, or (b) He created each person with an inherent bias—either toward accepting or rejecting Him. In both cases, God ultimately determines who will be in heaven.

---

2. bibleref.com/Matthew/16/Matthew-16-17.html

Who Chooses Salvation?

He must intervene to change a person's heart, therefore, He is truly saving them. But if He allows each person to choose freely, that choice is not an act of salvation but rather a privilege—an opportunity granted. Does God grant salvation as a privilege, or does He rescue sinners from an otherwise hopeless situation?

Picture this: *A traveler is lost in a vast wilderness—no map, no path, no stars to guide him. He's surrounded by deceptive trails that loop endlessly, each promising escape but leading nowhere. His feet are blistered, his hope fading. Suddenly, an eagle lands in front of him and locks eyes with him—piercing, purposeful. It turns and begins to walk, not fly, carving a path through the underbrush.*

Clearly, humans have insufficient ability to make an optimal decision. No matter if God grants a privileged free choice, no one can choose Him, or some inherently can and some cannot: those who refuse Him are spiritually dead and will suffer accordingly. Put another way, the spiritually dead will always reject and the spiritually alive will always accept. The only way to overcome this weakness is for God to make the decision of who to save. God rescues the spiritually dead from their inability to choose Him. God saves people who are yet His enemies by shining the light of His love and truth in their hearts.

God's Intentional Love

Though God creates all people with purpose, He shows a unique, redemptive love to His elect—a love that secures their salvation. All are born spiritually dead, alienated from God, and under the control of the devil (1 John 5:19). When God grants eternal life to His chosen people, they become a radically different creation—born of the Spirit and adopted as His children. God planned this in advance, so He did not make all people the same. Humanity is not made of identical clones like the stormtroopers from Star Wars.

If everyone were created the same, they would all make the same decision about Christ. The variability in outcomes proves a deciding factor exists. But who controls it? If humanity does, it would elevate us to god-like authority while diminishing God's sovereignty and cheapening His love. But people can't control the factor—doing so would require total independence from His sustaining power. Different outcomes are only possible because God purposely conforms them to His will (Ephesians 1:11).

God cannot share His glory with another "god" who has independent authority to oppose Him. He always accomplishes His purposes—never compromising His control (Isaiah 46:9-10). He exercises His sovereignty by:
- Creating each person intentionally, with no detail accidental or overlooked
- Choosing His children for salvation because they cannot save themselves

His authority is not passive—it shapes destinies, sustains creation, and brings about exactly what He intends.

God did not randomly create humanity; He did so with intention, knowing each person intimately before He formed them. His mercy and justice work together to save some while passing over others with perfect wisdom. Though we may not fully comprehend how this works, we can trust that God—being perfectly just and loving—manages the "fairness" of it all.

GOD'S LOVING FAVOR IS FAIR

What does it mean for God to be fair? Is fairness about sameness, or is it about loving people in their uniqueness? In human terms, fairness is often linked to equal opportunity, ensuring that everyone has the same chances and choices. But God's fairness operates on an entirely different foundation—one built on love, mercy, and sovereign favor.

Worldly Fairness vs. Divine Sovereignty

Worldly fairness requires human autonomy—the belief that individuals should have the power to shape their own destinies. But creatures do not possess the same freedom as their Creator. They cannot act independently of God's will or change their fate apart from His intervention. Every decision they make happens within the limits He sets.

Scripture affirms the truth that God is in control of every detail:
- John 15:5 — "Apart from Me you can do nothing."

Who Chooses Salvation?

- John 19:11 — "You would have no power over me if it were not given to you from above."
- Acts 4:27-28 — Even those who opposed Christ acted according to God's predetermined plan.

God maintains absolute control, ensuring that everything unfolds according to His sovereign will.

God's Favor In Creation

If I weren't a Christian but somehow understood the value of eternal life, I would make every effort to obtain it. Without realizing it is a gift, I'd attempt to "win" my place in heaven, perhaps even at the expense of others. I would strive to appear better, more deserving than others.

By God's great mercy, salvation is not a competition. God's choice cannot be influenced by personal effort. As Romans 9 teaches, His mercy is not earned—it is bestowed according to His divine purpose.

As a Christian, I understand that God chose me not because of my achievements or attempts to be lovable, but because He created me for eternal fellowship with Him. His choice reflects His love for me—how He uniquely designed my personality, abilities, and purpose. How precious this truth is!

I am thankful that my salvation is not contingent upon proving myself or striving to "win" favor. God chose me because He loves me. In heaven, no one will feel inferior or less loved than anyone else. We will rejoice together in the fullness of His grace and love.

Because God creates and chooses, His works are functional rather than equitable. A functional design is intentional, purposeful, and unique but an equitable design must be uniform. God creates a person, such as Esther, as a one-of-a-kind. She is valuable because God made her excellent as an individual, not because she has a right to be created equal.

Feeling truly loved is not possible without feeling the joy of being chosen (Romans 9:22-23).

God is assembling a functional body of Christ. Whoever God creates will function exactly as He plans, with each person designed intentionally for His purposes. They have different roles, abilities, giftings, and purposes. Each person is unique but no one person is superior to others because each part of a body is essential (1 Corinthians 12:12, Romans 12:4-5).

God has created a diverse range of people, each with different talents and abilities throughout history. No one has possessed all abilities. It is not right for a created being to complain about what she lacks, as if God made a mistake (SB#23, Pavlik, p. 20). Rather, He designed each person intentionally according to His will (Romans 9:20-21).

Paul likens God to a potter who molds clay to fulfill specific purposes. Romans 9 teaches that God favors some people over others—and because God is love, His favor must also be an expression of love (see John 21 for example).

Favoritism: Human vs. Divine

This raises an important question: if God favors some over others, how is that different from human favoritism, which we often call unfair?

Favoritism often carries a negative connotation because humans are imperfect and prone to unjust favoritism. But God's favor is not only fair—it is good. Unlike human favoritism, which often results in inequality or oppression, God's favor results from His perfect wisdom and love.

It is right for a created being to be satisfied with who she is, without comparing herself to others or demanding equality in abilities and opportunities (SB#23, Pavlik, p. 77). John the Baptist deferred to Jesus's role in salvation (John 3:22-36, Romans 12:3).

Favor is an integral part of love. Consider this practical example in marriage: A woman feels special when she is chosen above all others for marriage. Betrayal and infidelity, on the other hand, communicate rejection—telling her she was not truly unique or valued. Love, by its very nature, involves favor. A husband loves his wife above all others, which means he favors her exclusively.

Likewise, God chooses His people with divine love, setting them apart for Himself.

Who Chooses Salvation?

Assurance Of God's Love

People are either friends of God (children of God) or enemies of God (children of the devil). Everyone begins life as an enemy of God—hopelessly alienated from Him. If God had no special favor toward His chosen, He would have no motivation to die for them.

Doubting God's love is common despite assurances of His intimate love. Doubt often creeps in, even among believers:
- *Am I truly special to God?*
- *Am I really important to Him?*
- *Would He miss me if I didn't exist?*

Jesus reassures us: "Even the hairs on your head are all numbered" (Luke 12:7).

To be loved is to be favored. To be favored is to be chosen. This favor exists despite the hatred of God in our hearts before salvation. God intimately knows who we will become after He replaces our corrupt hearts (Jeremiah 1:5—"Before I formed you in the womb I knew you."). He chooses us in love, softening our hearts so that we can be friends—reconciled to Him through Christ.

Once we have the Spirit of sonship, we can cry Abba, Father (Romans 8:15). And once we have a Father, we are His forever. We were once strangers to grace—but now, chosen, loved, and secured, we will never be separated from His affections.

FOR REFLECTION AND DISCUSSION

1. Why must God be the one with the power to choose? Why is human choice inadequate? How might this be emotionally difficult to accept?
2. How does the distinction between a cheerleader and a coach further your understanding of God's role in salvation? How is God's sovereign control even greater than a human coach's?
3. How have personal experience, culture, and Scripture influenced your view of God?

4. Describe the difference between someone who accepts God and someone who rejects Him. What determines the outcome?
5. Can someone who is truly able to accept God still reject Him? Can someone who rejects God still accept Him? Under what conditions are these true or false?
6. How have you felt when you have shared the Gospel but the person did not become a believer? What are you responsible for when sharing the Gospel?
7. How does knowing you were chosen by God affect the way you view yourself—and how you relate to others?
8. Why is salvation not a lottery, but God's intentional choice?
9. If God's desire is for all people to be saved, why aren't all people saved?
10. What role does God's favor play in salvation, and how does it differ from human favoritism?
11. Why is it essential that God has the freedom to love people according to His wisdom rather than being constrained to love everyone the same?

CHAPTER 10

What Freedom Does Salvation Secure?

True freedom begins with recognizing what holds you captive. To be saved is to be set free from sin and death—so true freedom begins with understanding salvation. And, without certainty of that freedom, we cannot fully enjoy the peace it provides.

> And you will know the truth, and the truth will set you free.
> So if the Son sets you free, you are truly free.
> John 8:32, 36 NLT

Everyone desires freedom, yet not all "freedom" leads to life. God's freedom liberates believers from sin and evil, while worldly freedom seeks independence from Him. Believers long for peace and order, but non-believers pursue freedom from authority. A believer finds love and identity in God as a spiritual Father, while a non-believer strives to be her own god, mistaking autonomy for true liberation.

Picture this: A child is trapped in a burning house, disoriented by smoke. She can't see the exit, only shadows. Suddenly,

SECURE IN CHRIST

a firefighter bursts through the wall—not the door—grabs her, and carries her out.

Only God's truth, illuminated in the hearts of believers, sets them free. Truly free people see reality clearly, while the blind remain trapped in darkness. Because freedom depends on one's relationship to God, those who are separated from Him remain bound.

> For the Lord is the Spirit, and wherever the Spirit of the Lord is, there is freedom.
> 2 Corinthians 3:17 NIV

True freedom is not the pursuit of human autonomy but the result of walking in step with Holy Spirit. Without Him, we are helplessly enslaved to sin. We are truly free when God dwells within us—breaking through the barriers of darkness and lifting the veil so we can walk fully in His truth.

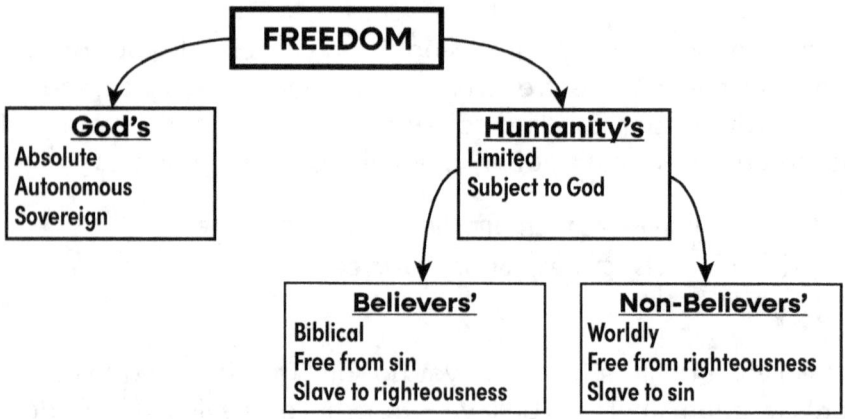

SOVEREIGN VS. HUMAN FREEDOM

Freedom exists in two distinct forms: God's sovereign freedom, which is absolute, and human freedom, which is limited by Him.

GOD'S ABSOLUTE FREEDOM

Only God possesses absolute freedom because He has always existed, is completely independent, and is accountable

What Freedom Does Salvation Secure?

to no one. He created everything, reigns sovereign over creation, and cannot be dethroned. Above all, He is good.

Absolute freedom is the ability to act without limitation or dependence—something only God possesses. No human has such autonomy. When we say God reigns supreme, we affirm that He has no competition—no challenger who could strip away His power.

God is both love and freedom. He is free because He is good and He answers to no one. His limitless creative power enables Him to accomplish all He wills. God's love requires absolute freedom—the ability to choose what serves a higher purpose.

Sin and addiction strip away freedom, leaving people trapped in spiritual bondage. But Jesus sacrificed His life to rescue His friends from slavery to sin.

> **There is no greater love than to lay down one's life for one's friends.**
> **John 15:13 NLT**

The Father, Son, and Holy Spirit share the same freedom because they live in perfect unity, never opposing one another. True freedom is impossible apart from God. Holy Spirit liberates His people by dwelling within them, granting them freedom from helpless captivity to sin.

HUMANITY'S LIMITED FREEDOM

All created beings possess limited freedom because they:
- depend on their Creator for existence
- can never escape that dependency
- are restricted by their Creator's sovereignty
- are accountable to their Creator

Since God alone possesses absolute freedom, humanity experiences only limited freedom—yet people continue to crave control and strive for autonomy.

If any created being were to possess absolute freedom, the result would be catastrophic. Infinite power without perfect character would lead to self-destruction under the weight of responsibility. If finite beings had absolute freedom without perfect wisdom, global-destruction would be imminent.

BIBLICAL VS. WORLDLY FREEDOM

Human freedom can be understood in two forms: biblical freedom, which leads to righteousness, and worldly freedom, which leads to sin. Biblical freedom means believers are freed from sin yet bound to righteousness, while worldly freedom means non-believers remain enslaved to sin yet free from righteousness.

BIBLICAL FREEDOM IS SERVANTHOOD TO GOD

Biblical freedom is active when Jesus sets believers free from:
- spiritual blindness and darkness
- sin and evil
- isolation and self-reliance

Those who receive this freedom become slaves to God's righteousness, which means they:
- surrender to God's control
- seek accountability with Him
- accept His loving care, guidance, and empowerment
- consider God an intimate friend

True freedom is permanent freedom from sin and death. As Galatians 5:1 declares, "It is for freedom that Christ has set us free."

Freedom can only exist in relationship with God, not apart from Him. It is the result of seeing, knowing, and experiencing God. Freedom is not a standalone concept—it flows from nearness to Him. The clearer one sees God, the closer one is to Him, the freer she becomes. Heaven is the ultimate fulfillment of true freedom—where God's presence reigns and sin is no longer possible.

WORLDLY FREEDOM IS A DECEPTIVE ILLUSION

Worldly freedom lacks a moral compass to choose good over evil. Non-believers define freedom as complete independence from everything, including God. In rejecting Him, the sinful person desires to be her own god.

Worldly freedom is when non-believers seek to be free from:
- reliance on God
- authority
- the love, light, and goodness of Jesus
- righteousness
- absolute truth

However, they remain slaves to sin, meaning they:
- value self-reliance above all
- surrender to Satan's control
- reject accountability and God's care
- consider God an enemy
- cannot stop sinning (evil thoughts and behavior)

Existence Without God Is Hell, Not Freedom

Worldly freedom leads to hell. Hell is not just suffering—it is remaining God's enemy, isolated from the source of life and love. Non-believers may think they are free, but their freedom is meaningless. Without God's power, love, and life, only emptiness and suffering remain.

Freedom only becomes meaningful and enjoyable when God gives Himself along with it. Without Him, there is only darkness, deception, and despair. Imagine having eyes made to receive light, but forever living in perfect darkness—those with physical blindness might understand the seriousness of spiritual blindness.

Many seal their fate by clinging to the illusion of independence from God—even though, apart from Him, true freedom is impossible.

Why did people want to crucify Jesus if He is good and loving? Because they cannot do otherwise—they are blinded by sin and unable to see who He truly is.

> Father, forgive them, for they do not know what they are doing.
> Luke 23:34 NIV

When people despise God, they attempt the impossible: possessing absolute freedom apart from Him. Satan deceives people into believing they can thrive apart from God, but this pursuit only keeps people in bondage to sin. In the Garden of Eden, the serpent convinced Adam and Eve that independence from God was beneficial (Genesis 3).

The devil's longing for power apart from God, for his own kingdom, is not freedom—it is rebellion. From the beginning, the devil has waged war for absolute freedom, attempting to claim God's sovereignty and establish himself as the supreme being. He leads a rebellion against God, misleading people into thinking they can be truly free apart from Him.

Those who desire separation from God cannot truly understand who He is. No believer who sees God clearly would ever desire separation from Him. Only through God's love can people truly love Him in return. The devil craves independence from God, and those who follow his deception remain in spiritual isolation, unable to find God's love apart from His intervention.

EVERYONE IS A SLAVE TO SOMETHING

Every person passionately serves one master—either sin or God. There is no middle ground or neutral option. A slave to sin cannot be righteous. A slave to God cannot be condemned for unrighteousness.

Paul makes it clear that every person is enslaved to something. Before salvation, individuals live under the rule of sin, leading to death (Romans 6:16, 20). Through spiritual birth, believers are set free from sin and become slaves to righteousness, to live in obedience to God (Romans 6:18-19).

What Freedom Does Salvation Secure?

> Don't you know that when you offer yourselves to someone as obedient slaves, you are slaves of the one you obey—whether you are slaves to sin, which leads to death, or to obedience, which leads to righteousness?
> Romans 6:16 NIV

Paul's point is: there is no neutral state—people either live under the dominion of sin or under the rule of God's righteousness. Humanity does not exist in some independent middle ground where people freely choose between good and evil. Instead:

- Without Christ, people inevitably sin, meaning their will is enslaved rather than truly free.
- With Christ, believers are liberated from sin's control—not into independence, but into belonging to God, where they desire His will above all else.

No one operates independently. Romans 6:18 declares that those who are in Christ have been set free from sin and have become slaves to righteousness, emphasizing that this transformation is a result of God's work, not human choice.

Salvation brings a complete transformation—believers become slaves to righteousness and are no longer ruled by sin's power (Romans 6:14). Believers are no longer bound to sin because they are dead to sin but alive to God in Christ Jesus (Romans 6:11).

While believers still struggle with sin due to their human nature, their spiritual identity has been permanently renewed. Their allegiance is now to God, and they are empowered by His grace to pursue righteousness. As Paul concludes in Romans 6:22, being slaves to God leads to holiness and, ultimately, eternal life.

Freedom Is Not For Fleshly Indulgence

Galatians 5 builds upon this truth by showing that Christian freedom is not about doing whatever one pleases but about living by the Spirit instead of the flesh.

- 5:1 NIV declares, "It is for freedom that Christ has set us free."

- 5:13 NIV warns, "...do not use your freedom to indulge in the flesh."

True freedom is found in joyful submission to righteousness, not through the false promise of autonomy. True freedom in Christ empowers believers to walk in the Spirit, bearing good fruit, instead of following sinful desires that lead to destruction.

We are not under law, but grace. Though the law cannot save, it still reveals God's holy standard and guides believers when paired with grace. When Paul speaks of "falling from grace" he refers to falling from freedom and returning to slavery (Galatians 5:4). Since we are truly free, we waste God's gift if we act like slaves to sin. Christ sacrificed to set us free from sin—this freedom must not be treated carelessly by submitting to slavery again.

The law cannot save, nor can a person will herself to freedom. She has a will, but it is powerless to free her from sin. We are born into darkness, unable to see Him, and therefore, unable to choose Him.

Together, Romans 6 and Galatians 5 present a biblical perspective on freedom. True freedom is not about independence but redemption—being transformed by Christ and strengthened to live in His righteousness.

DEPENDENCE ON GOD VS. THE ILLUSION OF AUTONOMY

True freedom does not exist apart from God—every person is either influenced by good or enslaved by evil. Every person is dependent on God, whether they are for Him or against Him. Even those who reject God remain dependent upon Him, because:
- No one exists except by God's creative power.
- God holds every molecule together.
- No one can create a desirable world where God is no longer needed.

Having god-like powers might sound appealing, but could anyone create a perfect world independent of God? We do not

What Freedom Does Salvation Secure?

have the ability to create even an imperfect world, let alone a perfect one.

People may claim they have free will, but they stumble in darkness until God illuminates their path. What good is "free will" in complete darkness? He gives us the ability to explore life, but we remain blind to His deeper reality unless He provides sufficient light and functioning spiritual eyes (John 3:3).

Even with light, we only discover what already exists—free will would not give us the power to escape God's reality (SB#24, Pavlik, p. 28). The universe has no hiding places that God doesn't know about.

> I can never escape from your Spirit!
> I can never get away from your presence!
> If I go up to heaven, you are there;
> if I go down to the grave, you are there.
> If I ride the wings of the morning,
> if I dwell by the farthest oceans,
> even there your hand will guide me,
> and your strength will support me.
> I could ask the darkness to hide me
> and the light around me to become night—
> but even in darkness I cannot hide from you.
> To you the night shines as bright as day.
> Darkness and light are the same to you.
> Psalm 139:7-12 NLT

True freedom is not found in independence but in complete alignment with God's truth. Separation from God means enslavement to one's own destructive desires. A human's will cannot be independent because God created it. God knows exactly what we will do before we do it. We cannot create, do, think, or feel anything new that God does not anticipate.

> You saw me before I was born.
> Every day of my life was recorded in your book.
> Every moment was laid out

before a single day had passed.
Psalm 139:16 NLT

Spiritual Slaves Deny Their Enslavement

All people start life as slaves, without true freedom. Since we are born into slavery, we do not know true freedom until God frees us. Earthly slaves want to be free from their oppressive masters. But what if people are enslaved by their own desires? Spiritual slaves to evil are subject to their corrupt natures. They cannot gain their freedom by self-effort because they cannot recognize their oppression. Their blindness is part of their bondage—they cannot seek freedom they don't believe they need. Only someone with the authority to free them can release them (John 8:33-37). God transfers believers from darkness to light, from slavery-to-sin to servitude-to-righteousness.

Picture this: *A narrow canyon cloaked in fog. Thorns claw at a battered sheep caught deep below. Above, the Shepherd stands. He leaps into the chasm—no hesitation, no negotiation—cutting through the thorns, pulling the sheep out. Light breaks through the mist.*

Believers' security rests in the stability of God's accomplished work, not human effort. The Gospel exists to set people free from sin and fear, leading believers into God's way of living. Consider the historical relationship between humanity and God:

- **The Will:** God created Adam and Eve in goodness, but without His internal guidance, they were vulnerable to deception and disobedience. Without an influencing nature they were like free agents. Their wills left them vulnerable, unable to prevent death or save them.
- **The Law:** Adam and Eve's disobedience led to spiritual death, enslavement to wrongdoing and a distorted view of God. Non-believers live without a connection to God. The law highlights their deficiency, but it can't save them.
- **The Spirit:** God dwells inside born-again believers providing a permanent guiding presence that prevents future separation. This is the only successful solution.

What Freedom Does Salvation Secure?

Adam and Eve were made in God's image (Genesis 1:27) and declared "very good" (Genesis 1:31), meaning they were without sin. However, their relationship with God was external rather than internal—they had direct fellowship with Him but did not yet possess His Spirit dwelling within them. This distinction explains their vulnerability to temptation in the Garden. They were innocent but, unlike born-again believers, not yet permanently sealed with God's Spirit.

Because of the Fall, humanity lost innocence, spiritual vitality, and connection with God. Salvation through Christ not only restores that broken relationship—it transforms believers by placing His Spirit within them (Ezekiel 36:26-27, John 14:16-17). This indwelling presence grants permanent spiritual life, on-board divine wisdom, and security, something Adam and Eve lacked before their fall.

God's Solution To Sin

God resolved vulnerability to evil by giving His Spirit to preserve believers—to guide them into truth and to protect them from falling away. Being a new creation means having God within to guarantee success. Our only hope is having God to constantly illuminate the path to righteous living. The only healthy spiritual walk is complete dependence and trust in Him.

God provides freedom to His children, but it is not the same as autonomy. **Believers gain freedom from sin only because they are slaves to righteousness.**

Life without God dwelling within will always fail. The tree of life symbolizes eternal life. God did not want humanity to live forever in their fallen state, so He blocked access to it until Jesus defeated sin and death. Scripture teaches that oneness with God is the only way life can be successful.

Salvation is not merely the assurance of a heavenly destination—it is a daily reality where God's permanent, indwelling presence transforms fear into faith, confusion into clarity, and striving into rest.

To become a believer is to lose something that is actually a gain. Moving from the "freedom" to engage in both good and evil to being able to only engage in good may feel restrictive, but in reality, it is the blessing of true freedom.

The effects of the fall are irreversible. **Humanity cannot fix its broken condition without God's intervention. Likewise, the effects of salvation are irreversible—people cannot break what God has truly fixed.** Salvation is not temporary or uncertain—it is God's definitive and eternal rescue. Jesus brings believers fully away from danger and into safety.

Four Possible Freedom States

A person exists in one of four states, defined by their vulnerability to good or evil:

1. **Vulnerable to spiritual life and death.** Adam and Eve were spiritually alive, but the possibility of spiritual death was real (Genesis 2:17). They were the only people to ever be in this state. After being deceived, they distrusted God, disobeyed His instructions, and died spiritually. God decided never to allow anyone to return to this state. Instead, He continued His plan for salvation (Genesis 3:15).
2. **Vulnerable to sin and sin's consequences.** These people are alienated from God due to sin. They are born spiritually dead and enslaved to sin, leaving evil as their only option. Self-righteousness is impossible.
3. **Vulnerable to righteousness (God), sin (evil), and the consequences of both.** Spiritually alive believers today walk by the Spirit, yet still contend with the flesh when they choose to sin. Through Christ's redemptive, transformative work, they are a new creation, immune to spiritual death. They are slaves to righteousness, even though sin remains possible. Jesus defeated death, allowing believers, now righteous, to eat from the tree of life and live forever, making a return to state 1 or 2 impossible.
4. **Vulnerable to righteousness.** Only Jesus currently fits into this state, but after He resurrects believers to glorified bodies, they will forever be with God and be like Him—incapable of sin or evil, free from all consequences of sin.

What Freedom Does Salvation Secure?

Non-believers are convinced they can manage life better without God. They value independence more than God Himself, believing they can be their own god. They are deceived, thinking they are in State 1 or 3 when they are actually in State 2.

Believers, allied with God, know they are in State 3 but long to be in State 4. They are learning how to live according to the Spirit rather than the flesh.

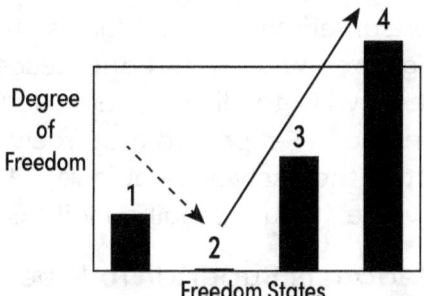

Because all are born spiritually dead, they lack the freedom that comes from being connected to God (State 2). Salvation alters a person's nature permanently, making her spiritually alive without vulnerability to spiritual death, as Adam and Eve were in State 1. Now, the believer, biased for good (State 3), understands that the only way to God is through Jesus Christ.

FREEDOM IS A BLESSING FREE WILL IS AN IDOL

Adam and Eve ate from the tree of the knowledge of good and evil. Eve believed she would gain wisdom and independence, yet she became worse off—knowing evil but powerless to resist it. This condition is a curse. God is holy and good, so He can know evil but will always resist it.

Free will cannot save anyone nor lead anyone into freedom. The human will does not operate in a vacuum—it is always primarily influenced by either God's Spirit (spiritual life) or the evil desires of the flesh (spiritual death). Neutrality is a myth. Non-believers are deceived into thinking their will is neutral and free, when in reality it is enslaved to evil. The desire for free will is an idol.

Freedom in Christ is superior to free will because free will cannot rescue anyone from slavery to sin. Jesus does not give people worldly free will—He gives true freedom, which realigns the will with God's truth. The correct measure of freedom is not the degree of autonomy, but the difference between bondage to sin and freedom in Christ.

Even believers sometimes wrongly insist that the ability to reject God through free will is good and necessary. Adam and Eve exercised their wills to disobey God, leading to spiritual death. That wasn't good—it proved that free will can never lead to salvation—left to themselves, people reject God. For human will to be of any value, it must be joined with God.

Freedom Is Superior To Free Will

True freedom isn't found in the ability to choose—it's found in the inability to desire what is evil. The human will is never neutral; it's either aligned with God or enslaved to sin. But even if the will could somehow exist in pure neutrality, it would still be powerless—unable to save, unable to love God, and unable to resist rebellion. The world's obsession with complete control over one's destiny is delusional and idolatrous.

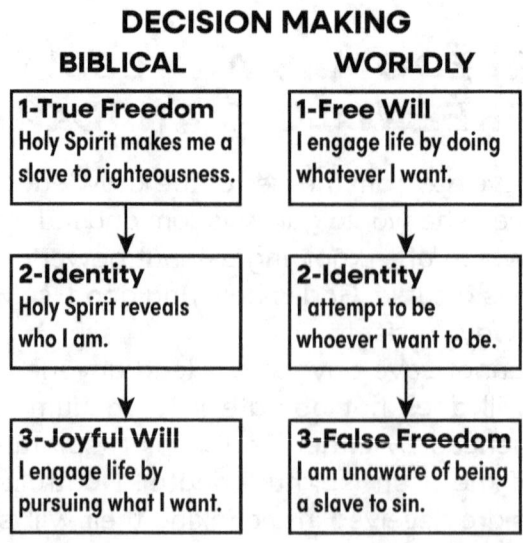

What Freedom Does Salvation Secure?

In the diagram, notice that non-believers get decision making backwards. They value free will as their god, believing autonomy is the highest human value. This mistake leads to eternal separation from Him—hell.

For believers, independence from God is no longer the goal. They seek joyful surrender to Him, living to serve and abide in His presence. Many things hold greater importance than independent free will—love, wisdom, and holiness for example. Having a "free" will without having God, is like moving quickly in the wrong direction—toward destruction. But because believers have Christ, they not only have His love, wisdom, and holiness, they have true freedom.

John 8 presents freedom in Christ as superior to human free will, revealing that true freedom is not the ability to choose whatever we desire, but the ability to live in truth and righteousness.

> "But we are descendants of Abraham," they said. "We have never been slaves to anyone. What do you mean, 'You will be set free'?" Jesus replied, "I tell you the truth, everyone who sins is a slave of sin. A slave is not a permanent member of the family, but a son is part of the family forever. So if the Son sets you free, you are truly free. Yes, I realize that you are descendants of Abraham. And yet some of you are trying to kill me because there's no room in your hearts for my message.
> John 8:33-37 NLT

Jesus teaches in John 8:34 that everyone who sins is a slave of sin, meaning human will, apart from Him, is not truly free—it is bound to rebellion, deception, and death. People may feel they have free will, but in reality, they are enslaved by sinful desires, unable to choose God on their own (Romans 3:11).

The Jews speaking in 8:33 were slaves of sin even though they were descendants of Abraham. Jesus tells them that slaves are not legitimate members of a household. Even though they were born in the house of Abraham, they were not a part of Jesus's family—the true spiritual family of God.

Jesus has the authority to set people free. He declares in John 8:36, "If the Son sets you free, you are truly free." This shows that true freedom comes not from our ability to choose, but from being liberated by Christ. When Jesus frees someone from sin's bondage, that person is no longer enslaved to sin but instead belongs to God, as Paul explains.

> But now that you have been set free from sin and have become slaves of God, the benefit you reap leads to holiness, and the result is eternal life.
> Romans 6:22 NIV

Worldly freedom can become an idol—an illusion worshiped instead of God. Many consider free will a supreme benefit, but in reality, the ability to reject a relationship with God is not a blessing—it is a curse. The inevitable consequence of so-called free will is separation from God.

No One Chooses To Reject God

Do we have the freedom to reject God? No. All people are born rejecting God, so rejecting Him out of free will is impossible. We cannot choose to do what already is. Instead of believing, "I can reject God if I want to," the truth is, "I was born rejecting God, and I cannot stop without His help."

Humanity exists in only one of two conditions. Those rejecting God have no ability to accept Him, and those accepting Him have no desire or ability in their spirit to reject Him. The flesh may still harbor rebellion, but in believers, it is counted as dead.

Once God enables a person to accept Him, could free will allow her to reject Him again? No—because every decision flows from either a righteous heart or a rebellious heart. A person set free by God can choose, but she never desires to separate from Him again. Likewise, a person enslaved to sin can choose, but she never desires to be joined to God.

We all make meaningful decisions. But what informs our decisions? It must come from one of two sources:
1. A spirit in tune with God's Spirit, walking in His truth.
2. A spirit in tune with the flesh, enslaved by worldly desires.

One leads to life and freedom, the other to bondage and destruction. Imagine these options:

a) The ability to walk freely but risk falling off a cliff to your death.
b) The assurance of safety amid limited freedom, knowing you can never fall.

Non-believers choose (a), valuing autonomy above divine security. Believers find peace in (b), resting in the assurance of God's sovereign protection.

God sets and communicates appropriate boundaries—defining where it is safe to walk and where it is not. Yet He goes beyond simply setting rules—He provides His Spirit as a helper who guides His people, preventing their destruction.

Why do some people believe salvation can be lost? The answer lies in how they value free will. When free will is valued more than connection with God, salvation is misunderstood. This failure occurs when they do not grasp the biblical teaching that those led by the Spirit are His slaves (Romans 6). To be human is to be a servant—always a slave to something.

To say that someone could lose salvation assumes human choice can overpower divine transformation. Believing salvation can be undone is to deny the completeness, power, and permanence of God's redemptive work.

FREEDOM IN CHRIST BY HOLY SPIRIT

Believers are united with Christ—one with Him as Holy Spirit dwells within them, granting them true biblical freedom.

By the power of Holy Spirit, believers are able to bear spiritual fruit. There are no limits to bearing spiritual fruit—no law restricts someone from being too loving or gentle (Galatians 5:22-23). True freedom is the ability to produce spiritual fruit—to share in the divine nature (2 Peter 1:4).

Degrees Of Freedom In The Spirit

Believers have been set free, are being set free, and will one day be completely free. Though this is guaranteed in Christ, we remain works in progress. Until Christ returns, freedom in the Spirit varies depending on a believer's spiritual maturity. Paul speaks of a progressive unveiling in 2 Corinthians 3:18, describing how believers are being transformed into Christ's image with ever-increasing glory. As faith deepens, so does the realization that we are already free.

> Now the Lord is the Spirit, and where the Spirit of the Lord is, there is freedom. And we all, who with unveiled faces contemplate the Lord's glory, are being transformed into his image with ever-increasing glory, which comes from the Lord, who is the Spirit.
> 2 Corinthians 3:17-18 NIV

Here are some freedoms believers gain and can experience:
- **Freedom from Condemnation:** At salvation, believers are freed from the penalty of sin (Romans 8:1-2).
- **Freedom from Legalism:** As believers understand grace, they no longer try to earn righteousness through works (Galatians 5:1).
- **Freedom from Sin's Power:** Through the Spirit, believers gain victory over sinful habits and desires (Romans 6:18).
- **Freedom in Worship and Relationship with God:** The veil is removed, allowing believers to experience intimacy with God (2 Corinthians 3:16).
- **Freedom in Spiritual Authority:** Mature believers walk in greater boldness, discernment, and power through the Spirit (Acts 1:8, 2 Timothy 1:7).
- **Ultimate Freedom in Eternity:** The fullest expression of freedom will come when believers are completely transformed in God's presence (Revelation 21:3-4).

True freedom is not found in autonomous self-rule but in surrender to God, where His truth shapes and empowers the believer. While the world defines freedom as independence and the ability to choose, Scripture reveals that every person is a slave—either to sin or to righteousness. The human will does not rescue anyone; rather, it highlights humanity's vulnerability. Before salvation, people are enslaved to sin, incapable of choosing God on their own. Only through Christ can they be set free, not for self-governed independence, but for joyful servanthood in righteousness. This transformation is not a limitation but a new creation—bringing believers into true spiritual liberty where their wills align with God's will, no longer bound by sin's deception.

The mistaken belief that free will is the highest human value leads to a dangerous misunderstanding of salvation. If free will allows a person to reject God, it is not a gift but a curse, reinforcing separation that leads to destruction. The Gospel does not offer the ability to choose God; it proclaims a definitive rescue out of utter helplessness, securing believers in God's righteousness through the indwelling Holy Spirit.

Salvation is far more than a "get out of jail free card"; it is the deepest granting of true freedom—a complete transfer from darkness to light, from slavery to sin into a life joyfully devoted to God. This freedom in Christ deepens as believers grow in faith, ultimately reaching its fullest expression in eternity, where they will dwell with God, incapable of sin, fully free at last.

FOR REFLECTION AND DISCUSSION

1. In your own words, what is freedom?
2. How does the Bible define freedom differently from how the world defines it?
3. Why is true freedom found in submission to God rather than in autonomous decision-making? How does freedom in Christ surpass the world's definition of independent choice?
4. How does salvation rescue believers from the false hope of autonomy? What does it mean to be a slave to righteousness rather than a slave to sin?
5. What does John 8 teach us about the reality of human will being enslaved to sin?
6. How and why did Adam and Eve fail? What lead them into bondage rather than true freedom?

7. In what ways does Holy Spirit enable believers to live in true freedom?
8. How does Galatians 5 describe the fruit of the Spirit as an expression of biblical freedom?
9. Why is complete freedom in Christ a gradual process? How does Holy Spirit free believers from sin's power while still requiring transformation?
10. Why do some people view free will as the highest human value? What dangers arise when people view free will as the path to true freedom?
11. What does ultimate freedom look like for believers in eternity?
12. To what degree are you living in biblical freedom, and what next step could deepen your walk in the Spirit?

CHAPTER 11

What Does Identity Teach Us About Salvation?

Life is not an independent journey where we craft our own identities apart from God—it is a process of discovering who we truly are within His reality (SB#24, Pavlik, p. 21). While many seek meaning through self-reliance, Scripture teaches us that true understanding comes through knowing God and His creation. The world operates within His sovereign design which shapes every aspect of existence, including salvation itself.

SEEING SALVATION THROUGH GOD'S CREATIVE WORK

From the beginning, God has actively revealed Himself through creation. The universe declares His majesty (Psalm 19:1), human nature reflects His image (Genesis 1:27), and history unfolds according to His will (Ephesians 1:11). Salvation is not merely a personal experience—it is a divine work that opens our eyes to the reality of His design.

There is an awe-inspiring depth to discovering God and His creation. When we step into His reality, we find ourselves immersed in a world of beauty, complexity, and intentionality. Each sunrise, each intricate detail of nature, each moment of human connection—all are reflections of His creativity and presence. To truly know God is to be drawn into the wonder of His handiwork, where every discovery leads to deeper awe and gratitude. This realization transforms how we see life: rather than striving for control or autonomy, we learn to embrace the gift of awareness, recognizing that we are part of something infinitely greater than ourselves.

Just as God's creative work reveals His design and purpose, it also establishes the boundaries of reality—leading every person toward either redemption or judgment. Every aspect of existence moves according to His will, and nothing escapes His sovereign plan. In the end, salvation and judgment are not arbitrary choices but inevitable outcomes woven into the fabric of creation itself.

Salvation does not exist in isolation. It is deeply connected to God's wisdom, sovereignty, and purpose. Through His creative work, believers come to understand salvation and embrace the freedom He has ordained.

AWARENESS INSTEAD OF AUTONOMY

No one wants to live in fear of losing what is important to them. The Gospel is Good News because it leads us into God's rest. Salvation is not the start of a journey with an uncertain destination—it's the beginning of a Spirit-secured walk into glory. It is an entrance into a new way of living, one that requires faith to endure God's sanctifying work, one that purges sin and lies from the believer's mind and heart. Only a true believer will persevere until that final entrance into heaven, after she passes from this earthly life.

This cleansing process is why we work out our salvation with fear and trembling—not in anxiety, but in awe of God who is in

What Does Identity Teach Us About Salvation?

control, knowing that we are not (Philippians 2:12-13). It's like an exhilarating ride on God's roller coaster: thrilling, unpredictable, but never unsafe—because catastrophic loss of salvation is not part of the journey.

God did not design the human will to oppose Him—He meant for us to cooperate with Him. Our sinful nature rejects Him, but once God kills it, only peace with Him remains. When our wills align with God's will, together they are unstoppable. In this sense, God does not need to coerce the human will onto His side—He simply frees it from sin so believers can serve Him wholeheartedly. Once the sinful nature is reckoned dead, having a "free will choice" to oppose God serves no purpose because rejecting love makes no sense.

God gives us awareness instead of autonomy. With spiritual awareness (faith, God-awareness), we can find meaning in His wisdom, love, and goodness. We are drawn to these because they resonate with the identity He created within us. Self-awareness allows us to discover who we truly are in Him, fostering gratitude for both God and His creation, which includes other people.

We respond to God's truth—we cannot create our own truth. Our human will is limited—we observe His handiwork, participate in His creation, but cannot design or alter it. While we make meaningful decisions, those decisions unfold within the reality God has already authored. The believer's aim is to walk in biblical freedom, not autonomous free will. God gifts us freedom from sin through union with Christ, but He does not hand over independent free will—and He doesn't need to.

The very fact that we must learn who we are suggests we have a Creator. If I do not know myself completely, God must. We grow in self-awareness, but we do not dictate our identity—God determined it from the beginning. If we do not control what motivates or inspires our decisions, feelings, thoughts, or actions, how can we claim to have "free will"? God established our desires and preferences at the moment of creation.

DISCOVERING AND TRUSTING GOD'S DESIGN OF IDENTITY

God establishes every human step, securing our paths, but people do not fully understand their own hearts. We are like music boxes—we can hear the melody but do not see the mechanics that produce it. We observe our actions, feelings, and thoughts but lack access to the deeper workings behind them. We act according to what is in our hearts, yet our identities remain outside of our control, somewhat of a mystery.

> The heart of man plans his way, but the Lord establishes his steps.
> Proverbs 16:9 ESV

Jesus has set us free—but what exactly does this mean? No human possesses unlimited power or the freedom to do anything she desires. Her freedom is shaped by her God-given identity, which defines and limits her abilities, creativity, and influence. Yet, within these boundaries, she experiences complete freedom—the freedom to fully embrace her true self, without being weighed down by negative comparisons or feelings of inferiority.

The true measure of freedom is not the ability to act without restraint, but the ability to love like God without the danger of sin and evil. To be a person is to have limits. Every person possesses unique talents, but no one possesses all talents.

We are relational beings, designed for fellowship, yet always following the design God has set in place. If we attempt to redefine or understand ourselves apart from Him, we only grow more confused about who we are.

When God created each of us, He gave us an identity—a set of instructions much like DNA (SB#24, Pavlik, p. 29). We follow these instructions, yet we do not have access to them. We cannot change who we are—we can only cooperate with the growth process God has set in motion.

> A man's steps are from the Lord; how then can man understand his way?
> Proverbs 20:24 ESV

What Does Identity Teach Us About Salvation?

Romans 8 reveals the depth of God's control and his unseen work to ensure His will prevails. God works behind the scenes in our hearts because we don't always know our inner-workings, God's exact plan, or the next best step.

> Likewise the Spirit helps us in our weakness. For we do not know what to pray for as we ought, but the Spirit himself intercedes for us with groanings too deep for words. And he who searches hearts knows what is the mind of the Spirit, *because the Spirit intercedes for the saints according to the will of God.* And we know that for those who love God all things work together for good, for those who are called according to his purpose. For those whom he foreknew he also predestined to be conformed to the image of his Son, in order that he might be the firstborn among many brothers. And those whom he predestined he also called, and those whom he called he also justified, and those whom he justified he also glorified.
> Romans 8:26-30 ESV, *emphasis mine*

The Spirit intercedes to guarantee God's will. Therefore, we know that when we drift, He will re-center us.

GOD'S REALITY IS FIXED, NOT UNCERTAIN

The Bible describes reality as absolute—fixed, stable, unchanging, and certain. By contrast, relative reality would be shifting, evolving, directionless, and uncertain. Absolute reality offers security because it is built on a firm foundation—God Himself, the Rock—not on shifting sands. God is purpose-driven and His plan flows from His purpose and power.

Just as God is unshakable, so is salvation for those He calls. Security requires this firm foundation—salvation cannot be built on human effort, but only on God's unchanging character and sovereign choice. His plan is unwavering, and His purpose is supported by His wisdom.

Identity, like reality, is also determined—not open. We are not meant to drift in uncertainty, but to stand firm in the truth of who we are in Christ. Paul warns against the instability of human wisdom:

> so that we may no longer be children, tossed to and fro by the waves and carried about by every wind of doctrine, by human cunning, by craftiness in deceitful schemes.
> Ephesians 4:14 ESV

Because God is unchanging, our identity, defined by Him, is also stable and reliable. This stability allows us to act with confidence and conviction, as we trust His sovereign design.

To know who we are, we must first remember who God is—and trust that His truth about us cannot change.

IDENTITY IS FIXED, NOT SELF-MADE

God defines our identity, which shapes our choices. Creatures do not define themselves; they are defined by their Creator. God crafts His people with perfect artistry and love. We cannot understand who we are without His forelove. Salvation reflects this truth—God calls, defines, and secures His people according to His resolute will.

Our identity—fixed by God's design—is whatever remains stable over time (SB#23, Pavlik, p. 8-9). Without His definition, we drift without purpose. We can appreciate and accept who we are only to the degree we know we are chosen, loved, and secure in Him.

Stability is not a limitation—it's a gift. Predictability, in God's hands, reflects purpose, not restriction. We don't want to be unstable, shifting, doubtful, or insecure. We need confidence and conviction. God is perfect—acting according to a fixed nature defines excellence. God has a pure identity. He does not evolve morally or any other way. He is already as excellent as He ever will be.

Acting from an unchangeable, fixed identity does not diminish life's joy—it maximizes it. God experiences perfect joy because He is completely fulfilled in His identity. Likewise, salvation is the gateway to fulfillment. In Christ, God enables believers to reach their fullest potential, designed for joy.

What Does Identity Teach Us About Salvation?

> These things I have spoken to you, that my joy may be in you, and that your joy may be full.
> John 15:11 ESV

God is stable—and we are made in His image. That means we are not random, nor undefined. An absolute design makes us knowable, relatable, and valuable.

God entrusts each person with distinct abilities—traits that aren't interchangeable and that reflect intentional craftsmanship. If I am designed for a purpose, it is not rigidity—it is reliability. That speaks of a Maker who is both deliberate and trustworthy.

Like an arrow aimed at a target, I want my life to fly true—without deviation. And to do that, I must believe what Scripture says: we are fixed, purposeful, and called according to design. Not static. Not stuck. But steadfast. Just like God.

God knows everything about His creatures, but we must discover who we are day by day. We don't know what we are going to do, or exactly how we choose what we do, but we are predictable to God. We can only know ourselves as we experience ourselves. We can only know other people, God included, as we experience them.

Living with limited knowledge requires dependence and faith. By faith, believers lean fully into God, trusting Him to work out life's details according to His sovereign plan.

What God creates, only He can recreate. We cannot alter our identity—but when God redesigns, He only perfects. In Christ, He remakes believers as new creations, made to live forever through spiritual oneness with Jesus. To be loved like this is infinitely better than possessing the option to reject Him.

A FIXED IDENTITY DOES NOT MAKE US ROBOTS

Along with a fixed identity, God provides Holy Spirit to be our dynamic spiritual guide. We are not puppets or robots but temples of the living God. Even though we function exactly as

He designed us to function, life is never boring. God Himself makes life exciting and new.

God avoids robotic constraint by mixing expansive variety and hidden treasures with purpose, certainty, and security.

The Creator's understanding is always superior to His creatures' understanding. God made us unique and knows us completely, including all future days He has ordained, but we cannot fully understand ourselves. This limitation makes life interesting and enjoyable as we pursue the mysteries of God and His creation (Psalm 139).

We are not robots because we are living beings with emotional needs. Our emotional needs, when properly expressed, reveal our dependence on God and drive us into His loving arms, where we find the fulfillment and security He provides through salvation.

Our God-given identity drives and limits our behavior, but it does not eliminate meaningful choices. What we do is predictable to God, just like anything humans create is predictable, such as a robot. But we can enjoy decisions.

Reality operates on two levels: divine certainty and human perception.
- God sees everything as fully complete. His plan is established from eternity.
- Humans see life unfolding moment by moment. We cannot see the future, making our choices genuinely significant.

From our limited perspective, we experience meaningful decisions because we do not know everything. But from God's perspective, all things move according to His sovereign will. He meets us within time, condescending to our understanding while retaining full authority.

Communication between God and humans requires divine accommodation. God reveals truth as we are able to comprehend it, yet He remains infinitely beyond our grasp. His ways are higher—some things remain mysteries beyond our understanding.

Though humans can choose, God remains in control as Creator. He knows those He has created with absolute certainty.

What Does Identity Teach Us About Salvation?

We experience decisions as real in the sense that we do not know all things, yet our path is fully known by Him. God hasn't given us any power that He can't see or adjust. His sovereignty doesn't diminish our story—it secures it.

GOD'S SOVEREIGN WILL IN SALVATION

Is there any part of creation, including the human will, that God does not have the power to change or influence? For God to have heaven the way He desires, He must have complete control over every aspect of creation.

Nothing can weaken God's sovereignty or strengthen our ability to save ourselves apart from Him. Satan deceived Adam and Eve into doubting God in the Garden of Eden and accepting a distorted image of Him. He took advantage of their vulnerability to spiritual death—and he continues using the same deception today, preying on our sinful nature. He deceives with half-truths:

- God is good, but not always good.
- He is powerful, but not all-powerful.
- He is loving, but not always loving.
- He is just, but not entirely just.
- And finally, He is in control, but not completely sovereign.

But believers know that God is entirely good, powerful, loving, just, and sovereign. He answers to no one and is responsible to no one, but we are accountable to Him. As created beings, we are responsible for following His decrees and laws. Salvation is His work from beginning to end; He aligns believers with His will during their earthly lives, and His work endures into eternity.

HUMAN WILL IS NOT FREE

God's sovereign will has sovereign freedom—it is completely free. Only God possesses this free will, also called autonomous free will. God is not a slave; He has no master. He does not depend on anyone. He is not accountable to anyone. But even He has an identity shaped by His righteous characteristics. While this might be confused as a limitation, it isn't. He is perfect—meaning He cannot become any better than He already is.

Each human will is not free but is enslaved either to sin or to righteousness. It depends entirely on God, its Creator. Although the human will can decide, those choices are inherently bound by its sinful or its redeemed nature.

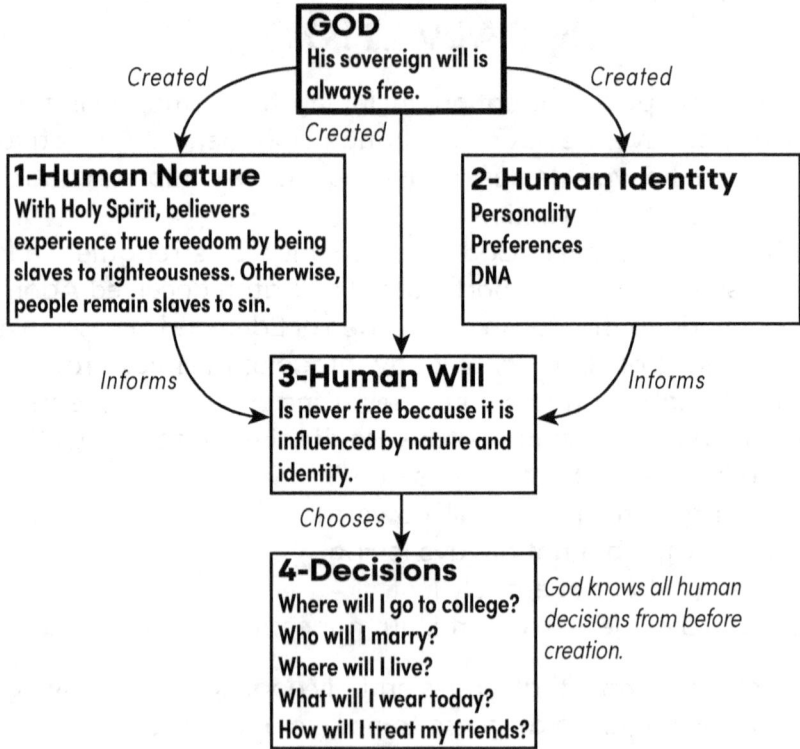

The will decides, but only with guidance—either from the law and Spirit to choose righteousness, or from the flesh to choose sin. The will is never free because it must always take direction from someone before it can decide. The will needs a coach—Holy Spirit—whispering in its ear:

> And your ears shall hear a word behind you, saying, "This is the way, walk in it," when you turn to the right or when you turn to the left.
> Isaiah 30:21 ESV

What Does Identity Teach Us About Salvation?

People always function as God created them to function. God creates humans with a nature, identity, and will. Nature and identity inform the will before it decides. In God's design, the will is at the end of the decision making process, completely dependent on the nature's degree of freedom and the identity's preferences.

GOD'S REALITY IS BIASED, NOT NEUTRAL

While humans can make decisions, they are never without bias. People will always act according to their strongest inclination (SB#5, Edwards, p. 148). God, as Creator, is the originating cause of these inclinations. The desire for autonomous free will—especially to reject God—originates solely from the sinful nature.

The problem is not simply choice, but sin, because sin always opposes God. The solution is not free will that gives people the option to take or leave Him; the true solution is the eradication of sin, which transforms the human bias from resisting God to desiring Him.

Bias shapes every decision. Since the Fall, there is no such thing as a purely neutral choice—without bias, choices would be entirely random, people would remain vulnerable to evil, or decision-making would be impossible. Bias must originate from somewhere—its ultimate source is God. He created the world with bias.

We should not be unbiased about danger. Rationally speaking, we should want to be biased against it. We should not be unbiased about love. We should want to be biased for it. Where does this bias come from? It must come from our Creator.

Sin is not rational because it is a bias for danger—a bias against God. Holy Spirit creates a bias for God. All humans are born into sin, separated from God from the very start. Without divine intervention, even if granted the opportunity to make a so-called free choice, people would remain bound to their sinful state, ultimately facing eternal separation from Him.

A person might intellectually or emotionally grasp the concept of paradise. However, if she is spiritually dead, she cannot truly see, accept, or choose it. Her ignorance—her bias against God—becomes the very obstacle in her path.

Every action is also determined by identity—God's design of a person's likes and dislikes. He planned for your personality to be exactly the way you are. Your talents and abilities aren't a mistake (SB#23, Pavlik, p. 20).

Desires Reflect Destiny

Non-believers do not want God. Believers want God only because Holy Spirit enables them to see Him. Believers' wills are constrained by God's preserving presence. They know God and experience His love so they will never desire to be separated from Him. Scripture affirms that God's love does not allow anything to separate us from Him (Romans 8:38-39).

Those who remain spiritually dead do not know fellowship with God. They neither value Him nor hold any value to Him, remaining His enemies forever. Conversely, those whom God chooses become His friends.

It is possible for people to love what enslaves them, when they are deceived. Pursuing personal desires may not feel like slavery, but apart from God's living water, all addictions are like dead, salty water—having a false appeal and never truly satisfying.

Knowing God is eternal life. Those in hell never knew God for who He truly is, and God does not know those who reject Him. As Jesus warns in Matthew 7:23, "I never knew you." Those who perish in their rebellion will never fully comprehend what they will never have.

Regarding heaven, everyone ends up where they ultimately want to be. No one will enter heaven apart from God's will—and no one who truly desires Him will be denied. His calling creates robust desire, and Jesus's sacrifice secures the outcome. This means all of the following are true:

- Whoever God wills to be with Him, will be in heaven.
- Whoever God does not will to be with Him, will not be in heaven.
- Whoever wants to be with God, will be in heaven.

- Whoever does not want to be with God, will not be in heaven.

God is throwing a party in heaven. Has He already invited you? If not, seek to understand the Gospel, then listen for His calling. The desire to seek the Kingdom is evidence that God is calling and drawing you to Himself.

GOD IS IN CONTROL

When we consider life from God's perspective, we begin to understand His omniscience and sovereignty. To be God is to rule over everything. He establishes His plans and ensures they are fulfilled according to His will. He is actively intervening in His creation to bring about His glorious purposes.

The human will is always limited by God's sovereign will. All creatures must ultimately submit to His authority—if not now, then eventually (Philippians 2:9-11). Some people view the human will as strong enough to counter God's will, but no one can thwart His plans.

God's saving work cannot fail due to a human's rebellious nature. Salvation has been eternally secured through Christ's death and resurrection. Whoever God wills to be saved, will be saved.

What can humans accomplish with their wills? We can control only what God permits us to control. Before any of us were born, He established the context of life—the framework of reality in which we exist. God always holds the home-field advantage; we live, act, and choose within His creation. All righteous decisions serve God directly, and He even makes all decisions meant for evil serve His ultimate purposes (SB#24, Pavlik, p. 28).

God's reality is not something we can shape—it's the foundation we're invited to stand on, or stumble over. True freedom is not found in rewriting reality, but in surrendering to the One who authored it.

This means that the scope of what we can accomplish by our own wills is severely limited. On our own, we are virtually powerless. We can do things, but apart from God, they are insignificant. Yet, when aligned with God inside of us, we are powerful.

How much control do we truly have over life's events? An autonomous human will is, at best, an illusion or, at worst, the devil's deception: "you can be free like God." We might feel or appear to be free, until we consider what we are enslaved to. What ultimately drives our behavior? While we might believe we are in control of many things, the reality is that God is fully in control, bringing everything into conformity with His will and purpose (Ephesians 1:11).

Only one being can be in total control. If God holds absolute authority, then no one else can rival Him. He has no formidable competition—nothing can defeat Him, He cannot be dethroned, and no one surpasses His power.

> The creature which conditions God is no longer God's creature, and the God who is conditioned by the creature is no longer God.
> SB#1, Gilmore, p. 191, quoting Karl Barth in The Humanity of God

In a world obsessed with self-definition, the Gospel invites us to rest in God's definition of us—loved, redeemed, and eternally secure. Our identity is not something we achieve, but a reality we receive. And when God names us, no one can rename us.

GOD CONTROLS WHO HAS FAITH

Our identity is deeply connected to our ability to perceive and respond to God. Just as our talents and inclinations are woven into who we are, so is our capacity for faith. No person generates faith independently—it is not the result of personal reflection or effort. Faith is the ability to recognize and embrace God's reality, gifted by Him rather than produced by human will.

This section reviews and builds on earlier discussions, reaffirming that salvation is entirely dependent on God's initiative.

Since humanity is spiritually dead, we are incapable of responding to the Gospel apart from God's complete intervention. Faith does not originate in the human heart but comes

What Does Identity Teach Us About Salvation?

from God, allowing His chosen people to believe and see truth. The Gospel message, combined with God's illuminating work, enables people to hear and see. Without divine revelation, spiritual blindness prevents any meaningful response.

Spiritual Blindness And Divine Illumination

Faith is like a spiritual flashlight, revealing the truth God chooses to unveil. Holy Spirit shines that light into a person's heart, enabling her to perceive what is otherwise hidden.

Faith is freedom because it is spiritual sight—allowing believers to walk in light and understanding while non-believers stumble in confusion because they are imprisoned in darkness.

God created the physical universe for all to see, but the secrets of His kingdom remain hidden, and not everyone has equal access to them. Most people are born with physical sight, but all people are born spiritually blind.

If people could fully see and freely choose between heaven and hell, how could anyone, with eyes wide open, willingly choose hell? They must be blinded, unable to recognize the best option. Only God is able to open their eyes. He is completely in control of who sees truth and who remains blind.

God controls understanding and wisdom by both shining and withholding light. Where God's light does not shine there is spiritual blindness. His light is always shining in believers' hearts so that only born-again, spiritually alive people can perceive spiritual truth correctly.

The physical world—under the influence of that evil ruler, Satan—is full of distractions that distort true reality. Faith enables believers to look beyond the physical world and know God as Spirit. However, even believers can become distracted by physical sight, losing focus on eternal truths.

Picture this: *A man spends his life studying stars through a telescope, mapping constellations, chasing patterns. One night, the sky opens and a radiant figure steps through the veil of space. Jesus reveals Himself as Creator of the heavens and earth. The man drops the telescope. He no longer needs it.*

Physical birth is not an offer; our wills are limited because we do not choose whether we want to be born. Likewise, spiritual birth—eternal life—is not an offer but a gift. When God gives faith to see, it is automatically received just like when someone turns on a light, she immediately benefits from it. Once received, eternal life cannot be cancelled. The person who sees the kingdom of God has been born again, and there is no way to "unsee" who God truly is. Upon seeing God, a person is changed forever—her heart gladly belongs to Him.

Jesus Himself is the gift, but awareness of the full extent and meaning of the gift only comes after receiving it. The spiritually blind cannot understand the gift and therefore have no interest in it. Believers can preach the Gospel, presenting the gift, but the spiritually dead cannot recognize it unless God grants them sight. Through preaching, believers shine the light, but only God can bring sight to the blind (Isaiah 4:27, Luke 4:18, Acts 26:18, Ephesians 1:18).

GOD MUST DRAW PEOPLE TO HIM

Saul's radical transformation into Paul illustrates how God's intervention in salvation is undeniable and absolute. Before encountering Christ, Saul actively opposed God's kingdom, persecuting believers with zealous determination. His nature was not neutral—it was fiercely set against God. Yet, when Jesus revealed Himself, Saul's resistance collapsed, and his new identity in Christ took over.

> 'Saul, Saul, why are you persecuting me? It is useless for you to fight against my will.' 'Who are you, lord?' I asked.
> And the Lord replied, 'I am Jesus, the one you are persecuting. Now get to your feet! For I have appeared to you to appoint you as my servant and witness. ... Yes, I am sending you to the Gentiles to open their eyes, so they may turn from darkness to light and from the power of Satan to God.'
> Acts 26:14-18 NLT

Saul did not choose salvation, nor was he given an option to accept or reject Christ. His conversion was the direct result of divine intervention, showing that human will does not lead to salvation. People have a will, but it is not free—before regeneration, it remains bound to sin and blindness, unable to recognize or desire God.

Non-believers' spiritually dead wills are not free at all, they are hopelessly biased to reject eternal life.

B. B. Warfield argued that our wills, left to themselves, will always reject eternal life. Salvation is not merely offered for acceptance or refusal—it is a gift that God gives decisively. Just as Lazarus had no power to resist being raised, and the man with the withered hand couldn't decline healing, spiritually dead souls do not initiate or even consent to their resurrection. God doesn't ask the dead if they wish to live—He commands life into being, and it comes (SB#1, Gilmore, p. 186, adapted from Warfield as quoted).

God must actively draw people into salvation, breaking through their resistance to bring them into His kingdom. Humanity is dead—unwilling and unable to respond without God's intervention. He draws through the Gospel, and people respond. While the human heart belongs to the individual, it is not free and it can only desire what God has shaped it to desire. Only God can raise the dead by breathing new life into a dead heart.

> **The Scriptures say that Abraham would become the ancestor of many nations. This promise was made to Abraham because he had faith in God, who raises the dead to life and creates new things.**
> **Romans 4:17 CEV**

Imagine that your heart stops beating. You have died, but there is still hope of being revived. Because you are dead, you are incapable of saving yourself. A doctor must attempt to restart your heart.

> **No one can come to me unless the Father who sent me draws him.**
> **John 6:44 ESV**

The Greek word for "draw" in this verse (elkuein: "to lead by inward power")[1] suggests a dragging force, implying resis-

---

1. blueletterbible.org/lexicon/g1670/kjv/tr/0-1

tance. For a person to become saved, Christ must pull her out of spiritual death, across the threshold into life. Only He has the ability to operate deep within the spiritual heart of a person. A person is saved only if God wills her to be saved, because the spiritually dead are completely passive in their resuscitation (SB#1, Gilmore, p. 185).

Martin Luther, in his book Bondage of the Will, had this same interpretation. The ungodly do not come to Christ by their own effort, even when they hear the Word. Instead, the Father must draw them inwardly by His Spirit, enlightening their hearts and bringing them to Christ. This is not a human-driven pursuit but a passive reception of divine grace (SB#9, Luther, p. 311).

Furthermore, Luther describes two kingdoms at war: Satan's kingdom, where all remain captive unless rescued by Christ, and Christ's kingdom, which resists Satan's rule. No one escapes Satan's grip by free will—only God's power can transfer a person into Christ's kingdom. This ongoing battle between darkness and light refutes the idea of free will, as humanity is either enslaved to sin or redeemed by grace.

> **We are compelled to serve in Satan's kingdom if we are not plucked from it by Divine power.**
> SB#9, Luther, p. 312

Imagine a figure sleeping in a war zone—not from laziness, but exhaustion, disorientation, and helplessness. Apart from the flashes of nearby impact, all is dark. A radiant figure kneels beside her, places a hand on her heart, and light begins to pulse from within. She awakens—a new creation.

CONCLUSION

Salvation and identity are inseparably linked. No person exists independently of God's creative design, and no one comes to faith apart from His sovereign calling. Before the moment of every soul's creation, God defines their purpose, inclinations, and ultimate destination. Rather than offering salvation as an option to be accepted or rejected, He grants it as a gift, ensuring that those He calls will receive eternal life.

A person's will is never autonomous. It is either enslaved to sin or bound to righteousness through Christ. While people experience decisions as their own, they remain shaped by their nature, inclinations, and God's will. The idea that individuals freely choose God contradicts Scripture—Jesus stated plainly that no one comes to Him unless drawn by the Father.

Those whom God calls recognize His truth, their spiritual blindness removed by His illuminating work. Salvation is not about weighing options or exercising independent choice—it is about being transformed by the love and authority of Christ. Believers are secure because their salvation is anchored in God's unshakable plan, not in their own fragile decisions.

We are not saved because we found God, but because He found us. Our identity, our sight, our faith—each is a gift flowing from His sovereign mercy. And because salvation begins and ends in Him, we have every reason to rest, rejoice, and believe without fear.

FOR REFLECTION AND DISCUSSION

1. Can God create a being with an independent will, one that does not depend on Him in any way? Why or why not?
2. What does it mean that salvation and judgment are woven into creation's DNA? How does this shape the way we see God's justice?
3. In what ways does Satan distort God's image in our minds, and how can believers combat these deceptions?
4. If humans can only control what God designed them to control, how does that challenge common views of free will?
5. If human free will were prioritized above God's will, how would that redefine truth, love, and grace?
6. What role does faith play in salvation, and how does God's illumination help people perceive the truth? When does He allow spiritual truth to remain veiled?

7. Why is bias inherent in both God and humans—and how does salvation reshape a believer's bias in a way that ensures eternal life remains eternal?
8. What does it mean to be defined by God rather than by personal choices or achievements?
9. If God defines a person's identity before birth, what does that imply about efforts at self-definition, personal ambition, and comparison to others?
10. How does comparing spiritual birth to physical birth reinforce the idea that salvation is entirely God's work?
11. How does Lazarus's resurrection illustrate that humans cannot participate in their spiritual birth?
12. In light of eternity, what is the true purpose of human choices, and how should that shape our daily decisions?
13. Imagine that God has removed all of your sin. What is left of you?

PART 4

God's Guaranteed Victory Secures Salvation

From the dawn of creation through every trial of evil and suffering, to the final capstone being laid in place, God architected His redemptive plan from beginning to end. Christ's resurrection and promised return ensure that every believer's salvation will be fully realized. Nothing can thwart the purposes of the One who conquered sin and death on our behalf. We wait in hope, assured that His final victory will bring us into everlasting glory.

CHAPTER 12

What Is Evil's Role In Salvation?

Is evil more like a nuisance that God must work around, or a scalpel in His hand, wielded with surgical precision? As a nuisance, evil would be an unfortunate byproduct of human free will, forcing God to take a tactical approach to contain evil's spontaneous activities. As a scalpel, God would strategically use evil to orchestrate eternal redemption.

Many people attribute evil to free will, arguing that God gave His creation the ability to choose between good and evil. Yet Adam and Eve did not make an informed choice—one grounded in true discernment or understanding of its consequences. Instead, they were deceived into mistrusting God. If their disobedience was the result of manipulation rather than deliberate rebellion, how can it rightly be attributed to free will? God allowed Satan to exploit their vulnerability—making the Fall not a celebration of autonomy, but a tragedy of deception.

To understand the role of evil, we must confront its origin. This chapter argues that evil was not an accident—but an intentional part of God's design from the beginning.

IS EVIL SPONTANEOUS OR PLANNED?

Evil has not always existed like God has. Some people believe evil arose spontaneously, as if it slipped into creation without God's permission, circumventing His control. Others believe God created evil for His sovereign purposes.

IF EVIL WAS SPONTANEOUS

This view suggests that God's plan was disrupted by an unforeseen rebellion, forcing Him to respond rather than reign. Evil, in this sense, becomes a rogue element—spontaneous, unchecked, and ultimately outside of God's intended order. However, this raises a troubling implication: If evil exists outside of God's will, then He is not fully in control.

If God is not fully in control, does this mean He depends on believers as crisis managers to help Him defeat evil? God delegates responsibility to believers such as preaching the Gospel, loving people into the kingdom, and overcoming darkness through prayer. They participate, but is the outcome dependent on their effort? If their efforts fall short, does that mean they are responsible for those who do not enter heaven? This perspective places the success of conversion primarily on human effort.

If salvation were left to chance—dependent on circumstances rather than divine purpose—then God would not be fully sovereign over redemption. This spontaneous approach assumes that God merely observes rather than directs salvation. But scripture portrays God as intentional and sovereign in calling people to Himself.

The weakness of this view is its inability to account for evil's role with clarity. It can't explain why some remain deceived while others are awakened to truth—why evil devours some but fails to keep others ensnared. What keeps one person asleep while another wakes up, alert and ready for action? Who can awaken a dead heart from spiritual slumber? Only Jesus can because He is the resurrection and the life (John 11:25).

DEISM COMPARED TO THEISM

Deism asserts that God created the universe but does not intervene in its affairs. He is like a watchmaker who sets creation in motion and then steps back, allowing natural laws to govern everything. Deists typically reject divine revelation, miracles, and ongoing interaction between God and humanity.

Theism, on the other hand, holds that God is actively involved in creation. He not only made the universe but continues to sustain, guide, and interact with His creation. Theism teaches that God is personally engaged and reveals Himself through scripture, miracles, and relationships with people.

In short, deism presents God as a distant architect, while theism embraces Him as a present and relational ruler. In the spontaneous view, God is passive and weak—He is able to be surprised. In the planned view, God is active, strong, and in control at all times.

Deism has far-reaching implications:
- Humans can choose God, and therefore also un-choose God.
- Humans are in control with God-like powers of autonomous free will.
- Instead of humans being in God's debt, God is in their debt.

But these things cannot be. The devil uses the illusion of choice to entice people to believe they control their destiny, when in truth, they are ensnared by deception. All independence from God is Bad News. The Good News is only possible because of God's sovereign mercy.

Luther rejects this Deistic framework. According to the editors of *Bondage of the Will*, Luther is a Theist:

> As a sinner, man is in the devil's kingdom, and can do nothing but choose to remain there; it is not in his nature to do anything else. As a creature, he is in the hand of God, who [either] leaves him under the power of sin, or rescues him from its clutches by renewing his nature, according to His own free and sovereign will.
>
> ...the creature can never make the Creator his debtor; man's destiny depends entirely upon the free decision of God. Thus, Luther

substitutes for Erasmus's Deistic doctrine of human 'free-will' and salvation by meritorious action a genuinely Theistic doctrine of Divine Lordship and salvation by sovereign mercy.
SB#9, Luther, p. 53

I did not choose God; God chose me. The Bible, Martin Luther, and my personal testimony align with the planned approach. God saves exactly who He wants saved. God is never surprised. Everyone who God wants to be in heaven will be there. God is fully capable of populating heaven with the people who fit His plans.

BECAUSE EVIL IS PLANNED

The planned approach asserts that evil was not an accident but an intentional part of God's design—not because He is capable of evil, but because its existence serves a greater purpose. Evil has not existed from eternity past, so God must have created it by some means or another.

Evil and suffering play a role in God's redemptive purpose. Through brokenness, humanity recognizes its need for God, leading us to seek His grace. The world's hardships are not arbitrary but serve a higher purpose in revealing God's mercy. Let's trace suffering back to its source:

- Suffering exists because of the curse.
- The curse exists because Adam and Eve disobeyed.
- Adam and Eve disobeyed because the serpent deceived them into mistrusting God.
- The serpent had the opportunity to deceive because God created evil and did not intervene.
- God created Adam and Eve as good, but vulnerable to evil.

God allowed the Fall—not to give humanity control over their eternal destination—but to prove that life without Him indwelling is doomed to error. God created us vulnerable to evil for a reason—to show us the depths of His grace.

What Is Evil's Role In Salvation?

> For God saved us and called us to live a holy life. He did this, not because we deserved it, but because that was his plan from before the beginning of time—to show us his grace through Christ Jesus.
> 2 Timothy 1:9 NLT

If He knew we would need grace, He must have known we would need saving. This supports that God planned salvation before He created the world.

God is telling a story, and every great story requires contrast—light and darkness, good and evil. A compelling narrative must include an adversary, not because the antagonist is equal to the hero, but because opposition allows the hero's qualities to shine more clearly. In the same way, God has allowed the existence of evil, not as an accident or an unforeseen crisis, but as part of His sovereign plan to reveal His love and justice.

In a story, the villain's darkness accentuates the hero's light, and through their struggle, the story's resolution becomes more powerful. Similarly, God's redemptive plan triumphs over evil, magnifying His glory. Because of both good and evil, there can be conflict then resolution, brokenness then redemption. If there were no struggle, no antagonist, no Fall, then salvation itself would lack meaning. God could have created a world where deception was impossible, but then there would be no need for His sacrifice.

Adam and Eve's vulnerability to deception indicates that the Fall was not a matter of free choice but part of a greater narrative. Because of the Fall, humanity became enslaved to sin, incapable of freeing itself. God allowed evil to prey on their vulnerability, knowing they would be lured into distrust, but also knowing that it would ultimately display the depths of His grace in salvation. In God's story, He redeems a people for Himself, securing them for His purposes and sustaining them by His power.

What Is Evil?

God could have prevented the Fall. He could have made Adam and Eve incapable of sin—but He didn't. He could have created Satan fully good, without any capacity for pride or rebellion, but He didn't. The fact that evil exists suggests that God allowed it—not passively, but intentionally—because it has a role to play in His ultimate plan. God could have even stopped Satan from deceiving Adam and Eve, but He didn't.

Some believers prefer to say that God "permitted" evil, as if it somehow emerged outside of His will—an unfortunate byproduct of human free will. But could a force so overpowering—one that causes its host to intentionally tempt, deceive, accuse, and destroy—really emerge on its own? Evil is a corrupting force—able to cause intelligent beings to become relentlessly motivated to oppose God and His children (Ephesians 6:11-12, 2 Corinthians 4:4, 1 Peter 5:8, James 3:15-16).

God is good but Satan is corrupted by evil. Satan is a counterfeit, not a counterpart. Unlike God, he lacks absolute creativity, authority, and power. He cannot invent, he can only imitate. God is self-existent and sovereign. But evil is dependent. It requires a host, a body it can possess and a will it can persuade.

Evil exists to mar what is beautiful. When it is active in the spiritually dead, it causes parasitic behavior, like a tick or a mosquito, draining a being's strength. It drives beings to attach to what is good, exploit vulnerability, twist truth into deception, and feed off of death and destruction.

Such a significant force points to God's intention, not spontaneous emergence. Evil must have been planned by God to serve His redemptive purposes. As a rogue force slipping past God's defenses, evil would weaken God's sovereignty. But as a governed force, evil magnifies His justice, mercy, and love. Our God, who is in control of everything, can be trusted with this scalpel.

It's far more compelling to understand evil as a tool in God's hands than a threat outside His control. Still, let's be clear: God is not the author of sin. He does not commit evil, nor is He tempted by it (James 1:13). But He is the author of a story in which evil exists precisely so that His mercy and justice can be revealed. That doesn't make evil inherently good—it makes it subject to a greater good. Evil is subordinate, never sovereign—contained and controlled, never rogue. Used, but never victorious. In God's hands, even evil-incited rebellion becomes the stage on which grace and justice reveal the beauty of salvation.

Christ's sacrifice was never a contingency plan to resolve an unexpected crisis. It was the original plan, designed before creation itself, to demonstrate God's love. Humanity's vulnerability to evil and disobedience did not surprise God. He knew what would happen and allowed it to unfold according to His greater purpose. Satan can never win, but God uses him to achieve His desired outcome. In God's redemptive plan, evil's influence over corrupt beings cannot suppress His glory.

The Gravity of God's Absence

God alone is the source of all spiritual vitality—wisdom, goodness, clarity, even the ability to will rightly. Scripture doesn't merely suggest this; it declares it.

> It is God who works in you to will and to act in order to fulfill His good purpose.
> Philippians 2:13 NIV

> Every good and perfect gift is from above.
> James 1:17 NIV

There is no self-generated insight or moral strength in humans, angels, or demons; all light is borrowed, and when God does not supply that light, that being—whether heavenly or earthly—inevitably retreats into sin, evil, and death.

One possible explanation for how evil exists is that it grows in the void of God's withdrawal. Just as darkness is simply the absence of light, evil is the absence of God's presence. When God created the universe, He did not fill every space with Himself, but left room for contrast—to cause evil to exist so that His goodness could be fully understood.

Evil is the absence of God's spiritual vitality. Spiritual death isn't a powerful rebellion but the hollow consequence of divine absence. Romans 1:24-28 reveals this sobering dynamic: when God "gives people over" to their desires, the result isn't liberation but deterioration. Their evil choices are not feats of autonomy—they're symptoms of spiritual disconnection.

This applies equally to humans, angels, and demons. Jude 1:6 speaks of angels who disobeyed God and await judgement day in a prison of darkness. They have no power over God and fell without His gracious favor. Likewise, Ephesians 2:1 describes humanity as "dead in trespasses and sins"—not energized rebels but lifeless souls cut off from their source. Evil activities, then, are not triumphs of independence but the collapse that follows when God does not supply spiritual life. Sin becomes foolish ruin rather than bold resistance. And assurance is possible not because of our grip on God, but because of His mercy, in His refusal to let go.

God Has Satan On A Leash

Because God is sovereign over everything He creates, nothing, including evil, can exist outside His control. Everything in the universe is dependent upon God, even evil. People can make decisions from evil intent and God can mean it for good (Genesis 50:20). This proves that evil is powerless when compared to God. Distrust, sin, and discouragement destroy—but under God's control, even setbacks become setups for greater glory.

God is the ultimate power source in creation—sustaining both good and evil, though He is aligned only with what is good. Evil functions within the boundaries of His will, but He remains entirely separate from it in nature. He carefully controls and contains evil's activities while remaining wholly good Himself (Job 1).

Evil doesn't just linger—it infiltrates. It behaves like a parasite: it exploits vulnerability by attaching itself to God's creation and filling the void where God has withheld His presence. It is not original, but reactive; not sovereign, but greedily opportunistic. When God leaves room for contrast, evil fills the space—not as a rival power, but as a distorted shadow of what is true. And that distortion results in rebellion.

Does it make a difference whether someone commits evil or simply withholds the good she ought to do? The Bible considers both to be sin (James 4:17). All sin comes from the spiritually corrupted flesh, but God is absolutely free and completely righteous.

What Is Evil's Role In Salvation?

Whatever God does is good by definition. If His actions appear to be evil, we must trust that He has a higher purpose for what He allows—a reason for acting that we cannot fully understand (Isaiah 55:8-9). God is not guilty of evil, for He is holy and His purposes transcend human understanding.

God's Sovereignty Over Evil

If evil exists within God's plan, then it must serve a greater purpose rather than being an accident or something outside His control. Scripture offers insight into this idea, particularly in passages that highlight God's sovereignty over both good and calamity. One such verse is Isaiah 45:7.

> I form light and create darkness; I make well-being and create calamity; I am the Lord, who does all these things.
> Isaiah 45:7 ESV

Some translations use the word 'evil' instead of 'disaster' or 'calamity', leading to debate about whether God actually creates evil. However, many scholars interpret this verse as emphasizing God's sovereignty over both blessings and judgment.

In the context of Isaiah 45, God is speaking about His control over nations, particularly His use of King Cyrus to fulfill His purposes. The verse does not mean that God is morally evil, but rather that He ordains calamity as part of His plan.

God did not create evil as an autonomous force, warring against Him outside His control. He directs all things toward His ultimate redemptive purpose.

God's Plan From The Beginning

If God is good and all-powerful, how and why does evil exist? Since God is in control of everything, He must have created the environment that allowed Adam and Eve to be deceived. He had to create the possibility of evil, leave humanity vulnerable to it, and allow Satan to tempt them. God must have intentionally introduced the possibility of rebellion. He could have created a world without evil, but instead, He created a world where evil exists for a reason (SB#3, Sproul Jr., p. 51-52).

There is a logical order to everything God planned before time began:
1. God has always existed.
2. God created everything as good. As part of His design, He introduced vulnerability to good and evil in angels and humans.
3. God introduced evil. Satan succumbed to it. Without God's sustaining power, beings decay into spiritual death (1 John 3:8).
4. God stood by while Satan deceived Adam and Eve. They died spiritually. Original sin is true because they represented all of us. Any human would have done the same.
5. God finished His plan for salvation through Jesus Christ. He rescues helpless people through His love and mercy.

God planned these steps ahead of time, before He created anything. He did this to demonstrate the riches of His love—so that those who experience His love can understand their uniqueness and value. His deliberate choosing before creation demonstrates that His plan was well thought out from the very beginning (Ephesians 1:4-5, 11, 2:7; Romans 8:29-30, 9:23; 2 Timothy 1:9; Titus 1:1-2).

> This letter is from Paul, a slave of God and an apostle of Jesus Christ. I have been sent to proclaim faith to those God has chosen and to teach them to know the truth that shows them how to live godly lives. This truth gives them confidence that they have eternal life, which God—who does not lie—promised them before the world began.
> Titus 1:1-2 NLT

God Aligns Believers' Wills With His

Should we resist evil if God is in control of everything? Of course. God has everything planned, but we don't know the entire plan. Also, we cannot sit idle by for very long because God's Spirit encourages us onward. We were created for a purpose: to join His cause. We experience the working of His plan in real time. He allows humanity to act within time, but He knows the future and ensures His plan will come to fruition. As

What Is Evil's Role In Salvation?

finite beings, we could not handle knowing the future while still needing to act in the present.

God's purposes unfold precisely as He intends. Even in a world where evil persists, His plan remains perfect and unshaken.

Rather than seeing evil as an intimidating, wild force, we should understand it as an illustrative contrast, allowing God to fully reveal His nature—justice, mercy, and love—in ways that would be impossible otherwise. He did not create evil to harm His people but to show them, in the most profound way possible, the depth of His love and the meaning of salvation.

DO PEOPLE CHOOSE HELL?

One of the challenging questions about salvation is whether people truly choose hell or if they remain lost because they lack the ability to choose God.

People suggest "free will choice" explains how non-believers end up in hell. This is a faulty and unnecessary effort to preserve God's integrity. God's character could be questioned if a person who desires heaven, who wants to be with God, is rejected by Him. But this never happens, because no one wants God. Those that do want Him are the ones who have already become born again.

Consider these three groups:
1. People who are ignorant of a better spiritual life.
2. People who actively choose independence of God.
3. People who actively choose to worship Satan.

All three groups of people are spiritually dead, with no group any better off than the other. Each path may look different, but the destination is the same. All three groups remain lost, demonstrating that free will is powerless to initiate salvation. **But God can reach anyone with the gift of eternal life because it is a transformation not a choice.**

All people believe they are choosing what is best at the time, even those who are most deceived. The battle is against the deception and darkness because free will saves no one. The ability to choose destruction, without the opportunity to learn from it, is no blessing—it is a curse. This reveals the deeper reality that deception and spiritual blindness prevent people from seeing God's goodness. Without His intervention, no one could freely choose Him.

Unsaved people do not want hell or God—they want to rule their own kingdom. Unfortunately for them, God does not provide this third option. The spiritually dead are pleased to reject God because of their sinful nature.

All unsaved people will end up in hell against their will. They must be cast into the fiery lake. They do not willingly walk in. Therefore, it's not that people choose hell, it's simply that they don't have ability or desire to choose God. What they fail to realize is that a heart that rejects God is a heart that embraces hell.

Recall from Chapter 4 the fertile and infertile view. Can a person find room for God's Word in her heart, before the Spirit makes it fertile? If she is barren can she have the ability to choose God? Hebrews 6 says "no" because even a person who experiences everything God has to offer can still reject Him. An infertile heart is unable to choose God.

Salvation is a gift. God must open the womb, open the eyes of the heart, for a person to be able to receive God's truth. The heart must first be regenerated—made fertile—before it can receive the seed—God's Word.

GOD'S LOVE AND THE EXISTENCE OF EVIL

The reality of election often challenges people's understanding of God's love. Election seems to contradict the idea that God's nature is wholly good, but a closer look reveals the depth of His intentionality in both election and love. If God is so loving, how could He choose some people, yet pass over or reject others?

God chooses through the Spirit like the wind blows—unseen, unpredictable, but perfectly directed. We can't discern a pattern, but God knows what He is doing. Everything He does is intentional—precisely the way He wills. Everyone in heaven delights in God's presence. And no one in hell longs for Him—they remain enslaved to bitterness, set up to remain opposed to Him for eternity.

There is peace in knowing that God is in control of salvation, determining beforehand exactly who will be redeemed according to His wisdom and purpose. If God decides, it is not only okay, it must be good. There is a method to the seeming randomness even though we can't identify it.

God actively chooses whom to save, ensuring that salvation is not arbitrary but guided by His sovereign will and purposes. Scripture repeatedly affirms that salvation is God's work, not a result of human effort. Ephesians 1:4-5 states, "He chose us in Him before the foundation of the world," reinforcing that salvation is an intentional act of divine election, not a matter of chance.

Many contend that love requires choice—that salvation must hinge on human free will, lest God be seen as forcing people into heaven. But since when does the Lord of the Sabbath ask permission to rescue us from evil? If evil serves God's redemptive design, then salvation is not negotiated through human decision. It is anchored in God's relentless commitment to reveal His love through redemption.

Picture this: *A diver plunges deep into the ocean, chasing a glimmering object. The pressure mounts, oxygen fades, and panic sets in. Just as the diver blacks out, a hand breaks through the water—pulling him upward. He awakens on the surface, gasping, surrounded by light and air.*

Jesus's death and resurrection were not a reaction—they were the culmination of a preordained plan. Through the cross, God reveals the depth of His love, showing that life is fellowship with Him and death is separation from Him—not merely as theological concept but as eternal reality.

If the thought of election feels harsh, consider that God cares for His children, but leaves the devil's children in the devil's care (Luke 9:60). Take comfort in the fact that God does not choose according to status or worth, but by grace—and His choice reveals a stunning reversal of worldly values:

> Brothers and sisters, think of what you were when you were called. Not many of you were wise by human standards; not many were influential; not many were of noble birth. But God chose the foolish things of the world to shame the wise; God chose the weak things of the world to shame the strong. God chose the lowly things of this world and the despised things—and the things that are not—to nullify the things that are, so that no one may boast before him. It is because of him that you are in Christ Jesus, who has become for us wisdom from God—that is, our righteousness, holiness and redemption.
> 1 Corinthians 1:26-31 NIV

God chose, through His mercy and wisdom, those the world considers insignificant or worthless. Your salvation is reality, because of His choosing.

WHY SALVATION IS NOT LEFT TO FREE WILL

If salvation depended on free will, would it be possible to know God for who He is, but still reject Him? If not God's doing, by what process can a hardened heart become soft, or blind eyes become seeing? If God provides some grace, but not enough to cause salvation, how much is the right amount?

What happens when the will is broken—directed by evil? Physical sight dominates. The heart resists. The mind doubts. Imagine if God does not determine who will be saved, but waits for the strong enough, wise enough, or lucky enough to choose Him. This would mean God does not guarantee saving anyone at best, and fails to save those He longs to redeem at worst. No one can achieve salvation on their own. No one trusts God for salvation on their own.

There is something deeply deficient in the person who rejects God—not intellectually, but spiritually. God must awaken her to see that a relationship with Him is good. The persuasion must increase until she desires Him—but the only way that happens is when God finally opens her eyes to the reality of who He is. And at that moment, she already believes. Free will contributed nothing.

What Is Evil's Role In Salvation?

The only way a person can see God clearly enough to "choose" Him is to have already been fully regenerated. But once a person is regenerated, they are by definition already "in love" with God. A child cannot resist her Creator's love. For salvation to work, God must fully reveal and communicate this love. Without a convincing love, how could someone make a valid choice? Once someone sees God clearly, rejection doesn't just become unlikely—it becomes unthinkable. It's not possible to "unsee" God's revelation of Jesus. Free will does not improve conversion rates or make salvation possible.

Non-believers might walk away from a distorted, incomplete view of God, but then are they truly rejecting God? How much grace is enough to give everyone a fair chance at believing? Does everyone receive the same amount? Too little, and people will reject God. Too much, and God has done all the work of salvation. What happens to those who die before they can "make a decision"?

If every person who wants to be in heaven will be there, and if everyone knows what heaven is, then why isn't everyone saved? There is a vast difference between understanding heaven as a concept and experiencing it as a reality. The first is merely intellectual knowledge—insufficient for salvation. A person who "chooses heaven" based on abstract understanding will eventually fall away because she never truly knew God.

A true believer is born again and knows heaven by experience, not theory. Holy Spirit moves understanding from mere concept to reality. A believer does not merely say, "I know about God"—she confidently says, "I know God. I have a relationship with Him."

Anyone who has truly known God's love would never abandon Him. But non-believers, still enslaved to sin, act irrationally regarding salvation and eternity. Their rejection is not simply poor decision-making—it is a result of spiritual blindness that only God can heal.

Car Analogy

Consider this analogy that more clearly shows that the human will is broken or irrational because of the sin nature.

SECURE IN CHRIST

You arrive at a car dealership looking for a car. The salesperson offers two options, Car A and Car B. There are no returns. After you choose, the car will be yours forever. If you don't make a choice, the dealer will assign you one by default.
1. **Car A** will reliably take you to your destination. It has a lifetime guarantee. It is free. It even has a loyal, competent driver.
2. **Car B** is guaranteed to be broken every time you want to use it. It has a large monthly payment that must be paid forever. You are responsible for driving it.

Which car would you choose? Is there really a choice? Wouldn't any rational person choose the first option?

Proponents of human free will expect that, even with a fully informed decision, some people would still prefer B over A, or Hell over Heaven—as if a soul could find satisfaction in a place prepared for weeping and gnashing of teeth. But no one deliberately chooses misery. Instead, a heart consumed by the desire for self-rule makes its home in Hell.

So what is happening inside a person that makes one embrace belief and another reject it? If salvation were truly a fair choice, everyone would choose Heaven. If God does not intervene, what blocks belief? And what awakens it?

The barriers to belief are not mere mistakes—they are deeply rooted conditions of the heart: a refusal to yield, a fear of surrender, a love of darkness, a soul wounded and guarded. These are not problems humans can fix. Left to themselves, people remain blind and unwilling. Unless God heals the heart, it will never open to Him.

If Car A represents Heaven and Car B represents Hell, why would anyone choose Hell? The answer is clear—salvation is entirely in God's hands. He chooses some but not others, ensuring that His greater plan unfolds exactly as He intends. Only He can breathe life into a dead heart. His wisdom in deciding how to populate heaven is more than enough (Romans 8:18).

What Is Evil's Role In Salvation?

CONCLUSION

A "decision" for Christ is not the cause of salvation, but the public response to what God has already done through regeneration. He created both the hearts that are vulnerable and the evil that preys upon them—but neither poses a threat to His plan. In His timing, He shines light into darkness and speaks life into what was barren.

Despite the existence of evil, God's grace and love are more than enough to overcome it. Evil is not a wild, uncontrollable force—it is a governed tool, serving His purposes. God does not wield evil recklessly; He uses it like a scalpel, with surgical precision. What seems like chaos to us is, to Him, carefully orchestrated. Evil cuts, yes—but only where and how God allows, never more. God's purpose is not destruction for destruction's sake, but refinement, contrast, and revelation.

This is our hope: the God who saves is also the God who rules over every shadow. Evil cannot win—it can only serve. It cannot hinder God's plan—it reveals the contours of His grace more vividly. In His hands, even evil and suffering have a role to play in eternal redemption and glory.

FOR REFLECTION AND DISCUSSION

1. Does God leave anything to chance, or does He intentionally direct everything?
2. Has evil ever operated outside God's control, or has it always functioned under His sovereignty?
3. What is God's purpose for evil? Consider both evil's impact and God's ultimate plan.
4. Has evil always existed? How did evil come into existence?
5. If God created evil intentionally, how does that affect your view of Him compared to a world where evil arose spontaneously? Which reality feels more consistent with God's holiness? Which is harder to accept emotionally?
6. If God created evil with purpose, what does that reveal about His justice and mercy?

7. How does contrast—light vs. darkness, good vs. evil—help us better grasp the meaning of salvation?
8. If evil thrives where God is absent, how does this shape our view of sin and human vulnerability?
9. How does Isaiah 45:7 expand or challenge your understanding of God's authority over both blessing and calamity?
10. If people do not actively choose hell but lack the ability to choose God, what does that reveal about the limits of free will—and how does the car analogy clarify this?
11. How does God's sovereignty ensure that both salvation and evil fulfill a greater good?
12. Considering that God planned your salvation before time began, does He work as purposefully before your spiritual birth as He does after it?
13. What or who is the originating source of suffering?
14. Would Jesus's sacrifice have happened if evil didn't exist?

CHAPTER 13

What is Suffering's Role In Salvation?

Everyone suffers. When loss strikes, when injustice lingers, or when pain feels endless, we instinctively search for meaning: *Why would a loving, powerful God allow this?* For believers at least, suffering has an end in sight.

Some see suffering as proof of God's absence. Others try to numb it, explain it away, or spiritualize it into silence. But the Bible does something different. It gives suffering a place—within the story of redemption itself.

This chapter is not about minimizing pain. It's about magnifying purpose. Through Scripture, we see that suffering is neither accidental nor wasted. It is necessary—transformed and even embraced by God—for our good and His glory.

Here, we'll explore how God works through pain. He doesn't sidestep suffering—He steps into it. We'll walk with Job, Joseph, and Jesus. We'll face the emotional dissonance between doctrine and sorrow, and press into a deeper vision of what salvation truly means.

HOLDING ONTO FAITH WHEN EMOTIONS CLASH WITH DOCTRINE

At times, doctrine tells us one thing while emotions scream another. The struggle is real—*how can God love me or I love God when He ordains my suffering?*

This tension lies at the heart of universal salvation debates—concerns not just about biblical interpretation but the clash between hard truth and human longing. *Why doesn't He save everyone? I can't process someone suffering for eternity.*

Yet, the Bible does not ask us to suppress our emotions but to bring them before God honestly. Job lamented, David pleaded, and Jesus Himself wept over death. God does not demand blind acceptance; He allows room to wrestle with truth.

The ultimate goal is to hold onto all truth while cultivating peace and trust in God. God's sovereignty over suffering is not meant to be a source of despair but an invitation to trust.

When emotions do not align with the truth, we must submit them to God in earnest lament until we exhaust ourselves of reliance on human wisdom and gain reliance on God. We must reach a point where we see the best option is surrender to God despite what happens in life.

Here is an example of sincere lament when relief is not in sight:

> I cry out to God; yes, I shout. Oh, that God would listen to me! When I was in deep trouble, I searched for the Lord. All night long I prayed, with hands lifted toward heaven, but my soul was not comforted.
> Psalm 77:1-2 NLT

We can cry out: *Why does God allow pain? Why does He permit rejection? Why doesn't He immediately intervene in suffering?* But through Job, Joseph, and Jesus, we see that suffering is never meaningless. When faced with grief and uncertainty, we hold onto the promise that He is sovereign, present, and working—even when we do not understand.

What is Suffering's Role In Salvation?

> Trust in the Lord with all your heart, and do not lean on your own understanding. In all your ways acknowledge him, and he will make straight your paths.
> Proverbs 3:5-6 ESV

So what do we do when our emotions rage against doctrine—when what we feel contradicts truth? How do we process this—wanting to love God but yet feeling hurt, disappointed with Him based on the implications of His truth? Don't drown in suffering. See beyond it to its purpose.

SUFFERING IS NOT AN END BUT A MEANS

There are purposes more enduring than pain. Suffering is not a believer's final destination, but a God-ordained path to a greater purpose.

The only way to endure suffering is to recognize that it does not last forever and that it accomplishes a purpose that cannot be had any other way.

When suffering feels senseless and unending, it distorts our understanding of God's character—tempting us to see Him as indifferent or even unjust. Some may become bitter toward Him, believing that His heart must hold some level of cruelty.

Bitterness, however, is more than simple frustration—it is hatred toward someone, fueled by unresolved pain. While we cannot judge God as evil, we can be real and honest about our emotions before Him.

HONEST EMOTION INSTEAD OF MISPLACED JUDGMENT

People should never hate God, if that is possible for them. He is the source of life and goodness—the best thing we have. To turn against Him would be to abandon the only option for hope and restoration.

Hatred of God wastes emotional energy and is ultimately a judgment against Him, implying that He is unjust or has wronged us. Since God is entirely righteous, this is a distorted view. Rather than projecting imperfect human motivations onto God, we must align our perspective with His revealed truth.

God does not "need" us, nor does He find fulfillment in our pain. He does not torture people for His pleasure, nor does He delight in suffering. But, all suffering has a purpose and it does not go unnoticed by God.

> You keep track of all my sorrows. You have collected all my tears in your bottle. You have recorded each one in your book.
> Psalm 56:8 NLT

For the child of God, pain will lead to something better. This is only possible because of Christ. Sometimes, God calls upon parents to walk with their child through suffering. For example, what if a child needs an operation that results in an immediate loss, but long-term stability? The child might be incapable of understanding the end goal, and so would resist surgery and feel betrayed by her parents. This situation is deeply painful.

If parents are capable of making such difficult decisions, then God certainly is. God's wisdom is infinitely higher than ours.

In our quest to understand how God can be sovereign over everything, including evil, we do not need to weaken His image by stripping away His agency or power. He can have full compassion and still make intentional decisions that result in suffering. Relying on human wisdom that alters His nature comes at a great cost.

RECONCILING SUFFERING WITH GOD'S LOVE

For many believers, the hardest question in faith is not simply why suffering exists, but how it can coexist with God's love. How can He claim to love us while deliberately introducing evil, knowing the pain it would cause? If suffering is intentional, does that mean God actively chooses to hurt people? This tension leads many to either question His goodness (give in) or resign themselves to accepting mystery without deeper understanding (give up).

But Scripture does not avoid these questions—it wrestles with them head-on. It reveals that love and suffering are not mutually exclusive, but deeply connected aspects of God's plan. For this to be acceptable to the human mind, we must be able to separate God's motives from the undesirable outcomes we observe and experience.

God is completely good and righteous. The existence of evil does not mean that God approves of it. God's loving patience allows for endurance in the face of evil, so that He can achieve greater purposes. God remains in control and does not flinch. He is not tempted by evil. He does not succumb to it. He cannot be manipulated or blackmailed by it. In God's hands, evil can only be used for His good purposes.

Has evil existed forever like God has? No, it has not. Then where did it come from? Did it arise spontaneously outside of God's control? There is no way it could have. Evil did not arise outside of God's control—He ensures it serves His purposes. While this may feel unsettling, there is comfort in knowing that evil is not a chaotic force beyond God's reach. Satan had to ask permission to afflict Job. Suffering exists not because God lost control of creation, but because He uses it to fulfill a purpose beyond immediate pain.

UNDERSTANDING LOVE REQUIRES OPPOSITION

To understand why God introduced evil and suffering, we must recognize the necessity of growth and testing. Love is not meaningful unless it is demonstrated through sacrifice and perseverance. Without sin, rebellion, or suffering, love would remain an abstract idea rather than a real, tested experience. True love is not merely an idea—it is tested, refined, and proven through adversity. We must be able to love despite evil. And God empowers us to persevere in love.

Consider a life without suffering. If Adam and Eve had never been deceived, if no one had ever sinned, and if humans had never experienced loss, would our understanding of love have the same depth? Would we grasp the magnitude of Christ's sacrifice? Would we understand grace if there were no need for it? Our understanding of love only becomes real when tested against hardship—when we experience brokenness and still choose devotion, when God allows pain but remains present, when redemption rises from destruction. Hope in the midst of suffering is only possible in the light of Jesus's promised future glory.

God did not cause suffering as an end in itself—He uses it as a contrast against which love and salvation would shine brightest. God means for us to look beyond suffering. What do we find when we look beyond it?

EXAMPLES OF THE FRUITS OF SUFFERING

Theology is essential, but it must be practical—especially when painful events intrude into our lives. In the midst of suffering, we need assurance that we matter to God, that He cares about the details of our lives.

God promises to work believers' suffering for good (Romans 8:28). Though this does not remove suffering, it assures believers that their pain carries purpose and is never wasted. While suffering cannot be reduced to simple explanations that make everything feel better, the following perspectives help believers find meaning amidst their pain.

While suffering feels cruel in the moment, it produces spiritual fruit that could not exist otherwise. Without suffering, many aspects of faith, character, and spiritual growth would remain incomplete. Above all, we must know Jesus as the sacrificial lamb.

People often wrestle with how God can be so loving, yet still allow evil and suffering. While suffering remains an endless reality for those who reject Christ and die in their sins, for believers, it is transformed into purposeful refinement and future glory. Though difficult to understand, suffering fits within God's greater plan in several significant ways:

What is Suffering's Role In Salvation?

Suffering Is Temporary

No pain lasts forever, and God promises restoration and healing in His time. Though suffering is painful, it is never wasted—it draws believers into deeper relationship with Him. Through suffering we see God more clearly and know Him more intimately. We suffer because we have weak, mortal bodies in a decaying world. To truly understand goodness and restoration, we must first experience brokenness. God allows suffering to contrast His redemption, deepening our appreciation of His grace.

Suffering Reveals The Impermanence Of This Life

Clinging to worldly comfort can lead us down a dangerous path toward complacency. Suffering shifts our focus toward eternal security, reminding us where true hope lies. Present suffering may feel overwhelming, but it cannot compare to the coming glory. It reorients our hearts toward eternity, anchoring our hope in what lasts forever (Romans 8:18).

Suffering Produces Dependence

Paul wrote, "My grace is sufficient for you, for my power is made perfect in weakness" (2 Corinthians 12:9). When life is free of hardship, people often fail to recognize their need for God. Suffering reminds believers of their dependence on Him.

Suffering And Love Are Compatible

God's love does not mean the absence of suffering. He permits hardship, but never abandons His people in it. His presence remains constant, guiding believers through trials.

Suffering Helps Define God

Jesus suffered more than anyone ever will. He understands suffering firsthand and does not ask His followers to endure anything He did not experience Himself.

Jesus Suffers With Us

Jesus walks with believers through suffering. Jesus does not ignore our pain; He intimately understands it as He intercedes on our behalf. He walks through our pain because He deeply cares for us as His body. Because believers are united with Christ, He shares in their suffering—not distantly, but intimately, as He intercedes and strengthens them.

Suffering Develops Perseverance

James 1:2-4 teaches that trials develop endurance, maturity, and completeness in faith. Hardship purifies faith, replacing distortion with deep trust in truth.

Suffering Precedes Glory

For believers, suffering refines faith, builds endurance, and leads to eternal glory (2 Corinthians 4:17). By suffering, we identify with Christ, and can experience His resurrection power. Because believers share in suffering, they will also share in glory (Romans 8:17, 1 Peter 4:13, Philippians 3:10).

Suffering Produces Compassion

Compassion from the heart produces empathetic and healing words. Those who have endured pain are better equipped to comfort others. Consider Joseph, who suffered betrayal and imprisonment, but later became a ruler who saved many lives. His pain prepared him for his purpose.

Suffering Leads To Redemption

Without suffering, salvation would not exist—Jesus's greatest act of love was accomplished through pain. Job, Joseph, and Jesus all demonstrate that suffering has a greater end—not just pain, but true transformation as evidence of true purpose.

JOB: TRUSTING GOD'S WISDOM IN TRIALS WE DON'T UNDERSTAND

Job was a righteous man—known for his devotion and integrity. He feared God, shunned evil, and lived a life that reflected unwavering faith. Yet despite his faithfulness, he endured suffering so severe that many would have turned away from God entirely. Because he did not, we know his relationship with God was genuine.

The story begins with a conversation in heaven. Satan approaches God and challenges Job's devotion, claiming that his faith is merely a result of God's blessings. "Does Job fear God for nothing?" Satan asks (Job 1:9). He argues that Job's loyalty is conditional—dependent on his prosperity. If those blessings were taken away, Satan insists, Job would curse God.

God permits Satan to test Job, but with limits. This detail is crucial: Satan's actions are not independent of God's sovereignty. Job's suffering, while devastating, does not occur outside of God's control.

In rapid succession, Job's life is overturned. His livestock and servants are destroyed, his children perish, and his health deteriorates. Boils cover his body, and he sits in ashes, scraping his wounds with a piece of broken pottery. His grief is unimaginable. Yet instead of cursing God, Job utters words that still challenge believers today:

> And he said, "Naked I came from my mother's womb, and naked shall I return. The Lord gave, and the Lord has taken away; blessed be the name of the Lord."
> Job 1:21 ESV

Job refused to believe God was untrustworthy. Despite his great loss, he maintained faith and worshiped. But he also poured out his grief and anger. Job demanded answers from God: *Why is this happening? Why do you allow suffering?*

> Though he slay me, I will hope in him; yet I will argue my ways to his face.
> Job 13:15 ESV

God responds—not with direct explanations, but with a revelation of His sovereignty. He asks Job where he was when He laid the earth's foundations, set the stars in the sky, and commanded the seas to halt at their borders (Job 38). The response is humbling—it is not suffering that Job must understand, but

God's wisdom itself. There is something beyond personal suffering. Suffering is never the end.

In the end, Job's fortunes are restored—not because he unraveled the mystery of his suffering, but because he learned to trust God beyond his comprehension. Job reminds us that trusting God does not require full understanding—only surrender to His wisdom.

JOSEPH: SEEING HOW GOD REDEEMS EVIL ACTIONS

Joseph's life is a striking example of how evil cannot disrupt God's plans. His suffering was caused by jealousy, betrayal, and injustice. His own brothers sold him into slavery out of envy, setting in motion years of hardship.

After being taken to Egypt, Joseph was bought by Potiphar, an officer of Pharaoh. Though Joseph proved trustworthy, his situation worsened when Potiphar's wife falsely accused him of assault—leading to his imprisonment.

Years passed, but Joseph was not alone—God was with him, even in prison. His ability to interpret dreams eventually brought him before Pharaoh, where he explained the meaning behind the ruler's disturbing visions: Egypt would experience seven years of abundance followed by seven years of devastating famine.

Through divine positioning, Joseph was able to save countless lives, including those of his family—the very brothers who betrayed him. When they arrived in Egypt seeking food, they unknowingly stood before Joseph, who now had the power to enact revenge. But instead of wrath, Joseph responded with grace:

> As for you, you meant evil against me, but God meant it for good, to bring it about that many people should be kept alive, as they are today.
> Genesis 50:20 ESV

What is Suffering's Role In Salvation?

Evil never has the final say—God's ability to redeem hardship is greater than any human betrayal. Joseph demonstrates how evil actions can be redeemed for good.

JESUS: EMBRACING SUFFERING FOR GOD'S PURPOSE

Jesus's suffering was unlike any other—it was not forced upon Him, but deliberately embraced for the sake of salvation.

Throughout His ministry, Jesus repeatedly foretold His death, warning His disciples that suffering was necessary for salvation.

The agony of the crucifixion was not merely physical—it was spiritual. He bore people's sin, facing complete separation from the Father for the first time (Matthew 27:46).

Unlike Job, Jesus understood His suffering completely. Unlike Joseph, He was not rescued from betrayal. His pain was not followed by earthly restoration—it led only to death.

But death was not the end. His suffering was not in vain. Three days later, His resurrection proved that suffering, when surrendered to God's purpose, leads to redemption. Jesus reveals that suffering, when embraced for God's purpose, leads to ultimate glory.

HOLDING ONTO JESUS IN SUFFERING

Job teaches us to trust God even when we don't understand. Joseph shows us that evil can be redeemed for good. Jesus reveals that suffering, when embraced for God's purpose, leads to ultimate glory.

Each suffered greatly, yet each experience led to something greater: assurance that God's "got this"—that despite evil, He brings restoration, redemption, and salvation itself. In God's hands, we can be sure that suffering produces something better, even if we cannot yet fully grasp the glory that awaits.

Suffering is not proof of God's absence—it is proof of His greater plan. These truths do not erase suffering, but they provide hope.

For believers, suffering has purpose because Jesus suffered, and we will be with Him in a place where there is no more pain. For non-believers, suffering in this life is only the beginning, but can yet have purpose too if it leads them to Christ. To complain about suffering in this life is too narrow a focus. The real concern should be where we will be for eternity.

God did not spare Jesus from suffering, He did not spare Job or Joseph, and He does not spare us—even though He is love. So, you're in good company. This reveals that love is not the absence of hardship, but God's presence within it.

Pain, loss, and trials are not punishments, nor are they proof that God lacks compassion. They are elements of a greater redemptive plan, working toward an eternal reality where suffering will no longer exist.

We may never fully understand why history must involve so much suffering, but, as believers, we can know it is never meaningless. Every trial, loss, and hardship carries the weight of eternal purpose, shaping faith and leading us closer to the God who remains sovereign—even in suffering.

> "So have no fear of them, for nothing is covered that will not be revealed, or hidden that will not be known. What I tell you in the dark, say in the light, and what you hear whispered, proclaim on the housetops. And do not fear those who kill the body but cannot kill the soul. Rather fear him who can destroy both soul and body in hell. Are not two sparrows sold for a penny? And not one of them will fall to the ground apart from your Father. But even the hairs of your head are all numbered. Fear not, therefore; you are of more value than many sparrows. So everyone who acknowledges me before men, I also will acknowledge before my Father who is in heaven, but whoever denies me before men, I also will deny before my Father who is in heaven."
> Matthew 10:26-33 ESV

Jesus shifted His followers' focus from momentary suffering to eternal glory, assuring them that God's sovereign plan accounts for every detail—even down to the hairs on their heads. His promise still stands: suffering is not the destination, but a bump we overcome on the road to everlasting life. This truth is reflected in John 21:18-19, where Jesus foreshadows Peter's death—revealing that even in suffering, God's plan is purposeful.

To walk in this truth, we must trade earthly reasoning for a heavenly perspective. In the depths of pain, we cling to the reality of God's love and power. And as that truth settles in, hardship begins to lose its grip and peace takes hold.

Paul highlights this truth in 2 Corinthians 4:16-18, reminding us that although our bodies may weaken, our spirits are renewed daily. Though our physical bodies decline, our spirits are not restricted by evil and suffering—we can, right now, grow, heal, and mature in our understanding of who God is.

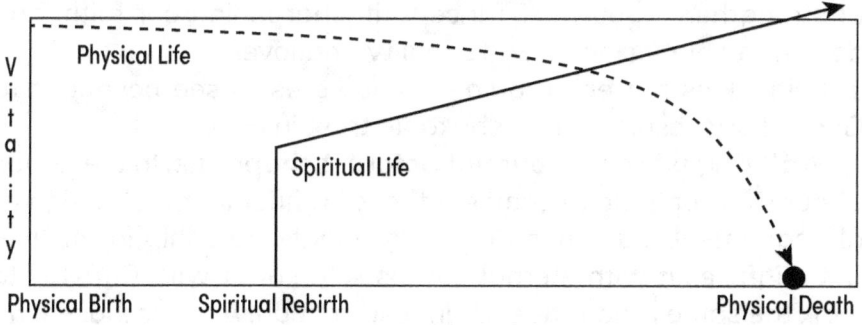

The power that raises believers from the dead is the same power that enables life everlasting.

> I also pray that you will understand the incredible greatness of God's power for us who believe him. This is the same mighty power that raised Christ from the dead and seated him in the place of honor at God's right hand in the heavenly realms.
> Ephesians 1:19-20 NLT

Our troubles are temporary, but the eternal glory they produce far outweighs them. When we fix our eyes on God rather than earthly suffering, we see beyond pain to His ultimate purpose.

> That is why we never give up. Though our bodies are dying, our spirits are being renewed every day. For our present troubles are small and won't last very long. Yet they produce for us a glory that vastly outweighs them and will last forever! So we don't look at the troubles we can see now; rather, we fix our gaze on things that cannot be seen. For the things we see now will soon be gone, but the things we cannot see will last forever.
>
> 2 Corinthians 4:16-18 NLT

Recognizing that we are created beings, fully dependent on our Creator, brings peace beyond human understanding. In our weakness, we cannot do anything but rely on His care. Trusting Him in suffering is not weakness—it is surrender to a wisdom far greater than ours.

Evil, though present, is powerless against God's greater plan. He does not allow it as an end in itself, but as a means of strengthening our resistance to it, sharpening our faith, and deepening our vision of God's reality and love.

Faith does not erase pain—it allows us to see beyond it to God's glory, resulting in unshakable trust in Him.

Suffering will end—but not before it shapes us. In the hands of our Creator, pain becomes a tool of refinement, not a sign of abandonment. Salvation doesn't eliminate hardship in this life, but it infuses it with eternal purpose. To suffer with Christ is to walk the same road that ends in resurrection. And for those who are His, glory is not a possibility—it's a promise.

FOR REFLECTION AND DISCUSSION

1. How does suffering align with God's love, and why does He allow His people to endure hardships?
2. What emotions surface when you think of God allowing your suffering?
3. Have you ever mistaken suffering for punishment? How does Scripture challenge that view?
4. How have you seen God's presence in pain you didn't initially understand?

What is Suffering's Role In Salvation?

5. Which biblical figure's suffering story resonates most with yours—Job, Joseph, or Jesus? Why?
6. Do you find it hard to reconcile God's love with His sovereignty over suffering? What helps?
7. How might suffering expose false hopes or misplaced security?
8. In what areas has your faith grown as a direct result of hardship?
9. How does knowing Jesus suffered willingly affect your view of your own pain?
10. What purpose might God be working through your present trial?
11. When have you resisted God's will because of fear of suffering?
12. If suffering brings about compassion, who is God calling you to comfort?
13. What happens when you fix your gaze on things unseen—especially in the midst of loss?

14) Write a lament that focuses on your suffering.

Laments are heart-felt cries to God in moments of pain—especially when He feels silent or absent. They allow us to express grief, fears, anger, and confusion honestly before Him.

Biblical lament is more than emotional release. It's profoundly spiritual—a faithful crying out to God that helps us move from sorrow to hope, from despair to trust, from numbness to joy. This shift doesn't always come with immediate relief or physical deliverance. Instead, it opens us to God's presence in the midst of our suffering.

Lament often begins in crisis—whether from physical illness, injustice, betrayal, or emotional turmoil. Scripture often describes these experiences metaphorically as "the enemy," and calls this threat to vitality, "death," even when life isn't physically at risk.

Take time to write your own lament. Follow the biblical pattern:

1. Cry out to God in honesty.

2. Name your pain or "enemy."
3. Ask boldly for help.
4. Offer—even faintly—to trust.
5. Wait patiently for God's answer.

Be comforted that circumstances do not have to change for you to feel closer to God. This is how you will find the assurance of God's love: not by pretending, but by pouring everything before a faithful God who hears.

CHAPTER 14

No Plan B: Where Else Can We Go?

Lord, to whom shall we go? You have the words of eternal life.
John 6:68 NIV

Faith shows us that trusting God is our Plan A—all other plans being futile. This hope does not put us to shame because God is in control. He doesn't need a do-over; He's got this.

God's plan has always been intentional, singular, and unchanging. There is no alternative path or contingency—only His perfect Plan A, guiding all things toward His ultimate purpose.

This concluding chapter explores the depth and breadth of that plan, revealing how God's sovereignty shapes every aspect of reality and leads His people into an eternal, perfected future.

The first part establishes the foundational truth that God's work is never random or reactive, but rather a deliberate movement from temporary existence to permanent glory. It examines humanity's transition from creation to redemption, showing how believers are not simply restored but elevated into a new, transformed reality through Christ.

The second part focuses on how these truths shape daily life, leading believers into a confident, joy-filled life that embraces God's wisdom while rejecting the enemy's distortions.

Picture this: *A man clutches a flickering candle in a pitch-black room. It's all he's ever known—dim, fragile, barely enough to see his own hands. Then, without warning, the wall before him vanishes. Morning light floods in. As he exits his prison, he sets the candle down, not even noticing it went out.*

GOD HAS ONLY A PLAN 'A'

God always and only brings His 'A'-game. Whatever happens is His Plan A—not a contingency or improvisation, but part of His perfect design. There is only what happens, not what could have been. He works all that happens for good (Romans 8).

God's plan is not reactive but eternally established. He does not adjust His will based on circumstances or human decisions; rather, all events—whether joyful or tragic—are woven into His singular, unchangeable purpose. What may seem to us like detours, mistakes, or unexpected turns are, from God's vantage point, part of His original design. His foreknowledge and wisdom ensure that nothing unfolds outside His control or requires an alternative course of action.

We often find ourselves asking, "What if?" We question decisions, wonder about missed opportunities, and mourn outcomes we wish had been different. But if God only has a Plan A, then there is no such thing as "what might have been." Regret and speculation have no place in a faith-driven perspective. Instead of being consumed by hypothetical scenarios, believers are called to trust that their present reality—no matter how difficult or confusing—was never outside God's intention. The absence of Plan B invites full surrender to what is, rather than striving for what might have been.

God's sovereignty means that there is only Plan A—nothing happens outside of His ultimate will. There are no alternate paths, no contingency Plan B, C, or D. What unfolds in history is exactly what God ordained, not what could have been.

This perspective removes uncertainty and regret. Since God's plan is fixed, human choices do not disrupt or alter His purpose. Even events that seem like mistakes or failures are still part of what was meant to happen, woven into His redemptive design. Just as God's plan is unchanging, so is the security of salvation. Those whom He has chosen and redeemed cannot fall away, for His purpose is fixed, and His promises never fail (John 10:28-29).

This understanding also alleviates worry about the future. Since Plan A accounts for all things, there are no surprises in God's creation. What may seem chaotic or unexpected is fully within His plan, ensuring that even suffering and challenges serve a higher purpose. Romans 8:28 reinforces this truth—God works all things together for good.

A key tension arises when considering sin. God does not long for sin—His holiness opposes it—yet it remains within His plan. He does not cause sin, but He uses it within His redemptive narrative. Without the Fall, there would be no need for Christ's sacrifice, and without human brokenness, there would be no revelation of grace. Thus, what "ought not to be" is still necessary for what "must be."

This perspective calls believers to shift their focus from uncertainty and regret to trust and worship. **Faith is not about hoping for a better alternative but embracing what is with confidence.** Instead of questioning why something happened, believers rest in the assurance that everything is unfolding exactly as it should. Instead of the defensive "Why?" ask the willing "What next?" This deepens surrender, removes anxiety, and enables a life lived in peace, knowing that God's unchanging Plan A is leading to ultimate redemption.

His design moves us—not just forward, but from the temporary to the permanent.

GOD IS LEADING HIS PEOPLE INTO PERMANENCE

The theme of temporary versus permanent runs deeply throughout Scripture, reflecting God's unfolding plan from creation to redemption. Many aspects of the first creation appear temporary, while the new creation offers permanence and fulfillment. Here are some key ways this contrast plays out in biblical theology.

Eden was a place of initial goodness but not eternal perfection. Adam and Eve's bodies appear temporary rather than intrinsically immortal. In contrast, the New Creation described in Revelation is an everlasting dwelling place where there is no death, sorrow, or corruption, marking a permanent fulfillment of God's design.

The contrast between the first Adam and the second Adam reinforces this theme. Adam was created from the dust, given life but vulnerable to sin and death. His body was natural and perishable. Christ, however, provides resurrection life through a spiritual, glorified body, one that is eternal and incorruptible. This shift from dust to glory highlights the transition from temporary to permanent.

Paul further emphasizes that flesh and blood cannot inherit the kingdom of God (1 Corinthians 15:50). Our current physical existence is temporary, while the resurrection body is permanent. Believers are promised glorified bodies that will never decay, aligning with God's ultimate plan for eternal life.

The Old Covenant, with its system of repeated sacrifices, was a temporary provision pointing forward to something greater. The New Covenant in Christ is eternal, with His sacrifice being once for all, removing the need for continual offerings.

The present world is also described as passing away, highlighting its temporary nature. However, the kingdom of God is eternal, promised as an everlasting reign that will never be destroyed.

Another significant shift is seen in God's presence. In the Old Testament, His presence was localized, dwelling in the tabernacle or temple. Through Christ and Holy Spirit, God indwells believers permanently, making them His dwelling place.

Rather than restoring the temporary features of the first creation, God is leading His people into permanence. Eden was good, but it was never meant to be the final stage—it was a starting point for something greater. The fact that the first creation didn't last suggests it was never intended to be the ultimate plan. Instead, God's purpose was always to transition us into a new, eternal reality where righteousness, communion, and life are permanent.

BELIEVERS ARE VERSION 2.0

Throughout history, theological discussions have explored the nature of Adam and Eve's will before the Fall. One perspective considers them as "free agents"—possessing the ability to make decisions, but lacking an internal guiding influence that would have safeguarded them from deception. Unlike humanity after the Fall, they did not have a sinful nature inclining them toward rebellion, nor did they have the indwelling presence of Holy Spirit to provide discernment. This left them in a state of moral naivety, lacking discernment, and therefore vulnerable to external influences such as the serpent's deception. Innocence alone is insufficient to sustain righteousness—true moral strength requires discernment from an internal safeguard.

God is sovereign over all events, including the Fall. Adam and Eve were foreordained to fall as part of God's larger redemptive plan, though their decision remained voluntary. This perspective suggests that God, in His wisdom, created them without an internal safeguard, allowing the Fall to unfold as He had planned, leading to the eventual necessity of redemption through Christ.

Adam and Eve were like a "version 1.0" of humanity—a foundational creation that was destined to fail in order to reveal the need for something greater. Their lack of an internal guide exposed human vulnerability, demonstrating that the human will alone was insufficient to sustain righteousness. This ultimately paved the way for Christ as the "second Adam," ushering in "version 2.0," where believers are transformed into a new creation with the indwelling presence of Holy Spirit as their internal guide—no longer vulnerable, but secure in grace.

This transformation is irreversible. Believers do not merely receive a temporary state of righteousness—they are eternally secure in Christ, sealed by Holy Spirit as a guarantee of their inheritance (Ephesians 1:13-14). Salvation is not conditional or uncertain; once God has redeemed someone, they remain His forever, fully secured in His sovereign purpose.

Having already subjected creation to the weakness of Version 1.0, God leaves no doubt that Version 2.0 will succeed (Romans 8:20).

Paul's contrast between Adam and Christ in 1 Corinthians 15:45 highlights this transition, with Adam as a "living being" and Christ as a "life-giving spirit." The new creation in Christ is not merely a restoration of what was lost in Eden, but an elevation to a higher spiritual reality—one in which God's people are empowered by His presence rather than left to navigate moral decisions alone. In heaven we will have superior spiritual, immortal bodies. This transformation suggests that God's ultimate intention was never just to return humanity to its original state, but to lead it into deeper communion with Him through the work of Christ. God never intended our physical bodies to last forever—only heavenly, spiritual bodies can last forever (1 Corinthians 15:42-54).

This progression from the first creation to the new creation not only defines humanity's redemptive journey but also provides insight into our present spiritual transformation. Through Christ, believers are no longer isolated in their moral choices but are empowered by His presence to walk in wisdom and truth. The indwelling Spirit serves as both a guide and a source of strength, shaping the believer into the image of Christ. This transformation does not merely prepare us for eternity but actively reshapes our lives now, giving us a foretaste of the greater spiritual reality that awaits us in heaven (2 Corinthians 4:16). In this final state, humanity will no longer struggle with the limitations of the first creation but will finally experience perfect communion with the Trinity.

This is the fulfillment of God's promise—to move us from the temporary and vulnerable to the permanent and incorruptible.

As believers embrace their identity as the new creation, they are called to live according to this elevated reality. No longer bound to self-reliance or external moral constraints, they are empowered by the indwelling Spirit to walk in righteousness, wisdom, and love. This transformation doesn't end at internal renewal—it is meant to radiate outward, shaping the way believers love, speak, serve, and move throughout the world. Through this renewed existence, humanity steps into a deeper communion with God, reflecting His glory and anticipating the fullness of redemption that awaits us in eternity.

This reality also calls believers into a life of active faith. Embracing the new creation is not just an internal transformation—it is lived out in every relationship, decision, and pursuit. As recipients of spiritual renewal, believers are called to extend grace and truth to others, living as ambassadors of reconciliation. Community becomes a vital aspect of this journey, as the redeemed people of God encourage one another and bear witness to the transformative power of Christ.

You are not version 1.0 improved. You are version 2.0 reborn—your spirit sealed by the Spirit and made for permanence.

Ultimately, this progression—from creation to redemption—reveals God's desire for communion with His people. It is an invitation to not only believe but to participate in spiritual life, stepping beyond mere restoration into something even greater. The new creation is not simply a return to Eden; it is an ascension into eternal unity with the Creator, where His people will finally experience the fullness of God's presence without sin's counterweight.

LIVING IN LIGHT OF GOD'S SOVEREIGNTY

Understanding salvation, faith, and identity through the lens of God's sovereign design reframes the Christian life. Rather than striving to define themselves or control their destiny, believers are invited to discover what God has already done. Life is not about reinventing truth—it is about walking in the reality He created, embracing His purpose, and finding fulfillment in Him. This perspective shifts the focus away from self-reliance and toward joyful dependence on the One who holds all things together.

Sharing the Gospel is an essential calling for every believer, but the responsibility for outcomes rests with God. Christians are called to proclaim the truth, but only He opens hearts and grants spiritual sight. This reality frees believers from anxiety over conversions, allowing them to trust in God's perfect plan while remaining faithful to His mission. As they share the message of salvation, they learn to rely not on persuasive words but on the Spirit's power.

If the Bible's purpose is to strengthen believers' assurance and convict non-believers, then the appropriate evangelical question is "Are you sure you'll spend eternity with your creator? If not, would you like to know how?"

Faith allows believers to cease attempts to control and instead surrender to God's leading. Prayer is not merely for personal desires, but for alignment with God's design. Prayers should reflect a longing for alignment with His Spirit, a fertile heart, wisdom, and deeper spiritual awareness. The Christian life moves beyond self-centered concerns and into a posture of surrender, valuing truth and love over personal rights (for example, the right to choose independence from God).

Rather than living in constant pursuit of God's favor, believers are already victorious in Christ. They do not need to earn His love or approval—it is theirs through grace. Christian living is not about proving worthiness but about walking confidently in the victory God has already provided. This confidence is balanced with humility and graciousness.

Knowing one's elevated worth in Christ should not foster arrogance but gratitude. The believer recognizes that every gift—from salvation to personal talents—originates in God's grace, shaping her identity with love rather than pride. A deep awareness of God's mercy produces compassion, leading believers to extend the same grace they have received to others.

One of the greatest freedoms believers experience is acceptance of whatever happens, knowing that God is always in control. Whether circumstances are positive or painful, every experience holds purpose and wisdom. Instead of fearing the unknown, Christians can view challenges as opportunities to grow in trust and understanding. There is always something to learn from everything that happens.

Because salvation rests in God's sovereignty, believers never have to fear losing it. Christ's sacrifice fully accomplished redemption, and nothing—neither sin, doubt, nor failure—can undo His saving work (Romans 8:38-39). This assurance brings profound peace, allowing believers to walk confidently in faith without fear of "being fired" by God.

> My goal is that they may be encouraged in heart and united in love, so that they may have the full riches of complete understanding, in order that they may know the mystery of God, namely, Christ, in whom are hidden all the treasures of wisdom and knowledge.
> Colossians 2:2-3 NIV

When we truly understand salvation through Christ, we know wisdom (Proverbs 4:7). That understanding transforms our perspective—and with it, our attitude. Joy is entirely separate from circumstances—it remains steady regardless of trials because it is rooted in eternal truth, not temporary struggles. Walking by faith allows believers to see beyond present difficulties, trusting that every moment is part of God's greater story.

God often teaches through contrasts, revealing deeper spiritual truths by placing opposites before us—good versus evil, sacrifice versus selfishness, trust versus self-effort. These lessons expose His wisdom and holiness, helping believers recognize His ways.

However, the enemy distorts these contrasts to deceive. He blurs the line between good and evil, making sin seem acceptable and rebellion appear liberating. He twists sacrifice into foolishness, convincing people to chase selfish desires. He pressures believers to trust in self-effort rather than God's provision, turning faith into striving. Even suffering, which God uses for refining, is falsely portrayed as failure rather than transformation. The enemy leads people to avoid hardship at all costs instead of trusting God's process. Recognizing these distortions is essential for spiritual maturity. By learning from God's contrasts, believers gain discernment and deepen their understanding of His truth.

The contrasts God gives not only reveal His wisdom but also help us navigate life with clarity. Understanding these contrasts prevents emotional confusion, strengthens discernment, and protects against deception. Mental and emotional health flourish when we rest in God's care, viewing challenges not as threats but as opportunities to grow in faith, resilience, and joy. The heart steadies and the mind clears.

A secure foundation in God's sovereignty provides stability in a world of uncertainty. When we recognize that our identity, salvation, and purpose are anchored in His control rather than our efforts, we experience profound emotional relief. Anxiety fades when trust replaces self-reliance, and peace grows as we embrace God's truth over the enemy's distortions.

This life is temporary, and we should not let earthly concerns consume us. What truly matters is where we are heading for eternity. True freedom is being released from fear and worry about life's uncertainties, knowing that Christ has secured an everlasting future. The weight of earthly struggle fades in comparison to the eternal joy found in knowing God. Jesus's sacrifice proves the depth of God's love. His elaborate plan, woven through history and scripture, demonstrates His care for His people. His faithfulness invites believers to trust fully, without hesitation.

God must truly love us because He has gone through all this elaborate planning to communicate it. At the end of the day, the most vital question remains: Where else can we go? Like Peter, every believer uses faith to realize that God alone is the source of life, truth, and security.

We may not understand every detail of the path. But this is the path God laid from before the world began—and the only one that leads home. We don't need another option when we already have Christ. There is no Plan B. He is the plan. To whom else shall we go? He alone holds the words of eternal life.

TRUTHS TO REST IN

- God has never changed course—He is still working Plan A.
- You are part of a redeemed creation, not a repaired experiment.
- The Spirit of God within you is evidence of His unstoppable purpose.
- Trust replaces regret. Peace replaces striving. Eternity replaces uncertainty.
- There is no plan more secure than the one that ends in His arms.

CLOSING PRAYER

Lord, Your plan is perfect—even when we don't understand it. You have always known the end from the beginning, and nothing takes You by surprise. Help us live as people who trust—not in what could have been, but in what You have already finished, and in what You will yet do. You are our only source of life. There is no other way. No other plan. No other love so faithful. We rest in You. Amen.

INVITATION TO CONNECT

Visit ChristianConcepts.com to connect with me online or subscribe to my blog.

I invite you to share feedback on this book and ask questions about what these truths mean for Christian living. If you want to facilitate group discussions using any of my books, I am available to support you as you help others.

SELECTED BIBLIOGRAPHY

The following works are listed in order of most relied on in this book.

1. Gilmore, John. *Sure Enough*. AuthorHouse, Bloomington, 2004.
2. Ferguson, Sinclair. *The Whole Christ*. Crossway, Wheaton, 2016.
3. Sproul Jr., R. C. *Almighty Over All*. Baker Books, Grand Rapids, 1999.
4. Murray, Andrew. *Abiding in Christ*. Bethany House, Minneapolis, 2003.
5. Edwards, Jonathan. *Freedom of the Will*. Edited by Paul Ramsey. Yale University Press, New Haven, 1957.
6. Gerstner, John H. *A Primer On Free Will*. Presbyterian and Reformed Publishing Company, Phillipsburg, 1982.
7. Hunt, Dave, and James White. *Debating Calvinism*. Multnomah Publishers, Sisters, 2004.
8. Strombeck, J. F. *Shall Never Perish*. American Bible Conference Association, 1936.
9. Luther, Martin. *Martin Luther on the Bondage of the Will*. Revell, Westwood, 1957.
10. Ironside, H. A. *Eternal Security*. Loizeaux Brothers, Neptune, 1986.
11. Ironside, H. A. *Hebrews, James, and Peter*. Loizeaux Brothers, Bloomington, 1986.
12. Rosscup, James E. *Abiding in Christ*. Zondervan, Grand Rapids, 1973.
13. MacDonald, William. *Once in Christ in Christ Forever*. Gospel Folio Press, 1997.
14. Gilbert, Greg. *Assured*. Baker Books, Grand Rapids, 2019.
15. Sproul, R. C. *Chosen By God*. Tyndale House Publishers, Wheaton, 1994.
16. Sproul, R. C. *Doubt & Assurance*. Baker Publishing Group, Grand Rapids, 1993.

17. Barrett, Matthew. *40 Questions About Salvation*. Kregel Publications, Grand Rapids, 2018.
18. Oliphant, J. H. *The Doctrine of the Final Perseverance of the Saints*. Frank H. Smith, Indianapolis, 1891.
19. Horton, Michael. *For Calvinism*. Zondervan, Grand Rapids, 2011.
20. Olson, Roger. *Against Calvinism*. Zondervan, Grand Rapids, 2011.
21. Sproul, R. C. *Willing To Believe: The Controversy Over Free Will*. Baker Books, Grand Rapids, 1997.
22. Calvin, John. *Commentaries on the Epistle of Paul to the Galatians and Ephesians*. Translated by William Pringle. Calvin Translation Society, Edinburgh, 1854.
23. Pavlik, Matt. *Confident Identity*. Christian Concepts, Centerville, 2017.
24. Pavlik, Matt. *To Identity And Beyond*. Christian Concepts, Centerville, 2018.
25. Kendall, R. T. *Once Saved, Always Saved*. Paternoster Press, Belfast, 1983.
26. Stanley, Charles. *Eternal Security*. Zondervan, Nashville, 2002.
27. Bavinck, Herman. *The Certainty of Faith*. Paideia Press, St. Catharines, Ontario, 1980.
28. Huegel, F. J. *Bone of His Bone*. Christian Books Pub House, Grand Rapids, 1997.
29. Barker, Harold. *Secure Forever*. BookBaby, 2011.
30. Levering, Matthew. *The Theology of Augustine*. Baker Academic, Grand Rapids, 2013.

ABOUT MATT PAVLIK

Matt Pavlik is a licensed professional clinical counselor, author, and committed follower of Christ since 1991. He brings decades of experience in Christian counseling and spiritual guidance to his writing, blending thoughtful theology and everyday insight. Matt earned his Master's in Clinical Pastoral Counseling from Ashland Theological Seminary and a Master's in Computer Science from the University of Illinois. He has counseled individuals and couples for more than 20 years at his Christian private practice, New Reflections Counseling (NewReflectionsCounseling.com).

Matt's books—*Confident Identity*, *To Identity and Beyond*, *Marriage From Roots to Fruits*, and the *Journal Your Way* series—explore God's sovereignty, the reality of identity, relational restoration, and emotional growth, all anchored in the truth of Scripture. His writing helps readers discover who God created them to be and experience the freedom and permanence found in salvation through Christ.

Matt and Georgette have been married since 1999 and live in Centerville, Ohio. They have four adult children. Matt blogs regularly at ChristianConcepts.com, where his ministry continues to equip believers with clarity, confidence, and spiritual direction.